PHP|ARCHITECT'S GUIDE TO
PHP DESIGN PATTERNS

by Jason E. Sweat

php|architect's Guide to PHP Design Patterns

First Edition: **July 2005**

ISBN **0-9735898-2-5**
Produced in Canada
Printed in the United States

Disclaimer

Bulk Copies

Marco Tabini & Associates, Inc. offers trade discounts on purchases of ten or more copies of this book. For more information, please contact our sales offices at the address or numbers below.

Credits

Written by	Jason E. Sweat
Published by	Marco Tabini & Associates, Inc.
	28 Bombay Ave.
	Toronto, ON M3H 1B7
	Canada
	(416) 630-6202
	(877) 630-6202 toll free within North America
	info@phparch.com / www.phparch.com
Edited By	Martin Streicher
Technical Reviewer	Marcus Baker
Layout and Design	Arbi Arzoumani
Managing Editor	Emanuela Corso

Biography
Jason E. Sweat

Jason graduated from Colorado State University in 1992 as a University Honor Scholar with a Bachelors of Science in Business Administration, concentrations in Computer Information Systems and Finance & Real Estate, and a minor in Mathematics.

He spent seven years working for a small engineering firm doing process control work in the steel industry. This let to extensive SQL development and Jason's first web development experience creating ASP pages. He changed employers and worked as a Senior Project Leader for a Fortune 100 industrial manufacturer, leading a team of developers for commercial applications, and acting as the web master for his business unit. His role changed again in January 2005, and Jason is now the Manager of eBusiness/Commercial Systems for the same business unit.

Jason has used PHP since 2001, where he was searching for a free‹as in beer ;) ‹substitute for IIS/ASP to create an accounting system for a home business. His Unix administrator pointed him towards Linux, Apache and PHP. He has since adopted PHP as an intranet development standard at work, as well as using PHP in a Unix shell scripting environment.

He was a co-author of PHP Graphics Handbook (Wrox 2003), has published several articles for the Zend website and for php|architect magazine, and has presented numerous talks on PHP at various conferences. Jason is a Zend Certified Engineer, and maintains a blog at http://blog.casey-sweat.us/.

Jason currently resides in Iowa with his wife and two children. He enjoys many activities with his family including camping, hiking and swimming. He also enjoys practicing the Japanese martial art of Aikido.

To my wife, Vicki, and to my children, Madeline and Caleb,
for putting up with "even more" time with Daddy on the computer.
Thank you for your support and love.

CONTENTS

4 The Singleton Pattern 75

5 The Registry Pattern 85

6 The MockObject Pattern 101

Introduction

HAVE YOU EVER STARTED to tackle a new feature in your application only to realize that its solution is strikingly similar to something that you've already implemented? If you've been a programmer for even a short time, the answer is probably "Yes" and it's likely that you'll reach for some existing code to bootstrap your new development. You might even realize that your solution is fundamental, an approach that can be applied widely and repeatedly, not just by you, but by all professional developers.

In fact, many programming problems are faced over and over again, and many fundamental solutions—or design patterns—have emerged to address them. Design patterns are a template for how to organize your code so you can take advantage of a tried-and-true design.

Design Pattern History

The term "design pattern" was originally coined in the field of architecture. Christopher Alexander, in his 1977 work, "A Pattern Language: Towns/Building/Construction," describes common issues of architectural design and explains how new, effective designs can be created through the aggregation of existing, well-known patterns. Alexander's concepts translate well into software development, where it's long been desirable to construct solutions from previously existing components.

All design patterns have several common characteristics: a *name*, a *problem statement*, and a *solution*.

- The *name* of a design pattern is important, because it allows you to instantly communicate the intent of your code with other programmers—at least programmers familiar with patterns—without going into too much detail.
- The *problem* is the domain where the pattern can be applied.
- The *solution* describes the implementation of the pattern. Good coverage of a pattern should discuss the pros and cons of the pattern's use.

A pattern is a useful technique to solve a given problem. A design pattern isn't a library—code to be included and used directly in your project—but rather a template for how your code can be structured. Indeed, a code library and a design pattern are applied much differently.

For example, a shirt you buy off the rack at a department store is a code library. Its color, style, and size were determined by the designer and manufacturer, but it meets your needs.

However, if nothing in the store suits you, you can create your own shirt—designing its form, choosing a fabric, and stitching it together. But unless you are a tailor, you may find it easier to simply find and follow an appropriate pattern. Using a pattern, you get an expertly-designed shirt in far less time.

Returning the discussion to software, a database abstraction later or a content management system is a library—it's pre-designed and already coded, and a good choice if it meets your requirements exactly. But if you're reading this book, chances are that off-the-shelf solutions don't always work for you. Yet you know what you want and are capable of realizing it; you just need a pattern to guide you.

One last thought: like a sewing pattern, a design is of little use on its own. After all, you can't wear a pattern—it's just a patchwork of thin paper. Similarly, a software design pattern is just a guide. It must still be tailored specifically to a programming language and your application's features and requirements.

The Goal of This Book

The goal of this book is not to present a comprehensive catalog of software design patterns or to develop any new design patterns or terminology, but rather to highlight a few of the existing, well-known design patterns. In particular, the book presents those patterns that I've found most useful for development of dynamic web applications and shows reference implementations for these patterns in PHP.

Object Oriented Programming

By the very nature of design patterns, a good deal of this book is based on the concepts and practices of Object Oriented Programming (OOP).

If you're not familiar with OOP, there are many resources—books, web sites, magazines, and classes—to help you learn more about it. Much of the OOP materials extol the benefits of *code reuse, robustness, encapsulation, polymorphism,* and *extensibility,* each of which is important and valuable. However, I believe the main benefit of OOP is how it encourages you to distill the problem at hand into manageable pieces. Designed and implemented in focused, small pieces, your code can be tested more thoroughly and is easier to understand and maintain.

Assumed Reader Skill Set

This book assumes that you're already fluent with PHP. In particular, it presupposes that you have a working knowledge of PHP and its syntax and understand the fundamentals of PHP's implementation of OOP. This book isn't intended to be an introduction to PHP programming, nor to OOP in PHP.

Because not all practitioners of OOP use the same terminology, where new terminology is introduced, it's defined in the text or in a sidebar.

PHP4 and PHP5

As I write this book, PHP5 has been released for some time but has yet to be widely adopted in the hosting community. In my own job, I've started to migrate new development of applications to PHP 5.0.3 and am very pleased so far with both its backwards compatibility with PHP4 code and its new object model, which is one of the significant new features of PHP5 and the main driver for my adoption.

There are many fine articles and tutorials dealing with the nuances of the change in the object model between PHP versions, but the short story is that PHP5 offers:

- Object handles (explained below, and further in Chapter 2: The Value Object Pattern)
- Better constructors (uniform name, changing $this not allowed)

- Destructors now exist
- Visibility (public, protected, private for methods and attributes)
- Exceptions (an alternative to triggering errors using the new `try{}` `catch{}` syntax)
- Class constants (defines using the class for a name space)
- Reflection (dynamic examination of classes, methods and arguments)
- Type hinting (specifying expected classes or interfaces for method arguments)

PHP5 also offers a few more obscure features:

- New magic methods (`__get()` and `__set()` allow you to control attribute access; `__call()` lets you dynamically intercept all method calls to the object; `__sleep()` and `__wakeup()` let you override serialization behavior; and `__toString()` lets you control how an object represents itself when cast as a string)
- Autoloading (allows the end user to try to automatically load the class the first time a reference to it is made)
- Final (do not allow a method or a class to be overridden by subclasses)

Object Handles

The best news in PHP5 is all objects are now defined by *handles,* similar to a system resource like a file or a database handle. *Passing an object to a PHP function no longer implicitly makes a copy of the object.*

To see the difference, consider the following two examples:

```
// PHP4 class
class ExampleP1 {
  var $foo;
  function setFoo($foo) {
    $this->foo = $foo`;
  }
  function getFoo() {
    return $this->foo;
  }
}
function changeExample($param) {
  $param->setFoo('blah');
  return $param->getFoo();
}
$obj = new ExampleP1;
$obj->setFoo('bar');
echo $obj->getFoo();  // bar
echo ChangeExample($obj);  //blah
echo $obj->getFoo();  // bar
```

In PHP4, the variable $param in changeExample() contains a *copy* of $obj. So, the function doesn't alter the value of $foo in the original object and the final $obj->getFoo() prints "bar."

In PHP5, because $obj is passed as a handle, the same changeExample() function does effect the original object. In other words, using handles, a copy isn't made and $param is the instance $obj.

```
// PHP5 class
class ExampleP2 {
  protected $foo;
  function setFoo($foo) {
    $this->foo = $foo;
  }
  function getFoo() {
    return $this->foo;
  }
}
$obj = new ExampleP2;
$obj->setFoo('bar');
echo $obj->getFoo();   // bar
echo ChangeExample($obj);   //blah
echo $obj->getFoo();   // IMPORTANT, produces blah
```

This issue becomes even more complicated when you pass the $this variable to other objects or functions inside of the object constructor.

What this boils down to is that in PHP4 you need to (nearly) always:

• Create an object by reference, as in $obj =& new Class;
• Pass an object by reference, like function funct(&$obj_param) {}
• Catch an object by reference function &some_funct() {} $returned_obj =& some_funct()

Now, there are some cases where you actually want to have a copy of the original object. In my PHP4 code, I *always* comment any non-reference assignment of an object as an intentional copy. In the long run, such a brief comment can save you or anyone else maintaining your code a great deal of headaches. Reference passing, object handles, and object copies are explored in greater detail in Chapter 2, "The Value Object Pattern."

Despite my personal preference to move towards PHP5 development, my feeling is that PHP4 will continue to be with us for quite some time and existing public projects should continue to support it. To that end, this book tries to provide equal footing to both versions of PHP. Whenever possible, both PHP4 and PHP5 versions of example code are provided and explained. Within each chapter, each code block that changes from one version of PHP to another has a comment of // PHP4 or

`// PHP5` to indicate the change. Subsequent blocks of code are in the same version of PHP, until the next switch is indicated.

Additional Resources and References

There are a number of great references available to help you learn more about design patterns. The "bible" of design patterns is *Design Patterns: Elements of Reusable Object-Oriented Software* by Erich Gamma, Richard Helm, Ralph Johnson and John Vlissides (his seminal work is often referred to as the "Gang of Four" or simply "GoF," in reference to the four authors). Throughout this book, the GoF names of patterns are used as the canonical source.

Following "Design Patterns," the next most useful book on design patterns for PHP web application developers is *Patterns of Enterprise Application Architecture* by Martin Fowler. Fowler's book details many patterns that are of use specifically in the task of developing web application, in contrast with the broader coverage of general patterns in GoF.

The Web offers many good resources for information on design patterns. One particular standout is the *Portland Pattern Repository* at `http://c2.com/ppr/`.

A good site for reference patterns implemented in PHP is *::phpPatterns()*, located online at `http://www.phppatterns.com/`.

Acknowledgments

I would like to thank my employer, where my role and responsibilities allow me to spend a portion of my time in this area I love, providing me with the knowledge and experience to have the confidence to write this book.

Another source of inspiration, ideas, and experience is the SitePoint (`http://www.sitepoint.com/`) forums. In particular, the regular contributors to the "Advanced PHP Forum" have a great wealth of experience and knowledge, which they regularly share in one of the most generous and helpful communities I've found on the Internet. It was through this resource I located SimpleTest (`http://simpletest.sf.net/`), WACT (`http://wact.sf.net/`) and numerous other PHP projects that I've found invaluable. I hope SitePoint continues to be a great resource for PHP developers for many years to come.

This book clearly could not have come into existence without the significant efforts and dedication of the PHP team, who developed a useful, easy to learn, and versatile language that's very well-suited to the ecological niche of web applications.

Finally, I'd like to thank Marco Tabini and the staff of php|architect. The magazine has been a source of many varied PHP topics, presented by professional developers with extensive knowledge to share. The conferences organized by Marco and company have been great as well.

1
Programming Practices

L EARNING A NEW TECHNIQUE means adopting new practices. This chapter introduces, or perhaps reinforces, several practices that you'll likely find very useful as you implement design patterns in your code.

Many of the practices summarized here are worthy of an individual chapter, even an entire book. You should consider this chapter an introduction to pattern-related practices with a PHP spin and look at the references listed throughout to investigate a topic further.

Testing Your Code

Probably no other coding practice is as important as *testing your code*. With good testing comes great freedom.

At first, that "motto" might strike you as counter-intuitive. If anything, you might assert, testing seems an *impediment* to freedom. To the contrary: if you can run tests that completely exercise your software's public interface, you can change the internals of your implementation without changing (or worse, breaking) existing applications. Testing validates the veracity and accuracy of your published interface, letting you readily change the inner workings of your code with complete confidence that it remains accurate and bug-free — that you've not introduced new bugs or reintroduced old bugs.

Before talking more about the benefits of testing, let's look at an example. All of the tests in this book use the SimpleTest PHP testing framework, available at http://simpletest.org/.

Consider this code:

```php
<?php
// PHP4
// the subject code
define('TAX_RATE', 0.07);
function calculate_sales_tax($amount) {
  round($amount * TAX_RATE,2);
}

// include test library
require_once 'simpletest/unit_tester.php';require_once 'simpletest/reporter.php';

// the test
class TestingTestCase extends UnitTestCase {
  function TestingTestCase($name='') {
    $this->UnitTestCase($name);
  }

  function TestSalesTax() {
    $this->assertEqual(7, calculate_sales_tax(100));
  }
}

// run the test
$test = new TestingTestCase('Testing Unit Test');
$test->run(new HtmlReporter());
```

The code defines a constant, TAX_RATE, and defines a function that calculates the amount of sales tax owed. Next, the code includes the required SimpleTest components: the unit tester itself and a "reporter" module that displays the results of the test.

The test itself, TestingTestCase, is a class that extends SimpleTest's UnitTestCase class. By extending UnitTestCase, all of the methods (except the constructor) within TestingTestCase that begin with the word Test are used as test cases — code that creates conditions to exercise your code and makes assertions about the results.

TestingTestCase defines one test, TestSalesTax(), which contains an assertEqual() assertion. This assertion passes if its first two arguments are equal and fails otherwise. (If you'd like to display an informative message if assertEqual() fails, pass a third argument, as in $this->assertEqual(7, calculate_sales_tax(100), "The sales tax calculation failed")).

The last two lines in the code create an instance of the test case and run it with an `HtmlReporter`. You can run this test case simply by browsing to its web page.

Running the test shows the test name, the details of any assertions that failed, and a summary "bar". (A green bar indicates success (all assertions passed), while a red bar indicates failure (at least one assertion did not pass).

The code above has an (intentional) error, so running it yields a failure such as this:

Testing Unit Test

Fail: TestSalesTax -> Equal expectation fails because [Integer: 7] differs from [NULL] by 7 at line [20]

1/1 test cases complete: **0** passes, **1** fails and **0** exceptions.

What went wrong in `calculate_sales_tax()`, a simple, one-line function? You may have noticed that the function doesn't return a result. Here's the corrected function:

```
function calculate_sales_tax($amount) {
   return round($amount * TAX_RATE,2);
}
```

Rerunning the test with the corrected code passes. "If the bar is green, the code is clean."

Testing Unit Test

1/1 test cases complete: **1** passes, **0** fails and **0** exceptions.

But a single test does not guarantee that the code is robust. For example, if you rewrote `calculate_sales_tax()` as `function calculate_sales_tax($amount) { return 7; }`, the test would pass, but would be correct only for the single dollar amount of 100. You can add additional `Test` methods to test other static values...

```
function TestSomeMoreSalesTax() {
  $this->assertEqual(3.5, calculate_sales_tax(50));
}
```

... or change `TestSalesTax()` to validate the results of a second (and third, and so on) value:

```
function TestSalesTax() {
  $this->assertEqual(7, calculate_sales_tax(100));
  $this->assertEqual(3.5, calculate_sales_tax(50));
}
```

Better yet, you might add another test that chooses values at random to give you more confidence in your code:

```
function TestRandomValuesSalesTax() {
  $amount = rand(500,1000);
  $this->assertTrue(defined('TAX_RATE'));
  $tax = round($amount*TAX_RATE*100)/100;
  $this->assertEqual($tax, calculate_sales_tax($amount));
}
```

`TestRandomValuesSalesTax()` introduces `assertTrue()`, which passes if the first parameter evaluates to the boolean value true. (Like the `assertEqual()` assertion, `assertTrue()` also takes an optional, additional argument to present an informative failure message.) So, `TestRandomValuesSalesTax()` asserts that the constant TAX_RATE has been defined and then uses that constant to calculate what the tax *should be* on the randomly selected amount.

   `TestRandomValuesSalesTax()` has a problem, though: it depends greatly on significant details from the actual implementation of the `calculate_sales_tax()` function, probably more than what's ideal for testing. Tests should be insensitive to the specifics of an implementation. Perhaps a better test might just be to establish a reasonable boundary and test for it. The following test assumes and asserts that sales tax rate will never be more than 20%:

```
function TestRandomValuesSalesTax() {
  $amount = rand(500,1000);
```

```
$this->assertTrue(calculate_sales_tax($amount)<$amount*0.20);
}
```

Making sure your code works is the primary benefit of testing, but there are additional, secondary benefits that you can realize by thoroughly testing your code:

- Testing forces you to write code that is easily testable. This leads to looser coupling, flexible designs, and good modularity.
- Writing tests forces you to explicitly clarify your expectations of how your code is to behave, distilling your design into sharper focus from the beginning. Writing tests forces you to consider the universe of possible inputs and the corresponding results.
- Tests are a very explicit way of communicating the intent of your code. In other words, test cases act as examples and documentation, showing exactly how a given class, method, or function should behave. In this book, I sometimes demonstrate the desired effect of code via a test case. By reading a test method's assertions, you can see how the code is intended to operate. A test case defines how code works in a non-ambiguous way.

Finally, if your *test suite*—your set of test cases—is very thorough, you can say your code is complete when all of your tests pass. Interestingly, that notion is one of the hallmarks of *Test Driven Development*.

Test Driven Development (TDD), also referred to as *Test First Coding*, is a methodology that takes testing one step further: you write your tests *before* you ever write any code. A nice, brief summary of the tenants of TDD is available at http://xprogramming.com/xpmag/testFirstGuidelines.htm, and a good introductory book on the strategy is "Test Driven Development: By Example" by Kent Beck. (The book's examples are in Java, but it's a quick read and gives you a very good overview and introduction to the subject.)

Agile Development

Recently, unit testing — in particular Test Driven Development — has been associated with agile development methodologies such as Extreme Programming (XP) that focus on rapid iterations of releasing functional code to customers and welcoming changing customer requirements as a natural part of the development process. Some good online resources for learning about agile development include:

- http://en.wikipedia.org/wiki/Agile_software_development
- http://agilemanifesto.org/
- http://www.extremeprogramming.org/

I hope you get infected after this discussion—"Test infected!" (This term, coined by Erich Gamma, is detailed in the article at http://junit.sourceforge.net/doc/testinfected/testing.htm.) As Gamma writes, you may feel that testing is cumbersome at first, but after you begin to build an extensive test suite for your software, you'll begin to have more confidence in all of your code.

Refactoring

Even the most thoughtful and skilled programmer cannot anticipate every nuance and subtlety of a software project. Problems crop up unexpectedly, requirements can and do change, and as a result, code is refined, shared, and obsoleted.

Refactoring is the practice of examining all of your code, looking for commonalities and similarities that can be unified and simplified to make the code easier to maintain and extend. Refactoring also includes recognizing when a design pattern can be applied to a problem—again to make solutions simpler.

Refactoring can be a simple as renaming an attribute or method, or can be as complex as collapsing an existing class. Changing your code to make it match one or more design patterns is another kind of refactoring—something you may do after reading this book.

Nothing explains refactoring better than an example.

Let's take two simple classes, CartLine and Cart. CartLine records the per unit price and the quantity of each item added to a shopping cart. For example, CartLine might record "four red polo shirts at $19.99 each." Cart is a container for one or more CartLine objects and performs calculations such as the total cost of all items in the cart.

Here is a simple implementation of CartLine and Cart:

```php
// PHP5
class CartLine {
  public $price = 0;
  public $qty = 0;
}

class Cart {
  protected $lines = array();
```

```
    public function addLine($line) {
      $this->lines[] = $line;
    }

    public function calcTotal() {
      $total = 0;
      // add totals for each line
      foreach($this->lines as $line) {
        $total += $line->price * $line->qty;
      }
      // add sales tax
      $total *= 1.07;
      return $total;
    }
  }
```

The first step in refactoring is to have adequate test coverage for your code. That ensures that your modified code does not produce different results from your original code. By the way, unless you change a requirement (the intended result of your code) or find a bug in a test case, your tests should not change.

Here is a sample test for CartLine and Cart, which won't change during refactoring:

```
function TestCart() {
    $line1 = new CartLine;
    $line1->price = 12; $line1->qty = 2;
    $line2 = new CartLine;
    $line2->price = 7.5; $line2->qty = 3;
    $line3 = new CartLine;
    $line3->price = 8.25; $line3->qty = 1;

    $cart = new Cart;
    $cart->addLine($line1);
    $cart->addLine($line2);
    $cart->addLine($line3);

    $this->assertEqual(
      (12*2 + 7.5*3 + 8.25) * 1.07,
      $cart->calcTotal());
  }
```

Looking at the code for CartLine and Cart, there are several "code smells"—curious looking and seemingly problematic code—that are likely candidates for refactoring. (Point your nose at http://c2.com/cgi/wiki?CodeSmell for more telltale code smells.) Two immediate candidates for refactoring are the comments and calculations related to line totals and sales tax. One form of refactoring, *Extract Method,* would pull these uglier pieces of code out of the flow of Cart::calcTotal()

and replace them with appropriately named methods that make the overall flow clearer.

For example, you might add two calculation methods, `lineTotal()` and `calcSalesTax()`:

```
protected function lineTotal($line) {
   return $line->price * $line->qty;
}

protected function calcSalesTax($amount) {
   return $amount * 0.07;
}
```

Now, you can rewrite `calcTotal()` as:

```
public function calcTotal() {
   $total = 0;
   foreach($this->lines as $line) {
      $total += $this->lineTotal($line);
   }
   $total += $this->calcSalesTax($total);
   return $total;
}
```

Since the changes made so far are significant (at least in the context of this example), it's beneficial to pause and run the test again to verify that the results are still correct. Remember, a green bar indicates success!

However, there are still some nagging doubts about the current code. One is the access of public properties in the new `lineTotal()` method. It's clear that the responsibility for calculating the line total doesn't belong in the `Cart` class, but should be in `CartLine` instead.

Refactoring again, add a `total()` method to `CartLine` to calculate the extended price of an item in the order ...

```
public function total() {
   return $this->price * $this->qty;
}
```

... then remove `lineTotal()` method from `Cart`, and change the `calcTotal()` method to use the new

`CartLine::total()` method. Then run the test again, looking for the green bar.

The newly refactored code is thus:

```php
class CartLine {
  public $price = 0;
  public $qty = 0;

  public function total() {
    return $this->price * $this->qty;
  }
}

class Cart {
  protected $lines = array();

  public function addLine($line) {
    $this->lines[] = $line;
  }

  public function calcTotal() {
    $total = 0;
    foreach($this->lines as $line) {
      $total += $line->total();
    }
    $total += $this->calcSalesTax($total);
    return $total;
  }

  protected function calcSalesTax($amount) {
    return $amount * 0.07;
  }
}
```

Now the code no longer requires inline comments, because the code itself documents what is happening much better. The new methods better encapsulate the calculation, allowing more flexibility in the future if the calculation must change (say, to consider different sales tax rates). In addition, the classes are now more balanced, maintaining code in better alignment with each classes role.

This example is obviously trivial, but hopefully you can extrapolate and envision what this can do for your own code.

When coding, you should be in one of two modes: adding features or refactoring. When adding features, write tests and add code. When refactoring, change only existing code, making sure all that all relevant tests still run correctly.

The primary reference on refactoring is *Refactoring: Improving the Design of Existing Code* by Martin Fowler. To be so bold as to summarize Fowler's book in a few bullet points, the steps in refactoring are:

- Identify the code in need of refactoring.
- Have test coverage for the code.
- Work in small steps.
- Run your tests after each step. Code and test in quick iterations — which is much easier in an interpreted language like PHP as compared with compiled languages.
- Use refactoring to make your more readable and to improve performance.

Other Practices

There are several other practices that are worthy of mention and valuable to incorporate into your own coding habits.

UML

The *Unified Modeling Language* (UML, a synthesis of the notations of Booch, Rumbaugh, and Jacobson) is a programming language- and vendor-independent notation for describing object oriented programming concepts. General information on UML can be found at http://www.uml.org/.

There are many aspects to UML, but the two most relevant for PHP developers are the *class diagram* and the *sequence diagram*.

The class diagram describes one or more classes and how the classes relate to each other in your program. Each class is represented by a box with up to three divisions: the first division is the name of the class; the second division enumerates the classes attributes (variables); and the last division lists the class's methods. The visibility of attributes and methods are designated with + for public, — for private, and # for protected.

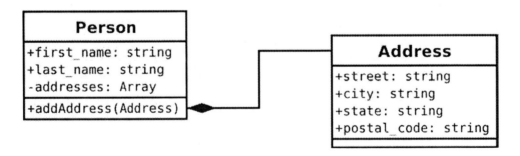

The sequence diagram illustrates the typical interaction of objects in the code for a particular task or event. A sequence diagram conveys when different methods are called, by whom, and in what order (hence the name, "sequence diagram"), and are incredibly useful instruments to communicate interactions between sets of objects to other developers.

In my own work, I typically use both kinds of diagrams to sketch out designs, but rarely formalize them into project documentation. Often, the relationships between objects change as your knowledge of the system evolves and as user requirements change, and the diagrams can age quickly. That being said, "A picture is worth a thousand words." These diagrams can be very useful in communicating the design of a system to new developers and can serve as documentation for developers that use your software.

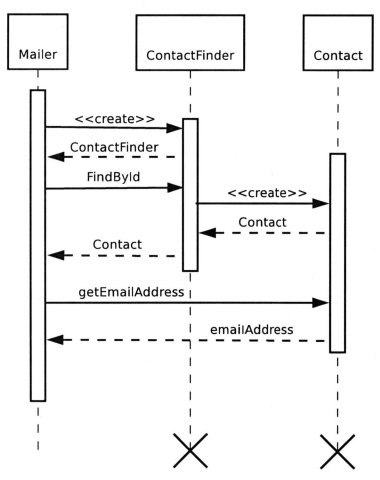

Source Control

"Save code early and often" is another valuable developer mantra. Even if you're the sole developer on a project, you should maintain everything under source control.

While there are many source control solutions available, two are standouts: *CVS* (https://www.cvshome.org/) and *Subversion* (http://subversion.tigris.org/). CVS is a very popular solution, used by both the PHP and Apache projects. Meanwhile, Subversion is rapidly becoming a popular alternative, because the project's design has overcome several of CVS's shortcomings (particularly in the areas of atomic commits and moving/renaming directories and files). However, fewer projects run Subversion servers.

I have adopted use of CVS for projects at work, and the chapters and code in this book were maintained in a Subversion repository.

Source Code Documentation

If you flip through the pages of this book, you may notice some distinctly formatted comment blocks similar to:

```
/**
 * funny multi-line comments
 * @something what is this?
 */
```

These are *docblocks* and are used by programs like *phpDocumentor* (http://phpdocu.sf.net/) to automatically generate application programming interface (API) documentation for your PHP projects.

Docblocks are specifically formatted multi-line comments that start with /**, continue on each subsequent line with a leading *, and are terminated by */, with white space allowed before each prefix (which allows docblocks to be indented at the same level as your code).

The @something represents a "tag," which clarifies information when the documentation is converted to the parsed format. An example of a tag is @private, which was used in PHP4 to mark a method or attribute of a class as private, since the language did not provide that capability natively (all functions and variables are public in PHP4).

Source code documentation such as docblocks serve both as a useful reference and as an advertisement for open source projects. One example (that I help to maintain) is the SimpleTest API documentation at http://simpletest.org/.

2

The Value Object Pattern

In all but the simplest applications, most objects have an "identity." An important business object, such as a `Customer` or a `SKU`, will have one or more attributes—an ID, or a name and an email address, say—that differentiate it from other instances of the same class. Moreover, an object with an identity "persists": it's a singularity that exists across the entire application. To you, the programmer, "Customer A" is "Customer A" everywhere, and changes to "Customer A" endure for as long as your application is running.

But an object need not have an identity. Some objects merely describe the characteristics of other objects.

For example, it's common to use an object to represent a date, a number, or money. A `Date`, `Integer`, or `Dollar` class is a handy—and inexpensive—encapsulation, easily copied, compared, or created when needed.

At first blush, small descriptive objects may seem a cinch to implement: they're just (tiny or small) classes, no different in structure than a `Customer` or `SKU`. That's almost right, but "almost right" leads to bugs.

Consider the following implementation of a dollar that's almost right (the class is named BadDollar because it's not an ideal implementation). See if you can find the bug.

```php
// PHP5
class BadDollar {
  protected $amount;
  public function __construct($amount=0) {
    $this->amount = (float)$amount;
  }
  public function getAmount() {
    return $this->amount;
  }
  public function add($dollar) {
    $this->amount += $dollar->getAmount();
  }
}
```

```php
class Work {
  protected $salary;

  public function __construct() {
    $this->salary = new BadDollar(200);
  }

  public function payDay() {
    return $this->salary;
  }
}

class Person {
  public $wallet;
}
```

```php
function testBadDollarWorking() {
  $job = new Work;
  $p1 = new Person;
  $p2 = new Person;

  $p1->wallet = $job->payDay();
  $this->assertEqual(200, $p1->wallet->getAmount());
  $p2->wallet = $job->payDay();
  $this->assertEqual(200, $p2->wallet->getAmount());

  $p1->wallet->add($job->payDay());
```

```
        $this->assertEqual(400, $p1->wallet->getAmount());

        //this is bad - actually 400
        $this->assertEqual(200, $p2->wallet->getAmount());

        //this is really bad - actually 400
        $this->assertEqual(200, $job->payDay()->getAmount());
    }
```

So, what's the bug? If the test case didn't make the problem apparent, here's a hint: employees $p1 and $p2 share the same BadDollar.

First, instances of Work and Person are created. Then, assuming that each person initially has an empty wallet, Person::wallet is set to the BadDollar object returned by Work::payDay().

Remember your "friend" the PHP 5 object handle? Because of it, $job::salary, $p1::wallet, and $p2::wallet, three *conceptually different* objects with different "identities," actually all *refer to the same object.*

So, the second pay day, $job->payDay(), which was intended just to fatten the wallet of $p1, inadvertently pays $p2 again and changes the base $salary of $job. Hence, the last two assertions fail:

```
Value Object PHP5 Unit Test
1) Equal expectation fails because [Integer: 200] differs from [Float: 400] by 200
        in testBadDollarWorking
        in ValueObjTestCase
2) Equal expectation fails because [Integer: 200] differs from [Float: 400] by 200
        in testBadDollarWorking
        in ValueObjTestCase
FAILURES!!!
```

The Problem

So, how do you implement a *lightweight,* or easy to construct, descriptive object like Date or Dollar?

The Solution

Lightweight objects should behave like PHP integers: if you assign the same object to two different variables and then change one of the variables, the other variable should remain unaffected. And indeed, this is the goal of the *Value Object* pattern.

Implementing *Value Object* differs between PHP 4 and PHP 5.

As you saw above, PHP 5's (new) method of referring to objects via a handle—a paradigm we typically try to emulate with references in PHP 4—is an issue. To solve that problem and implement a proper `Dollar` *Value Object*, make the $amount attribute—and, in the general case, all attributes of a *Value Object—immutable,* or unchangeable. While PHP does not provide immutability as a facility of the language, you can combine attribute visibility and getter and setter methods to simulate it adequately.

In contrast, PHP4 (almost) treats all objects like *Value Objects,* because the PHP4 assignment operator = makes a copy of the object if you omit the reference operator &. To implement *Value Objects* in PHP 4, simply break your carefully-cultivated habit of always creating, passing and catching objects by reference.

Terminology - Immutable

The dictionary definition of immutable is "not capable of or susceptible to change". In programming, the term denotes a value that does not change once it's been set.

PHP 5 Sample Code

Since we started with PHP 5 code, let's flesh out a PHP 5 Value Object implementation and build a better `Dollar` class. Naming is very important in OOP: selecting a single currency type as the name of this class explicitly declares that it doesn't handle multiple forms of currency.

```php
class Dollar {
  protected $amount;

  public function __construct($amount=0) {
    $this->amount = (float)$amount;
  }

  public function getAmount() {
    return $this->amount;
  }

  public function add($dollar) {
    return new Dollar($this->amount + $dollar->getAmount());
  }
}
```

Using `protected $amount` so the attribute `Dollar::amount` is not accessible from outside of the class itself is the first step towards making `Dollar::amount` immutable. `protected` (and `private`) denies direct access to the attribute.

Normally, when you use this OOP idiom, you create a "setter" function like `public setAmount($amount) { $this->amount = $amount; }`. In this case, no setter function has been defined since `Dollar::amount` is set during the instantiation of the object. `Dollar::getAmount()` is an accessor method, giving public access to the `Dollar` objects amount as a `float`.

The most interesting change is in the `Dollar::add()` method. Instead of changing the value of `$this->amount`, thereby altering the state of the existing `Dollar` instance, the method creates and returns a *new* instance of `Dollar`. Now, even if you assign this object to multiple variables, each is insulated from changes made to any other.

Immutability is key to the *Value Object* pattern. Any change to the amount of a *Value Object* is accomplished by creating a new instance of the class with the different desired value. Above, `$this->amount` never changes.

To review briefly, the fundamentals of the ValueObject pattern in PHP 5 are:

1. Protect the attributes of a *Value Object* so direct access is forbidden.
2. Set the object's attributes in the constructor.
3. Provide no "setter" functions, which otherwise allow attributes to be altered.

These three steps create an immutable value—one that can not change after it's initially set. Of course, you should also provide "getters," or methods to access a *Value Object's* attributes and provide any functions that are germane to the class. A *Value Object* need not be a simple structure, either; it can hold important business logic as well. Let's look at that next.

In Context Example

Let's explore the *Value Object* pattern in the context of a larger example. Let's begin an implementation of a game of Monopoly, building upon the PHP 5 `Dollar` class created above.

The first class is `Monopoly`, a frame to build on:

```php
class Monopoly {
  protected $go_amount;
  /**
   * game constructor
   * @return void
   */
  public function __construct() {
    $this->go_amount = new Dollar(200);
  }
  /**
   * pay a player for passing "Go"
   * @param  Player $player  the player to pay
```

```
   * @return void
   */
  public function passGo($player) {
    $player->collect($this->go_amount);
  }
}
```

So far, the Monopoly class is very minimal. The constructor creates $go_amount, an instance of the Dollar Value Object class, set to $200. $go_amount is used by passGo(), which takes a Player as an argument and tells the Player to collect() $200.

Player should be next. The Monopoly class calls a Player::collect() method with one argument, a Dollar, to add that Dollar amount to the player's cash balance. In addition to that method, let's add the method Player::getBalance() to access a player's cash reserve current to validate that the Player and Monopoly objects are working,

```
class Player {
  protected $name;
  protected $savings;
  /**
   * constructor
   * set name and initial balance
   * @param  string $name the players name
   * @return void
   */
  public function __construct($name) {
    $this->name = $name;
    $this->savings = new Dollar(1500);
  }
  /**
   * receive a payment
   * @param  Dollar $amount the amount received
   * @return void
   */
  public function collect($amount) {
    $this->savings = $this->savings->add($amount);
  }

   * return player balance
   * @return  float
   */
  public function getBalance() {
    return $this->savings->getAmount();
  }
}
```

Given `Monopoly` and `Player`, you can now write a test case for what's been implemented so far. `MonopolyTestCase` might look like:

```
class MonopolyTestCase extends UnitTestCase {
  function TestGame() {
    $game = new Monopoly;
    $player1 = new Player('Jason');
    $this->assertEqual(1500, $player1->getBalance());
    $game->passGo($player1);
    $this->assertEqual(1700, $player1->getBalance());
    $game->passGo($player1);
    $this->assertEqual(1900, $player1->getBalance());
  }
}
```

If you run `MonopolyTestCase`, you should get a green bar. Time to continue adding features.

Another important concept in Monopoly is paying rent. Let's write a test case first (a la Test Driven Development) to set the goals for the next round of coding:

```
function TestRent() {
    $game = new Monopoly;
    $player1 = new Player('Madeline');
    $player2 = new Player('Caleb');
    $this->assertEqual(1500, $player1->getBalance());
    $this->assertEqual(1500, $player2->getBalance());

    $game->payRent($player1, $player2, new Dollar(26));
    $this->assertEqual(1474, $player1->getBalance());
    $this->assertEqual(1526, $player2->getBalance());
}
```

Looking at the test, the `payRent()` method needs to be added to the `Monopoly` class to allow one player to pay rent to another.

```
Class Monopoly {
  // ...
  /**
    * pay rent from one player to another
    * @param Player $from the player paying rent
    * @param Player $to   the player collecting rent
    * @param Dollar $rent the amount of the rent
```

```
    * @return void
    */
   public function payRent($from, $to, $rent) {
     $to->collect($from->pay($rent));
   }
 }
```

payRent() effectuates the transaction between two players, $from and $to. Player::collect() already exists, but the Player::pay() method must be added to let $from pay() a Dollar amount to $to. Player::pay() might look like:

```
class Player {
   // ...
   public function pay($amount) {
     $this->savings = $this->savings->add(-1 * $amount);
   }
 }
```

Unfortunately, you can't multiply an object by a number in PHP (unlike some programming languages, PHP does not allow for the overloading of operators, which might allow for a construct like this). Instead, add a debit() method to Dollar to perform subtraction.

```
class Dollar {
   protected $amount;
   public function __construct($amount=0) {
     $this->amount = (float)$amount;
   }
   public function getAmount() {
     return $this->amount;
   }
   public function add($dollar) {
     return new Dollar($this->amount + $dollar->getAmount());
   }
   public function debit($dollar) {
     return new Dollar($this->amount - $dollar->getAmount());
   }
 }
```

Given Dollar::debit(), Player::pay() remains simple:

```
class Player {
  // ...
  /**
   * make a payment
   * @param  Dollar $amount the amount to pay
   * @return Dollar the amount payed
   */
  public function pay($amount) {
    $this->savings = $this->savings->debit($amount);
    return $amount;
  }
}
```

`Player::pay()` returns the `$amount` paid so the statement in `Monopoly::payRent()` of `$to->collect($from->pay($rent))` works properly. This can help in the future if you refine the "business logic" to not allow a payment greater than the player's balance. (Such a circumstance would then return the players balance and perhaps raise a "BankruptException" to calculate a modified payment instead of the full amount. The `$to` player would still want to collect as much as possible from player `$from`.)

Terminology — Business Logic

Mentioning "business logic" in the context of modeling a board game may seem odd. The business here does not refer to companies engaged in the act of commerce, but rather to the concept of application-specific requirements in the domain the application is addressing. Think of the definition of business as "an immediate task or objective," as in "What is your business here?",

Of course, given the problem domain for Monopoly, perhaps the connotations of "business logic" apply just the same.

PHP 4 Sample Code

Unlike PHP 5, PHP 4's copy-by-value object semantics work naturally with the *Value Object* pattern. However, because PHP 4 does not support property or method visibility, implementing a Value Object in PHP 4 has its nuances as well.

If you recall, the "Object Handles" section of the Preface of this book presented three "rules" to "nearly always" apply when working with objects in PHP 4 to simulate PHP 5's object handles:

1. Create objects by reference (`$obj =& new Class;`)
2. Pass objects by reference (`function funct(&$obj_param) {}`)

3. Catch by reference (`function &some_funct() {} $returned_obj =& some_funct()`)

The *Value Object* pattern is one significant exception to the "nearly always" part of these rules. Just ignore the rules and you'll always get a copy of the PHP 4 object (the equivalent of the PHP5 "clone" operation, described at http://www.php.net/manual/en/language.oop5.cloning.php.

While PHP 4 makes object copying a breeze—its an inherent behavior in the language—immutability can only be realized by convention. To create *Value Objects* in PHP 4, never create or catch *Value Objects* by reference, and prefix all "private" property or method names prefixed with an underscore (_). By convention then, variables that hold *Value Object* attributes should be with an underscore to indicate it's private.

Here is the `Dollar` class in PHP 4:

```
// PHP4
class Dollar {
  var $_amount;
  function Dollar($amount=0) {
    $this->_amount = (float)$amount;
  }
  function getAmount() {
    return $this->_amount;
  }
  function add($dollar) {
    return new Dollar($this->_amount + $dollar->getAmount());
  }
  function debit($dollar) {
    return new Dollar($this->_amount - $dollar->getAmount());
  }
}
```

And here is a test case that demonstrates you can not make an immutable property in PHP4:

```
function TestChangeAmount() {
  $d = new Dollar(5);
  $this->assertEqual(5, $d->getAmount());
  //only possible in php4 by not respecting the _private convention
  $d->_amount = 10;
  $this->assertEqual(10, $d->getAmount());
}
```

Again, in all PHP 4 objects, prefix private variables with an underscore, and do access such private properties and methods directly.

Business Logic in ValueObjects

Value Objects need not be restricted to be simple structures of data with minimal accessor methods; they can contain valuable business logic as well. Consider the case where you want to divide money equally among a number of people.

If the amount is divisible exactly, you might return an array of `Dollar` objects, with each containing one of the equal portions. But what happens when the amount to be divided does not divide equally into round numbers of dollars and cents?

Let's start coding with a few simple test cases:

```
// PHP5
function testDollarDivideReturnsArrayOfDivisorSize() {
  $full_amount = new Dollar(8);
  $parts = 4;
  $this->assertIsA(
    $result = $full_amount->divide($parts)
    ,'array');
  $this->assertEqual($parts, count($result));
}
```

(i) **assertIsA**

The **assertIsA()** assertion lets you test if a particular variable is an instance (or descendant) of a named class. You can also use this assertion to validate against PHP base types like **string**, **number**, or **array** as well.

A `Dollar::divide()` method could pass this test by being coded as...

```
public function divide($divisor) {
  return array_fill(0,$divisor,null);
}
```

... so it'd be better to add more specifics:

```
function testDollarDrivesEquallyForExactMultiple() {
  $test_amount = 1.25;
  $parts = 4;
  $dollar = new Dollar($test_amount*$parts);
  foreach($dollar->divide($parts) as $part) {
```

```
        $this->assertIsA($part, 'Dollar');
        $this->assertEqual($test_amount, $part->getAmount());
    }
}
```

Now, instead of just being the correct size array, the returned array must be populated with `Dollar` objects of the correct amount. The implementation can still be a one liner:

```
public function divide($divisor) {
    return array_fill(0,$divisor,new Dollar($this->amount / $divisor));
```

The last feature to code is the possibility of rounding errors caused by a divisor that does not divide evenly into the `Dollar` amount. That's a sticky point: does the first portion or the last portion get the extra penny if there's a rounding issue? How can that be tested independent of the implementation?

One means is to specify the end goal of the code explicitly: the size of the array should be equal to the number of parts, no part should differ more than $0.01 from any other part, and the sum of all the part's amounts should equal the value of the amount being dividing.

This expressed as a test case is:

```
function testDollarDivideImmuneToRoundingErrors() {
    $test_amount = 7;
    $parts = 3;
    $this->assertNotEqual( round($test_amount/$parts,2),
                           $test_amount/$parts,
                           'Make sure we are testing a non-trivial case %s');
    $total = new Dollar($test_amount);
    $last_amount = false;
    $sum = new Dollar(0);
    foreach($total->divide($parts) as $part) {
        if ($last_amount) {
            $difference = abs($last_amount-$part->getAmount());
            $this->assertTrue($difference <= 0.01);
        }
        $last_amount = $part->getAmount();
        $sum = $sum->add($part);
    }
    $this->assertEqual($sum->getAmount(), $test_amount);
}
```

assertNotEqual

The **assertNotEqual()** assertion fails if the first two arguments passed to it satisfy a PHP == conditional test. You can use it in test cases whenever you need to make sure two values are different.

With some test cases in hand, how does Dollar::divide() shape up?

```
class Dollar {
  protected $amount;
  public function __construct($amount=0) {
    $this->amount = (float)$amount;
  }
  public function getAmount() {
    return $this->amount;
  }
  public function add($dollar) {
    return new Dollar($this->amount + $dollar->getAmount());
  }
  public function debit($dollar) {
    return new Dollar($this->amount - $dollar->getAmount());
  }
  public function divide($divisor) {
    $ret = array();
    $alloc = round($this->amount / $divisor,2);
    $cumm_alloc = 0.0;
    foreach(range(1,$divisor-1) as $i) {
      $ret[] = new Dollar($alloc);
      $cumm_alloc += $alloc;
    }
    $ret[] = new Dollar(round($this->amount - $cumm_alloc,2));
    return $ret;
  }
}
```

This code works, but still has some issues. Consider boundary conditions like changing the beginning of testDollarDivide() to $test_amount = 0.02; $num_parts = 5;. Or consider what happens when you don't provide an integer divisor?

The methodology to solve issues like these? Use the Test Driven development cycle: add a test case, observe for failure, code to allow the new test case to pass, and refactor if needed. Repeat as necessary.

3

The Factory Pattern

I N OBJECT-ORIENTED PROGRAMMING, the most common way to create an object is with the new operator, the language construct provided to do just that. But in some cases, new can be problematic. For instance, the creation of many kind of objects requires a series of steps: you may need to compute or fetch the object's initial settings; you might have to choose which of many sub classes to instantiate; or perhaps you have to create a batch of other helper objects before you can create the object you need. In those cases, new is a "process" more than an operation—a cog in a bigger machine.

The Problem

How can you create such "complex" objects easily and conveniently—without cut-and-paste programming?

The Solution

Create a "factory"—a function or a class method— to "manufacture" new objects. To understand the value of a factgory, think about the difference between ...

```
$connection =& new MySqlConnection($user, $password, $database);
```

... spread throughout your code, and the more concise ...

```
$connection =& create_connection();
```

The latter code snippet centralizes the code to create a database connection in the create_connec-tion() "factory," and, following the analogy earlier, transforms the process of creating the database connection to a simple operation—an operation just like new. The *Factory* pattern injects "intelligence" to object creation. It encapsulates the creation of an object and returns the new object to the caller.

Need to change the structure of an object and how it's created? Just go to the object's factory and change the code *once*. (The *Factory* pattern is so useful, it's *foundational*, meaning that it appears again and again in many other complex patterns and applications.)

Sample Code

The *Factory* pattern encapsulates the creation of objects. You can create a *Factory* within the object itself or in an external *Factory* class—the exact implementation depends on the needs of your application. Let's look at an example of a *Factory*.

The application code below repeats the same code to create a database connection in multiple places:

```php
// PHP4
class Product {
    function getList() { $db =& new MysqlConnection(DB_USER, DB_PW, DB_NAME);
      //...
    }
    function getByName($name) { $db =& new MysqlConnection(DB_USER, DB_PW, DB_NAME);
      //...
    }
    //...
}
```

Why is this bad? Connection parameters are spread all over, and while I've shown the parameters as constants, implying you have a way to define them centrally and globally, the solution is obviously not optimal:

- While you can change the values of the parameters easily, you cannot add or change the order of parameters without changing (at least) two sections of code.
- You cannot easily instantiate a new class to use another kind of database connection, say a PostgresqlConnection.
- It is difficult to separately test and validate the behavior of the connection object.

The code would be much improved with the use of a *Factory*:

```
class Product {
  function getList() {

    $db =& $this->_getConnection();
    //...
  }
  function &_getConnection() {
    return new MysqlConnection(DB_USER, DB_PW, DB_NAME);
  }
}
```

The class method _getConnection() centralizes the otherwise repetitious new MysqlConnection(DB_USER, DB_PW, DB_NAME) calls found in the class's other methods.

Here's another variation of a *Factory*, this one a static call to a *Factory* class:

```
class Product {
  function getList() {
    $db =& DbConnectionBroker::getConnection();
    //...
  }
}

class DbConnectionBroker {
  function &getConnection() {
    return new MysqlConnection(DB_USER, DB_PW, DB_NAME);
  }
}
```

DbConnectionBroker::getConnection() produces the same result as the previous *Factory*, but has a distinct advantage: it replaces the repeated new `MysqlConnection(DB_USER, DB_PW, DB_NAME)` calls in every method *in every class* that uses the database.

Yet another variation is a call to a *Factory* class that's been previously associated with the object:

```
class Product {
  var $_db_maker;
  function setDbFactory(&$connection_factory) {
    $this->_db_maker =& $connection_factory;
  }
  function getList() {
    $db =& $this->_db_maker->getConnection();
    //...
  }
}
```

Lastly, a *Factory* can be implemented as a procedural function, a reasonable way to achieve global visibility for the *Factory*:

```
function &make_db_conn() {
  return new MysqlConnection(DB_USER, DB_PW, DB_NAME);
}

class Product {
  function getList() {
    $bar =& make_db_conn();
    //...
  }
}
```

Here's a UML class diagram for an idealized implementation of the *Factory*:

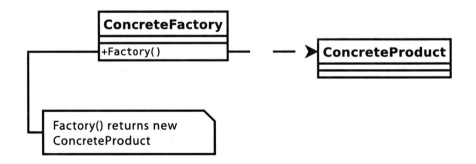

Adding a Little Color

To go into the *Factory* pattern in more detail, let's take a small segue and build a simple class that can serve as an example for the rest of the chapter. Let's build a class to output an HTML RGB color in hex. The R, G, and B values are passed in as three arguments to the constructor and a function `getRgb()` returns a string of the hex color value.

As before let's follow the Test Driven Development (TDD) methodology: write a test, write the code to satisfy the test, refactor if needed, and repeat.

Here's a very simple initial test:

```
function TestInstantiate() {
  $this->assertIsA($color = new Color, 'Color');
  $this->assertTrue(method_exists($color, 'getRgb'));
}
```

The code to satisfy this test looks just like the pseudo-code you might sketch out on a white board while designing the class:

```
class Color {
  function getRgb() {}
}
```

(This `Color` class might look like a baby step, but TDD is an iterative process. Code in very small increments when necessary—perhaps when you're initially learning a new concept or when you're struggling with a particular implementation.)

Next, the `getRgb()` method should return the hex string based on the red, green, and blue values passed when the `Color` object is created. Specify that with a test:

```
function TestGetRgbWhite() {
  $white =& new Color(255,255,255);
  $this->assertEqual('#FFFFFF', $white->getRgb());
}
```

Per TDD, you write the simplest possible code to satisfy your test, not necessarily the code that satisfies your sense of aesthetic or the code you think is the proper implementation.

The simplest implementation of the Color class that passes this test is:

```
class Color {
  function getRgb() { return '#FFFFFF'; }
}
```

This Color isn't very satisfying, but it does represent incremental progress.

Next, let's add an additional test to force the Color to save some state information inside the object for a more realistic implementation:

```
function TestGetRgbRed() {
  $red =& new Color(255,0,0);
  $this->assertEqual('#FF0000', $red->getRgb());
}
```

So what must change in Color? The constructor must take the red, green, and blue arguments and store them in instance variables. Color also requires a method to convert decimal integer numbers to hexadecimal. Some code to implement those requirements might look like:

```
class Color {
  var $r=0;
  var $g=0;
  var $b=0;

  function Color($red=0, $green=0, $blue=0)
  {
    $this->r =$red;
    $this->g = $green;
    $this->b = $blue;
  }
  function getRgb() {
    return sprintf('#%02x%02x%02x', $this->r, $this->g, $this->b);
  }
}
```

The constructor is very simple: collect the red, green, and blue values passed into the constructor and store them in instance variables. The getRgb() method uses sprintf() to convert the values to hexadecimal.

To gain still more confidence in the code, you can test it with more values. This test runs with the code as-is:

```
function TestGetRgbRandom() {
  $color =& new Color(rand(0,255), rand(0,255), rand(0,255));
  $this->assertWantedPattern(
    '/^#[0-9A-F]{6}$/',
    $color->getRgb());
  $color2 =& new Color($t = rand(0,255), $t, $t);
  $this->assertWantedPattern(
    '/^#([0-9A-F]{2})\1\1$/',
    $color2->getRgb());
}
```

assertWantedPattern

The **assertWantedPattern()** assertion tries to match its second parameter to the PCRE expression in the first parameter. If there's a match, the assertion passes; otherwise it fails.

Building on the power of regular expression matching, the **assertWantedPattern()** assertion can allow for flexible tests.

All of these tests detail how the Color class behaves under normal, expected circumstances. But every well-designed class should also account for boundary conditions. For example, what should happen if a negative number is passed into the constructor as a color value? What happens for numbers greater than 255? What happens for non-numeric data? A good test suite for Color would account for these boundary conditions in the tests.

```
function testColorBoundaries() {
  $color =& new Color(-1);
  $this->assertErrorPattern('/out.*0.*255/i');
  $color =& new Color(1111);
  $this->assertErrorPattern('/out.*0.*255/i');
}
```

assertErrorPattern

The **assertErrorPattern()** assertion allows you to specify a PCRE expression that should match a PHP error. If the error doesn't materialize or doesn't match the specified pattern, the assertion fails.

With those tests in place, Color could be further implemented as:

```php
class Color {
  var $r=0;
  var $g=0;
  var $b=0;

  function Color($red=0, $green=0, $blue=0) {
    $red = (int)$red;
    if ($red < 0 || $red > 255) {
      trigger_error("color '$color' out of bounds, "
        ."please specify a number between 0 and 255");
    }
    $this->r = $red;
    $green = (int)$green;
    if ($green < 0 || $green > 255) {
      trigger_error("color '$color' out of bounds, "
        ."please specify a number between 0 and 255");
    }
    $this->g = $green;
    $blue = (int)$blue;
    if ($blue < 0 || $blue > 255) {
      trigger_error("color '$color' out of bounds, "
        ."please specify a number between 0 and 255");
    }
    $this->b = $blue;
  }

  function getRgb() {
    return sprintf('#%02x%02x%02x', $this->r, $this->g, $this->b);
  }
}
```

This code passes the test, but the "cut-and-paste" style of the code should smell bad to you. In TDD, a rule of thumb is to code the simplest possible solution and if you need the same code *twice*—wince—but duplicate the code. However, if you need the same a *third* or more times, then refactor. So, Color is a great candidate for *Extract Method* refactoring.

Refactoring — Extract Method

When you have two or more sections of code that can be assimilated, combine the sections of code into a separate method named according to its purpose. Extract method refactoring is most powerful when the same section of code is repeated several times in one or more methods in your class.

```
class Color {
  var $r=0;
  var $g=0;
  var $b=0;
  function Color($red=0, $green=0, $blue=0) {
    $this->r = $this->validateColor($red);
    $this->g = $this->validateColor($green);
    $this->b = $this->validateColor($blue);
  }
  function validateColor($color) {
    $check = (int)$color;
    if ($check < 0 || $check > 255) {
      trigger_error("color '$color' out of bounds, "
        ."please specify a number between 0 and 255");
    } else {
      return $check;
    }
  }
  function getRgb() {
    return sprintf('#%02x%02x%02x', $this->r, $this->g, $this->b);
  }
}
```

Factories to Hide Object State Setup

Let's add a *Factory* to Color that makes creating new instances easy. Really easy. Let's add a method that creates a Color given a *name*—after all, who can remember the RGB values of his or her favorite color?

Factory objects or functions don't have to be named "Factory." Factories are pretty obvious whenever you read code. Instead, it's better to use a meaningful name that expresses how the *Factory* corresponds to the problem you're solving.

In this example code, I am going to call the Color *Factory* CrayonBox. The static method CrayonBox::getColor() takes a text string containing the name of a color and returns a Color object with the appropriate values set.

Here's the desired behavior as a test case:

```
function TestGetColor() {
  $this->assertIsA($o =& CrayonBox::getColor('red'), 'Color');
  $this->assertEqual('#FF0000', $o->getRgb());
  $this->assertIsA($o =& CrayonBox::getColor('LIME'), 'Color');
  $this->assertEqual('#00FF00', $o->getRgb());
}
```

The test case validates that each returned object is an instance of the class `Color` and that its `getRgb()` method responds with the correct string. The "red" used for the test was all lowercase, so the second case, "LIME," is passed as all uppercase to make sure the code is case-insensitive.

To be safe, let's also add an additional test to explore boundary conditions that should not work. The `TestBadColor()` method expects an invalid color name to trigger a PHP error containing the name of the bad color and expects the *Factory* to return the color black instead.

```php
function TestBadColor() {
    $this->assertIsA($o =& CrayonBox::getColor('Lemon'), 'Color');
    $this->assertErrorPattern('/lemon/i');
    // got black instead
    $this->assertEqual('#000000', $o->getRgb());
}
```

A sample implementation of a `CrayonBox` class to fulfill these tests might be:

```php
class CrayonBox {
    /**
     * Return valid colors as color name => array(red, green, blue)
     *
     * Note the array is returned from function call
     * because we want to have getColor able to be called statically
     * so we can't have instance variables to store the array
     * @return   array
     */

    function colorList() {
        return array(
            'black'   => array(0, 0, 0)
            ,'green'  => array(0, 128, 0)
            // the rest of the colors ...
            ,'aqua'   => array(0, 255, 255)
        );
    }

    /**
     * Factory method to return a Color
     * @param   string   $color_name   the name of the desired color
     * @return   Color
     */
    function &getColor($color_name) {
        $color_name = strtolower($color_name);
        if (array_key_exists($color_name,
                $colors = CrayonBox::colorList())) {
            $color = $colors[$color_name];
            return new Color($color[0], $color[1], $color[2]);
        }
        trigger_error("No color '$color_name' available");
```

```
        // default to black
        return new Color;
    }
}
```

This is obviously a very simple factory, but it does simplify object creation (using text names for colors rather than RGB values) and shows how the internal state of an object can be established at the time the object is created but before the client code calling the factory receives the new object.

Factories to Promote Polymorphism

Controlling the internal state of returned objects is important, but promoting *polymorphism*— returning objects of varying classes with the same interface—is an even more powerful capability of the *Factory* pattern.

Let's revisit the Monopoly example and implement the game's real estate properties. In the game, you get a deed when you purchase a property; the deed contains a number of basic facts about the property that are used throughout game play. Further, there are three different types of properties: streets, railroads, and utilities. All three kinds of properties have some aspects in common: each can be owned by a player; each has a price; and each generates rent for its owner whenever other players land on it. But some aspects of each kind of real estate are very different. For example, the formula for calculating rent depends on the type of property.

The following code can act as a base real estate property class:

```
// PHP5
abstract class Property {
  protected $name;
  protected $price;
  protected $game;

  function __construct($game, $name, $price) {
    $this->game = $game;
    $this->name = $name;
    $this->price = new Dollar($price);
  }

  abstract protected function calcRent();

  public function purchase($player) {
    $player->pay($this->price);
    $this->owner = $player;
  }

  public function rent($player) {
    if ($this->owner
      && $this->owner != $player) {
      $this->owner->collect(
```

```
            $player($this->calcRent())
            );
        }
    }
}
```

Here, the *Property* class and the method `CalcRent()` are declared *abstract*.

Terminology — Abstract Class

An abstract class is a class that cannot be instantiated directly. An abstract class contains one or more abstract methods that must be overridden in a subclass. Once all of the abstract methods have been realized by actual methods, the subclass can be instantiated.

Abstract classes make good prototypes for families of similar classes.

`calcRent()` must be overridden in a subclass to make a concrete class. Hence, each subclass of `Property`, `Street`, `Utility`, and `Railroad`, must define a `calcRent()` method.

An implementation of those latter three (sub)classes might be:

```
class Street extends Property {
    protected $base_rent;
    public $color;
    public function setRent($rent) {
        $this->base_rent = new Dollar($rent);
    }

    protected function calcRent() {
        if ($this->game->hasMonopoly($this->owner, $this->color)) {
            return $this->base_rent->add($this->base_rent);
        }
        return $this->base_rent;
    }
}

class RailRoad extends Property {
    protected function calcRent() {
        switch($this->game->railRoadCount($this->owner)) {
        case 1: return new Dollar(25);
        case 2: return new Dollar(50);
        case 3: return new Dollar(100);
        case 4: return new Dollar(200);
        default: return new Dollar;
        }
    }
}

class Utility extends Property {
```

```
    protected function calcRent() {
      switch ($this->game->utilityCount($this->owner)) {
      case 1: return new Dollar(4*$this->game->lastRoll());
      case 2: return new Dollar(10*$this->game->lastRoll());
      default: return new Dollar;
      }
    }
  }
}
```

Each subclass extends the `Property` class and includes its own `protected ClacRent()` method. Since all of the abstract methods are defined, each subclass can be instantiated.

To set up the game, all of the Monopoly properties have to be created. Since this is the chapter on the *Factory* design pattern—and because the property types in Monopoly have much in common—you should be thinking about a polymorphic *Factory* to create all of the necessary objects.

Start by creating a `Property` factory class. Where I live, the County Assessor handles property taxes and deeds, so I named my `Property` factory `Assessor`. Next, the factory has to manufacture all of the Monopoly properties. In a real application, all of the Monopoly assets might come from a database or a configuration file, but for this example, let's just hard code an array with the relevant data:

```
class Assessor {
  protected $prop_info = array(
    // streets
    'Mediterranean Ave.' => array('Street', 60, 'Purple', 2)
    ,'Baltic Ave.'       => array('Street', 60, 'Purple', 2)
      //more of the streets...
    ,'Boardwalk'         => array('Street', 400, 'Blue', 50)
    // railroads
    ,'Short Line R.R.'   => array('RailRoad', 200)
      //the rest of the railroads...
    // utilities
    ,'Electric Company'  => array('Utility', 150)
    ,'Water Works'       => array('Utility', 150)
    );
}
```

The `Property` subclasses require an instance of `Monopoly` as part of the constructor. For now, simply make a setter function and define an instance variable, $game, to hold it in the `Assessor` class.

```
class Assessor {
  protected $game;
  public function setGame($game) { $this->game = $game; }
```

```
    protected $prop_info = array(/* ... */);
}
```

Although you'd likely prefer a database of records over such an array, there are times when long lists of parameters are unavoidable. If you run into such an occasion—such as here—consider the "Introduce Parameter Object" refactoring.

Refactoring — Introduce Parameter Object
Methods with long lists of parameters are complex and therefore prone to error. You can replace naturally grouped sets of parameters with an object encapsulating those parameters. For example, "start date" and "end date" parameters could be replaced with a **DateRange** object.

In the case of Monopoly, what might a parameter object for the real estate properties, say, PropertyInfo, look like? The intent is to pass each properties array into the constructor of the PropertyInfo class and receive a new object. Intent implies design, and according to TDD, that means a test case.

Here is a sample test that begins to sketch a PropertyInfo class:

```
function testPropertyInfo() {
    $list = array('type','price','color','rent');
    $this->assertIsA(
      $testprop = new PropertyInfo($list), 'PropertyInfo');
    foreach($list as $prop) {
      $this->assertEqual($prop, $testprop->$prop);
    }
}
```

This test verifies that each PropertyInfo has four public attributes and validates the exact order of the array parameters.

But because the RailRoad and Utility classes don't require color or rent information when instantiated, another test is needed to verify that PropertyInfo can also be instantiated given a shorter list of parameters:

```
function testPropertyInfoMissingColorRent() {
    $list = array('type','price');
    $this->assertIsA(
```

```
    $testprop = new PropertyInfo($list), 'PropertyInfo');
  $this->assertNoErrors();
  foreach($list as $prop) {
    $this->assertEqual($prop, $testprop->$prop);
  }
  $this->assertNull($testprop->color);
  $this->assertNull($testprop->rent);
}
```

assertNoErrors()

assertNoErrors() validates that no PHP errors have occured. If any errors are present, the assertion fails.

assertNull()

assertNull() passes if the first parameter passed is null. Any other valid PHP value causes the assertion to fail. Like most other SimpleTest assertions, you can optionally pass a failure message as a second parameter.

A `PropertyInfo` class to satisfy the two previous tests might look like:

```
class PropertyInfo {
  const TYPE_KEY  = 0;
  const PRICE_KEY = 1;
  const COLOR_KEY = 2;
  const RENT_KEY  = 3;
  public $type;
  public $price;
  public $color;
  public $rent;
  public function __construct($props) {
    $this->type  =
      $this->propValue($props, 'type',  self::TYPF_KFY);
    $this->price =
      $this->propValue($props, 'price', self::PRICE_KEY);
    $this->color =
      $this->propValue($props, 'color', self::COLOR_KEY);
    $this->rent  =
      $this->propValue($props, 'rent',  self::RENT_KEY);
  }
  protected function propValue($props, $prop, $key) {
    if (array_key_exists($key, $props)) {
      return $this->$prop = $props[$key];
    }
  }
}
```

So, `PropertyInfo` can now act as a parameter object for the various `Property` classes, and `Assessor` has the data needed to create valid `PropertyInfo` objects.

It's time to creates new instances of the `PropertyInfo` class based on the data from our `Assessor->$prop_info` array.

Such code might look like:

```php
class Assessor {
  protected $game;
  public function setGame($game) { $this->game = $game; }
  public function getProperty($name) {
    $prop_info = new PropertyInfo($this->prop_info[$name]);
    switch($prop_info->type) {
    case 'Street':
      $prop = new Street($this->game, $name, $prop_info->price);
      $prop->color = $prop_info->color;
      $prop->setRent($prop_info->rent);
      return $prop;
    case 'RailRoad':
      return new RailRoad($this->game, $name, $prop_info->price);
      break;
    case 'Utility':
      return new Utility($this->game, $name, $prop_info->price);
      break;
    default: //should not be able to get here
    }
  }
  protected $prop_info = array(/* ... */);
}
```

This code is functional, but brittle. Consider what happens if you pass a key that doesn't exist in the `$this->prop_info` array. Because the instantiation of the `PropertyInfo` object is embedded in the code, there is no effective way to test the created object. A better solution is to create a *Factory* method to facilitate creation of the `PropertyInfo` objects. Hence, the next step is to write a test for the `PropertyInfo` factory method in the `Assessor` class.

There is a problem, however: this method shouldn't be a part of the public API of the `Assessor` class. How then can it be tested?

There are a couple of approaches here, and delving into any requires a fair amount of testing theory. Briefly, you can perform *black box testing* or *white box testing*.

Black Box Testing

Black Box Testing treats the tested object as a "black box," where the specification (the published API) is known, but nothing of the actual implementation of the object is known. Testing therefore focuses only on the inputs and outputs to the public methods of the object.

White Box Testing

White Box Testing is the opposite of Black Box Testing, in that it assumes the tester has both knowledge of and access to all of the code for the tested object. The goal of this style of testing is typically complete code coverage and extensive failure condition testing. See http://c2.com/cgi/wiki?WhiteBoxTesting for a good introduction to this style of testing.

To avoid straying too far off topic, though, is there a compromise between Black Box and White Box Testing to enable use of TDD? One option is to make the method public during development and protected upon release (commenting out any effected tests). This is not a very satisfying approach, so an alternative is to subclass the object and make the method public in the testing subclass.

Here's the subclass approach:

```
class TestableAssessor extends Assessor {
  public function getPropInfo($name) {
    return Assessor::getPropInfo($name);
  }
}
```

The advantage of this solution is you can have the correct `Assessor` public API, but still allow for test coverage through the `TestableAssessor` subclass. Additionally, any other code you might introduce specifically for test coverage would not be present in your normal run-time version of `Assessor`.

The disadvantages include testing an additional class, which could introduce additional problems due to the additional complexity. And since you're specifying the behavior for the object's internal API, your tests become brittle if you ever refactor this internal structure again.

Weighing the pros and cons, a test case is the correct way to go for this example, so let's get started.

```
function testGetPropInfoReturn() {
  $assessor = new TestableAssessor;
  $this->assertIsA(
    $assessor->getPropInfo('Boardwalk'), 'PropertyInfo');
}
```

To ensure that all calling code passes valid key values, use an *exception*. SimpleTest is currently a PHP4 based testing framework, so it doesn't have any built-in features to test for exceptions, but you can easily work around this in a test case.

```
function testBadPropNameReturnsException() {
  $assessor = new TestableAssessor;
  $exception_caught = false;

  try { $assessor->getPropInfo('Main Street'); }
  catch (InvalidPropertyNameException $e) {
    $exception_caught = true;
  }
  $this->assertTrue($exception_caught);
  $this->assertNoErrors();
}
```

Finally, the implementation of *Assessor* can be completed:

```
class Assessor {
  protected $game;

  public function setGame($game) { $this->game = $game; }

  public function getProperty($name) {
    $prop_info = $this->getPropInfo($name);
    switch($prop_info->type) {
    case 'Street':
      $prop = new Street($this->game, $name, $prop_info->price);
      $prop->color = $prop_info->color;
      $prop->setRent($prop_info->rent);
      return $prop;
    case 'RailRoad':
      return new RailRoad($this->game, $name, $prop_info->price);
      break;
    case 'Utility':
      return new Utility($this->game, $name, $prop_info->price);
      break;
    default: //should not be able to get here
    }
  }

  protected $prop_info = array(/* ... */);

  protected function getPropInfo($name) {
    if (!array_key_exists($name, $this->prop_info)) {
      throw new InvalidPropertyNameException($name);
    }
    return new PropertyInfo($this->prop_info[$name]);
  }
}
```

The method `Assessor::getPropInfo()` represents the logical introduction of a `PropertyInfo` factory as a protected method of the `Assessor` class. The `Assessor::getProperty()` method is the public factory that returns one of our three `Property` subclasses, depending on what property name is requested.

Factories for Lazy Loading

Another significant benefit to using a *Factory* is the ability to perform *lazy loading*. Where this scenario comes into play most often is when a factory can instantiate a number of subclasses that are defined in separate PHP source files.

Terminology — Lazy Loading

The term lazy loading refers to not performing expensive operations (generally IO operations like including PHP files or querying a database) before they are absolutely required by the script.

A common technique with web sites is to have multiple web pages dynamically controlled through a single script. Consider blog software that might have different pages for viewing the recent entries, a single entry with comments, a comment submitting page, an archive navigation page, a page for the administrator to edit page, and so forth. You might encapsulate the logic to generate each of these in a class, and use a *Factory* to load both the class definition and the object. Each of these classes might be stored in a separate file in a 'pages' subdirectory of your application.

The code to implement a lazy loading page factory might look like:

```php
class PageFactory {
  function &getPage() {
    $page = (array_key_exists('page', $_REQUEST))
      ? strtolower($_REQUEST['page'])
      : '';
    switch ($page) {
    case 'entry':   $pageclass = 'Detail';    break;
    case 'edit':    $pageclass = 'Edit';      break;
    case 'comment': $pageclass = 'Comment';   break;
    default:
      $pageclass = 'Index';
    }
    if (!class_exists($pageclass)) {
      require_once 'pages/'.$pageclass.'.php';
    }
    return new $pageclass;
  }
}
```

You can take advantage of PHP's dynamic nature and use run-time logic to determine the class name you wish to create. In this case, an HTTP request parameter, page is evaluated to determine which page has been requested. You can implement lazy loading by not loading all possible "page" classes during every script execution, but instead including the class definition only when you are about to create the new object. This occurs in the conditional require_once above. This technique is not as important on a system with a PHP accelerator—a byte code cache—because the cost of including the additional source code is negligible there. Otherwise; it's a good performance enhancer for most typical PHP hosted environments.

For a more detailed look at *lazy loading*, read *Chapter 11—The Proxy Pattern*.

Issues

The *Factory* pattern is reasonably simple and very powerful. You may have examples of this pattern in your code already, and you will soon notice many more. The GoF book includes several additional related construction patterns: *AbstractFactory* and *Builder*. An *AbstractFactory* handles families of related components and the *Builder* pattern is designed to facilitate construction of complex objects.

In many of this chapter's examples, a parameter was passed to the *Factory* method (e.g. CrayonBox::getColor('red');). The GoF refer to this as a "parameterized factory" and it is fairly typical of the *Factory* methods I have seen in PHP web applications.

You have now been introduced to the *Factory* pattern, a technique for managing creation of new objects within your code. You have seen how the *Factory* pattern can centralize the creation of complex objects or even substitute objects of different classes. Factories support the very important principal of polymorphism in OOP.

4

The Singleton Pattern

I N NEARLY EVERY OBJECT-oriented program, there are usually one or two resources that are created once and shared for the duration of the entire application. For example, a database connection in an e-commerce application is one such resource: it's initialized when the application launches, is used to effectuate all transactions, and is finally disconnected and destroyed when the program ends. In your code, there's no need to conjure a database connection each and every time; that's a hassle and very inefficient. Instead, your code can simply re-use the connection that's already been established. The challenge then is how do you refer to the connection (or to any other unique perennial resource, such as an open file or a queue).

The Problem

How do you ensure that an instance of a particular class is exclusive (it's always the lone instance of that class) yet is also readily-accessible?

The Solution

Of course, a global variable is an obvious solution, but it's also a Pandora's Box (The saying, "Good judgment comes from experience, but experience usually comes from poor judgment" comes to mind.) Any portion of your code can modify a global variable, causing endless aggravation debugging any number of serendipitous problems. In other words, the state of a global variable is always questionable. (A good description of the global variable dilemma can be found at http://c2.com/cgi/wiki?GlobalVariablesAreBad.)

When you need an exclusive instance of a particular class, use the aptly-named *Singleton* pattern. A class based on the *Singleton* pattern properly instantiates and initializes one instance of the class and provides access to the exact same object every time, typically through a static method named getInstance().

Getting the exact same instance every time is critical and worthy of a test:

```
// PHP4
function TestGetInstance() {
  $this->assertIsA(
     $obj1 =& DbConn::getInstance(),
     'DbConn',
     'The returned object is an instance of DbConn');
  $this->assertReference(
     $obj1,
     $obj2 =& DbConn::getInstance(),
     'Two calls to getInstance() return the same object');
}
```

> **(i)**   **assertReference**
> **assertReference()** ensures that the two passed parameters are references to the same PHP variable.
>
> In PHP4, this asserts the two tested parameters are in fact the same object. **assertReference()** may be deprecated as SimpleTest is migrated to PHP 5.

This test method makes two assertions: that the value returned from calling the static DbConn::getInstance() method is an instance of the DbConn class and that a second call to getInstance() returns the *same* reference, which implies it's the very same object.

Besides asserting the expected behavior of the code, the test also demonstrates the proper (PHP4) usage of getInstance(): $local_conn_var =& DbConn::getInstance();. The local variable is assigned the result of the static method call by reference (=&).

There's one other test to write, at least for now: verify that instantiating a *Singleton* class directly via new causes an error of some kind. Here's that test:

```php
function TestBadInstantiate() {
  $obj =& new DbConn;
  $this->assertErrorPattern(
    '/(bad|nasty|evil|do not|don\'t|warn).*'.
    '(instance|create|new|direct)/i');
}
```

The code creates an instance of the DbConn class by using new directly, which should cause a PHP error. To make the code less brittle, a PCRE pattern is provided to match the error message. (The exact wording of the error message is relatively unimportant.)

Sample Code

The *Singleton* is an interesting pattern. Let's explore its implementation in both PHP4 and PHP5, starting with PHP4.

A "Global" Approach

Conceptually, a global variable makes an ideal *Singleton*, but a global variable is unpredictable: there's no guarantee that it contains the exact same object over the entire course of your script. However, you can mitigate the problem of "unrestrainted access" to a global variable by never referencing the global directly. For instance, this code "hides" the reference in a global variable with a very long unique and descriptive name.

```php
class DbConn {
    function DbConn($fromGetInstance=false) {
        if (M_E != $fromGetInstance) {
            trigger_error('The DbConn class is a Singleton,'
            .' please do not instantiate directly.');
        }
    }
    function &getInstance() {
        $key = '__some_unique_key_for_the_DbConn_instance__';
        if (!(array_key_exists($key, $GLOBALS) && is_object($GLOBALS[$key])
            && 'dbconn' == get_class($GLOBALS[$key]) )) {
            $GLOBALS[$key] =& new DbConn(M_E);
        }
        return $GLOBALS[$key];
    }
}
```

You may be wondering about the default parameter $fromGetInstance in the DbConn constructor. It provides (pretty weak) protection from instantiating the object directly: unless the default value is changed to *e* (the PHP math constant M_E = 2.718281828459), the code triggers an error. The getInstance() method calls new DbConn(M_E), creating the object in the correct manner.

Expressed as a UML class diagram, the solution looks like this:

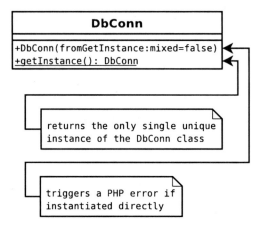

If you don't care for this "secret parameter"-style guard, another option is to create a global token to validate you're creating the object from the getInstance() method. This moves the guard condition from "something you know" to "something in the environment."

Here's a sample of how the constructor guard code might look like with a global semaphore:

```php
class DbConn {
    function DbConn() {
        $token = '__some_DbConn_instance_create_semaphore__';
        if (!array_key_exists($token, $GLOBALS)) {
            trigger_error('The DbConn class is a Singleton,'
                .' please do not instantiate directly.');
        }
    }
    function &getInstance() {
        static $instance = array();
        if (!$instance) {
            $token = '__some_DbConn_instance_create_semaphore__';
            $GLOBALS[$token] = true;
            $instance[0] =& new DbConn;
            unset($GLOBALS[$token]);
        }
        return $instance[0];
    }
}
```

Tip
PHP4 allows you to change the value of **$this** in the constructor. In the past, I have used **$this = null;** when I had a construction error, ensuring the invalid object could not be used by further code. While useful in PHP4, it's not compatible with PHP5, so in the interest of future-proofing your code, this technique is no longer recommended.

Another important aspect of the code is the use of the reference operator, &. There are two locations where the use of & is required. The first is in the function definition, prior to the function name, which indicates the `return` is a reference. The second is the assignment of the new `DbConn` object to the `$GLOBALS` array. (Both uses emphasize the point mentioned in the preface and the *ValueObject* chapter: in PHP4 code, you nearly always want to create, pass, and return objects by reference, leading to a proliferation of & reference operators in your code.)

The conditional check in the `getInstance()` method is written to always run without warnings, even at the `E_ALL` error reporting level. It verifies there's an object of the class `DbConn` in the appropriate spot in the `$GLOBALS` array, else it creates the object there. The method then returns the object that may or may not have been created on this iteration through the method, but by the time the method is finished, you're sure you have the one valid instance of the class, and that it's been initialized correctly.

A Static Approach
One problem with the global variable solution, even with the global variable access hidden within `getInstance()`, is you still have the potential to corrupt the global variable inadvertently, simply because the variable is potentially in scope anywhere in your script.

A cleaner solution is to use a static variable inside of the getInstance() method to store the *Singleton*. A first cut at the code might look like:

```
class DbConn {
  // ...
    function &getInstance() {
      static $instance = false;
      if (!$instance) $instance =& new DbConn(M_E);
      return $instance;
    }
}
```

Alas, the Zend 1 engine in PHP4 doesn't store references in static variables (see http://www.php.net/manual/en/language.variables.scope.php#AEN3609). A workaround is to store a

static array, and place the reference to your *Singleton* instance in a known index of that array.
getInstance() method might then look like:

```
class DbConn {
    function DbConn($fromGetInstance=false) {
        if (M_E != $fromGetInstance) {
            trigger_error('The DbConn class is a Singleton,'
                .' please do not instantiate directly.');
        }
    }
    function &getInstance() {
        static $instance = array();
        if (!$instance) $instance0 =& new DbConn(M_E);
        return $instance0;
    }
}
```

This code simply chooses the first element of the static $instance array to hold the reference to our
Singleton DbConn instance.

This code is much tighter than the global version, though it does it does rely on a bit of PHP
boolean magic: an empty array evaluates to false in a conditional check. As in the previous version
of the DbConn class, reference operators are required in the function definition and in the assignment.

The Singleton in PHP5

A *Singleton* in PHP5 is much simpler to implement, because PHP5 provides and enforces visibility
for variables and functions inside of classes. By making the DbConn::__construct() method private, no code can directly instantiate the class. Expressed in a UML diagram, a PHP5 DbConn
singleton looks like:

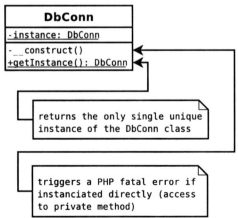

Combining the static method variable to hold the instance and the private constructor to prevent inadvertent construction, you now have a class like:

```
class DbConn {
  /**
   * static property to hold singleton instance
   */
  static $instance = false;
  /**
   * constructor
   * private so only getInstance() method can instantiate
   * @return void
   */
  private function __construct() {}
  /**
   * factory method to return the singleton instance
   * @return DbConn
   */
  public function getInstance() {
    if (!DbConn::$instance) {
      DbConn::$instance = new DbConn;
    }
    return DbConn::$instance;
  }
}
```

Issues

Now that you've seen several possible implementations of the *Singleton* design pattern, let's look at some of the tradeoffs you should consider when looking at implementing this design pattern.

First, a *Singletons* isn't a "better" global variable. For example, if a method requires a *Singleton*, pass it as a parameter to make its usage plainly obvious.

Also, you may be tempted to lump "utility functions" of all sorts into a *Singleton* class because of its "global" availability to your application. Avoid this, limiting the *Singleton*'s methods to the functions that are purposeful for the class.

More discussion related to these issues is available online at:

* http://c2.com/cgi/wiki?SingletonGlobalProblems
* http://c2.com/cgi/wiki?GlobalVariablesAreBad

The Monostate Pattern: Stealth Singletons

Occasionally, I've wanted a class where all of the instances of that class share a global state — in other words, any instance of the class returns the exact same information. Similar in behavior to a

Singleton, this is a design pattern called the *MonoState* (http://c2.com/cgi/wiki?MonostatePattern).

In PHP, you can use a neat trick with references to bind global data to an instance variable to achieve a *MonoState*.

As an example, let's create a class to provide global application configuration. No matter what instance of this *MonoState* class you access, you get the same values.

Here are those requirements expressed as a test:

```php
// PHP4
function TestApplConfig() {
  $this->assertIsA(
    $obj1 =& new ApplicationConfig, 'ApplicationConfig');
  $this->assertIsA(
    $obj2 =& new ApplicationConfig, 'ApplicationConfig');
  $test_val = '/path/to/cache'.rand(1,100);
  $obj1->set('cache_path', $test_val);
  $this->assertEqual($test_val, $obj2->get('cache_path'));
}
```

The test creates two different instances of the *MonoState* class, changes one, and then verifies that the other instance was indeed affected by the change.

Here is the code to implement the *MonoState*:

```php
class ApplicationConfig {
  var $_state;
  function ApplicationConfig() {
    $key = '__stealth_singleton_state_index__';
    if (!(array_key_exists($key, $GLOBALS)
        && is_array($GLOBALS[$key]))) {
      $GLOBALS[$key] = array();
    }
    $this->_state =& $GLOBALS[$key];
  }
  function set($key, $val) {
    $this->_state[$key] = $val;
  }
  function get($key) {
    if (array_key_exists($key, $this->_state)) {
      return $this->_state[$key];
    }
  }
}
```

The core of this trick is $this->state =& $GLOBALS[$key;]. After making sure $GLOBALS[$key] is an array, the code binds a reference to the global array to the class variable $this->state. From then on, any changes to $this->state are seamlessly reflected in the global array and therefore in any other instance of the class.

This trick can be used with any of PHP's superglobal arrays and is particularly effective with $_SESSION for the user notification queue. A *MonoState* can store a series of messages to present to the user for use throughout your code (but you might redirect to another page prior to actually displaying the messages). $_SESSION is a good place to store these messages so that the messages persist after redirection.

5

The Registry Pattern

Because it's generally considered "good form" to avoid the use of global variables, objects are usually passed from one code segment to another as parameters. But the problem with passing instances is that objects sometimes end up as "tramp data," passed into one function only to be passed again to another function which truly needs the object.

To make writing, reading, and consuming code simpler, it's best to minimize the number of different objects and consolidate knowledge of how to get to a myriad of other widely-used objects into a single, well-known object.

The Problem

How can you get references to objects through a single, well-known, object?

The Solution

The *Registry* design pattern is like an "object phone book"—a directory—that stores and retrieves references to objects. (PHP associative arrays perform a similar "phone book" function, and in fact, the heart of a *Registry* implementation can center around PHP's powerful arrays.) The features of a *Registry* are most often encapsulated in a *Singleton* (see *Chapter 4*), making the *Registry* a definitive source of information for your entire application.

> The primary reference on the *Registry* pattern is *Patterns of Enterprise Application Architecture*, where Martin Fowler describes the pattern using Java as the implementation language.
>
> Marcus Baker wrote a detailed article on using the *Registry* pattern in PHP, which is available on the phpPatterns.com site at (http://www.phppatterns.com/index.php/article/articleview/75/1/1/). Baker also focuses on testing considerations and demonstrates more of the Test Driven Development methodology.

Sample Code

As Martin Fowler mentions in his chapter on the *Registry* pattern, you can implement the pattern in a number of ways and offer a variety of interfaces. Let's explore that notion and build several variations of the *Registry* pattern in PHP4.

Let's start with writing code to store and retrieve instances of objects and provide global access to the *Registry*. An instance variable caches the objects, and the *Registry* itself is a *Singleton*.

As always, tests capture the requirements. This first test verifies that the *Registry* is a *Singleton*.

```
// PHP4
class RegistryPHP4TestCase extends UnitTestCase {
  function testRegistryIsSingleton() {
    $this->assertIsA($reg =& Registry::getInstance(), 'Registry');
    $this->assertReference($reg, Registry::getInstance());
  }
}
```

Given what you've learned from the previous chapter on the *Singleton* pattern, you should be able to quickly write a `Registry` class that passes this test. Here's a `Registry` class that satisfies the test (ignoring the code required to enforce no direct object creation):

```
class Registry {
  function &getInstance() {
    static $instance = array();
```

```
        if (!$instance) $instance[0] =& new Registry;
        return $instance[0];
    }
}
```

A simple static array is sufficient to record the single instance.

Next, let's turn to the specific features of the *Registry*. A registry should provide get() and set() methods to store and retrieve objects using some key and should also offer an isValid() method to determine if a specific key has been set.

The very easiest of these three methods is the latter. Here are two test cases for isValid():

```
class RegistryPHP4TestCase extends UnitTestCase {
    function testRegistryIsSingleton() { /*...*/ }
    function testEmptyRegistryKeyIsInvalid() {
        $reg =& Registry::getInstance();
        $this->assertFalse($reg->isValid('key'));
    }

    function testEmptyRegistryKeyReturnsNull() {
        $reg =& Registry::getInstance();
        $this->assertNull($reg->get('key'));
    }
}
```

(i) **assertFalse()**
assertFalse() is simply the negation of **assertTrue()**: it passes if the first parameter evaluates to a PHP boolean false.

Per Test Driven Development, do the minimum coding possible to satisfy your existing tests and then add more tests if you haven't satisfied all of the class' requirements. Here's the simplest amount of code that satisfies the previous test:

```
class Registry {
    function isValid() {
        return false;
    }
    function get() {
    }
    function &getInstance() {
        static $instance = array();
        if (!$instance) $instance[0] =& new Registry;
```

```
        return $instance[0];
    }
  }
```

Admittedly, the code snippets for isValid() and get() aren't very inspired, but all of the tests do pass. Time to add some more meaty tests.

```
class RegistryPHP4TestCase extends UnitTestCase {
  function testRegistryIsSingleton() { /*...*/ }
  function testEmptyRegistryKeyIsInvalid() { /*...*/ }
  function testEmptyRegistryKeyReturnsNull() { /*...*/ }

  function testSetRegistryKeyBecomesValid() {
    $reg =& Registry::getInstance();
    $test_value = 'something';
    $reg->set('key', $test_value);
    $this->assertTrue($reg->isValid('key'));
  }
}
```

To satisfy testSetRegistryKeyBecomesValid(), the Registry class must have some means of tracking if a particular key has been stored using set(). The obvious implementation is to use a PHP associative array as an instance variable and use PHP's array_key_exists() function to determine if the index of interest has been created yet. Here's a possible next step for Registry:

```
class Registry {
  var $_store = array();

  function isValid($key) {
    return array_key_exists($key, $this->_store);
  }
  function set($key, $obj) {
    $this->_store[$key] = $obj;
  }
  function get() {
  }
  function &getInstance() {
    static $instance = array();
    if (!$instance) $instance[0] =& new Registry;
    return $instance[0];
  }
}
```

By initializing the $_store variable when it's declared, there's no need for a constructor method.

(With no proper visibility in PHP4, the code follows the convention of prefixing a private variable with an underscore.)

The tests pass again; time to move on to the final feature: given a key, the `Registry::get()` operation needs to return a reference to the specified object. Here's a test that captures that intent:

```php
class RegistryPHP4TestCase extends UnitTestCase {
  function testRegistryIsSingleton() { /*...*/ }
  function testEmptyRegistryKeyIsInvalid() { /*...*/ }
  function testEmptyRegistryKeyReturnsNull() { /*...*/ }
  function testSetRegistryKeyBecomesValid() { /*...*/ }

  function testSetRegistryValueIsReference() {
    $reg =& Registry::getInstance();
    $test_value = 'something';
    $reg->set('key', $test_value);
    $this->assertReference($test_value, $reg->get('key'));

    //another way to test the reference
    $test_value .= ' else';
    $this->assertEqual(
      'something else'
      ,$reg->get('key')
      );
  }
}
```

And here is a complete implementation of the `Registry` class:

```php
class Registry {
  var $_store = array();
  function isValid($key) {
    return array_key_exists($key, $this->_store);
  }
  function &get($key) {
    if (array_key_exists($key, $this->_store))
      return $this->_store[$key];
  }
  function set($key, &$obj) {
    $this->_store[$key] =& $obj;
  }
  function &getInstance() {
    static $instance = array();
    if (!$instance) $instance[0] =& new Registry;
    return $instance[0];
  }
}
```

The `Registry::get()` method returns a reference. Similarly, the `$obj` parameter of the `Registry::set()` method is defined to be pass by reference and a reference is assigned to `$this->_store[$key]`. The combination of these `get()` and `set()` methods and the proper use of reference allows the `assertReference()` assertion in `testRegistry()` test to pass.

> The **Registry::get()** code could be written **return @$this->_store[$key;]**, however, it's best to avoid the error suppression operator. Moreover, the code using the error suppression operator would be ambiguous, requiring more time to digest if you have to revisit the code again later. The **array_key_exists()** function makes it clear what error is being avoided.

In PHP5, object handles come to the rescue again, saving you from the hassle of object reference passing. In fact, *Registry* implementations become trivial because you can access associative arrays without worrying about the possibility of a fatal error from not passing the object by reference. Using PHP5, you can also mix objects and literals in *Registry*.

An Example

So what might a *Registry* look like in action? In web application development, it's fairly typical to have a single database connection (hence the widespread use of a *Singleton* for managing that connection). But, say, for legacy reasons, that your application's customer database is separate from your online orders database and that your database analyst (DBA) has moved older orders to an archive database, again, completely separate from your customer database and the (current and recent) orders databases. How can you manage those three database connections easily, without coding three different *Singletons*? Use a *Registry*.

```
class DbConnections extends Registry {}
```

> **Tip**
> When you integrate a design pattern into your code, the name of your class should still reflect it's role or function in your application, not necessarily the pattern's name.
>
> Referring to code using a pattern name is good for communication with programmers outside of your project; within your project, however, the names of your classes should be appropriate to the domain of your application and be well understood by your colleagues.
>
> *Continued ...*

Tip: *Continued...*
Throughout the rest of this chapter the example class names reflect the patterns name and the specific implementation being developed, not a role in an application. This is done for clarity of the example, not as an example of a good naming convention.

DbConnections is a *Singleton* and since it inherits from the Registry class, DbConnections combines all of the benefits of the two patterns.

The following code snippet creates and stores a connection to each of the databases in the *Registry*.

```
// initial setup, somewhere near the start of your script
$dbc =& DbConnections::getInstance();
$dbc->set(
  'contacts',
  new MysqlConnection('user1', 'pass1', 'db1', 'host1'));
$dbc->set(
  'orders',
  new MysqlConnection('user2', 'pass2', 'db2', 'host2'));
$dbc->set(
  'archives',
  new MysqlConnection('user3', 'pass3', 'db3', 'host3'));
```

With the *Registry* loaded with data, it's ready to be used.

```
// domain model classes
class Customer {
  var $db;
  function Customer() {
    $dbc =& DbConnections::getInstance();
    $this->db =& $dbc->get('contacts');
  }
  //...
}
class Orders {
  var $db_cur;
  var $db_hist;
  function Contact() {
    $dbc =& DbConnections::getInstance();
    $this->db_cur =& $dbc->get('orders');
    $this->db_hist =& $dbc->get('archive');
  }
  //...
}
```

One class models the customer database and the other class models both the historical and current orders databases. Obtaining the right connection is two lookups: one to find the *Registry* and one to find the object associated with the key.

Implementing the Registry as a MonoState Object

As mentioned earlier, there are a number of possible implementations for the *Registry* pattern.

The first variation realizes the *Registry* as a *MonoState* object (the *MonoState* pattern was covered briefly at the end of *Chapter 4—The Singleton Pattern*). With this design, any instance of the *Registry* would need access to the same array. Let's call the new class RegistryGlobal to distinguish it from the Registry class that was just developed and to reflect the nature of the implementation. Here's a test to flesh out the idea (it should look very familiar):

```
class RegistryGlobalPHP4TestCase extends UnitTestCase {
  function testRegistryGlobal() {
    $reg =& new RegistryGlobal;
    $this->assertFalse($reg->isValid('key'));
    $this->assertNull($reg->get('key'));
    $test_value = 'something';
    $reg->set('key', $test_value);
    $this->assertReference($test_value, $reg->get('key'));
  }
}
```

The implementation should look reasonably familiar as well:

```
class RegistryGlobal {
  var $_store = array();
  function isValid($key) {
    return array_key_exists($key, $this->_store);
  }
  function &get($key) {
    if (array_key_exists($key, $this->_store))
      return $this->_store[$key];
  }
  function set($key, &$obj) {
    $this->_store[$key] =& $obj;
  }
}
```

The isValid(), get(), and set() methods are identical to the methods of the Registry class developed earlier.

Next, let's write a test to verify that the RegistryGlobal class functions as a *MonoState*:

```php
class RegistryGlobalPHP4TestCase extends UnitTestCase {
  function testRegistryGlobal() { /*...*/ }
  function testRegistryGlobalIsMonoState() {
    $reg =& new RegistryGlobal;
    $reg2 =& new RegistryGlobal;
    $this->assertCopy($reg, $reg2);
    $test_value = 'something';
    $reg->set('test', $test_value);
    $this->assertReference(
        $reg->get('test')
       ,$reg2->get('test'));
  }
}
```

ⓘ | **assertCopy()**
The **assertCopy()** assertion is the negation of **assertReference()**, so if the two variables passed are not references, the assertion passes.

Here, the test creates two instances of the RegistryGlobal class, verifies they're not references to the same object, sets a value in one *Registry*, and finally validates that the same object is returned by both instances. If the tests pass, the RegistryGlobal class exhibits *MonoState* behavior.

```php
define('REGISTRY_GLOBAL_STORE', '__registry_global_store_key__');
class RegistryGlobal {
  var $_store;
  function RegistryGlobal() {
    if (!array_key_exists(REGISTRY_GLOBAL_STORE, $GLOBALS)
      || !is_array($GLOBALS[REGISTRY_GLOBAL_STORE])) {
      $GLOBALS[REGISTRY_GLOBAL_STORE] = array();
    }
    $this->_store =& $GLOBALS[REGISTRY_GLOBAL_STORE];
  }
  function isValid($key) {
    return array_key_exists($key, $this->_store);
  }
  function &get($key) {
    if (array_key_exists($key, $this->_store))
      return $this->_store[$key];
  }
  function set($key, &$obj) {
    $this->_store[$key] =& $obj;
  }
}
```

The real magic in this alternative is the line $this->_store =& $GLOBALS[REGISTRY_GLOBAL_STORE;], where the reference operator binds the global array to the instance variable $_store. This is the key to *MonoState* implementations: each time $this->_store is used in the object, the actual effect is mirrored to the global variable.

But it hardly makes sense to recommend a solution based on global variables. A static class variable would be a better solution, if only PHP4 provided such a feature. Yet, is there a way to use references to implement a static class variable in your own code?

The tests can be similar to the RegistryGlobal tests:

```
class RegistryMonoStatePHP4TestCase extends UnitTestCase {
  function testRegistryMonoState() {
    $this->assertCopy(
       $reg =& new RegistryMonoState
      ,$reg2 =& new RegistryMonoState);
    $this->assertFalse($reg->isValid('key'));
    $this->assertNull($reg->get('key'));
    $test_value = 'something';
    $reg->set('key', $test_value);
    $this->assertReference($reg->get('key'), $reg2->get('key'));
  }
}
```

To make your own class static variable, bind a reference to a *function static variable* to a class instance variable.

```
class RegistryMonoState {
  var $_store;

  function &_initRegistry() {
    static $store = array();
    return $store;
  }

  function RegistryMonoState() {
    $this->_store =& $this->_initRegistry();
  }

  function isValid($key) {
    return array_key_exists($key, $this->_store);
  }

  function &get($key) {
    if (array_key_exists($key, $this->_store))
      return $this->_store[$key];
  }
```

```
function set($key, &$obj) {
    $this->_store[$key] =& $obj;
  }
}
```

The `initRegistry()` method contains a static variable, `$store`, initialized to an array. This static variable is returned by reference. In the constructor, the `$_store` instance variable is set to the returned reference from the `initRegistry()` method and thus to the static array. Voila! A PHP4 class static variable.

Implementing with Class Static Variables

In PHP5, there's no need to implement your own class static variables, because the language supports the concept of static class variables directly. Thus, PHP5 simplifies the implementation a bit. Also, reference and objects no longer have the meaning they had in PHP4, but `assertReference()` handles this distinction, passing the test if two variables refer to the same object handle.

Here's the familiar Registry test case modified for PHP5:

```
// PHP5
class RegistryMonoStatePHP5TestCase extends UnitTestCase {
  function testRegistryMonoState() {
    $this->assertCopy(
        $reg = new RegistryMonoState
      ,$reg2 = new RegistryMonoState);
    $this->assertFalse($reg->isValid('key'));
    $this->assertNull($reg->get('key'));
    $test_value = new TestObj;
    $reg->set('key', $test_value);
    $this->assertReference($test_value, $reg2->get('key'));
  }
}
```

And here's the PHP5 version of the *Registry* class using static class variables.

```
class RegistryMonoState {
  protected static $store = array();

  function isValid($key) {
    return array_key_exists($key, RegistryMonoState::$store);
  }

  function get($key) {
    if (array_key_exists($key, RegistryMonoState::$store))
```

```
        return RegistryMonoState::$store[$key];
    }

    function set($key, $obj) {
        RegistryMonoState::$store[$key] = $obj;
    }
}
```

An interesting side effect of coding the *Registry* in PHP5 this way is you can actually use both instance and static method calls with the same set of code. Here is a test case that proves that—it uses static method calls only.

```
class RegistryMonoStatePHP5TestCase extends UnitTestCase {
    function testRegistryMonoState() { /*...*/ }

    function testRegistryMonoStateStaticCalls() {
        $this->assertFalse(RegistryMonoState::isValid('key'));
        $this->assertNull(RegistryMonoState::get('key'));
        $test_value = new TestObj;
        RegistryMonoState::set('key', $test_value);
        $this->assertIdentical($test_value,
            RegistryMonoState::get('key'));
    }
}
```

Now that you've seen how the static call interface looks in PHP5, let's code the same interface in PHP4. As in the previous PHP4 "static class variable" emulation, this implementation needs to use the "function static returning a reference" trick.

The test for PHP4 static call interface looks similar to the PHP5 version of the test.

```
// PHP4
class RegistryStaticPHP4TestCase extends UnitTestCase {

    function testRegistryStatic() {
        $this->assertFalse(RegistryStatic::isValid('key'));
        $this->assertNull(RegistryStatic::get('key'));
        $test_value = 'something';
        RegistryStatic::set('key', $test_value);
        $this->assertReference($test_value, RegistryStatic::get('key'));
    }
}
```

And here is an implementation that satisfies the test:

```
class RegistryStatic {

  function &_getRegistry() {
    static $store = array();
    return $store;
  }
  function isValid($key) {
    $store =& RegistryStatic::_getRegistry();
    return array_key_exists($key, $store);
  }
  function &get($key) {
    $store =& RegistryStatic::_getRegistry();
    if (array_key_exists($key, $store))
      return $store[$key];
  }
  function set($key, &$obj) {
    $store =& RegistryStatic::_getRegistry();
    $store[$key] =& $obj;
  }
}
```

The key to this implementation is having the getRegistry() method return a reference to a static array. The line $store =& RegistryStatic::_getRegistry(); in subsequent functions sets the local variable $store by reference to this static array, granting all of the functions static access to the array and allowing all of the methods to be called statically.

There is another way to achieve the same effect without using the PHP4 static class variable trick: combine the original *Singleton*-based Registry class with a wrapper class to allow for static method calls. This class has an identical test to the testRegistryStatic(), but is implemented like this:

```
class RegistryStatic {
  function isValid($key) {
    $reg =& Registry::getInstance();
    return $reg->isValid($key);
  }
  function &get($key) {
    $reg =& Registry::getInstance();
    return $reg->get($key);
  }
  function set($key, &$obj) {
    $reg =& Registry::getInstance();
    $reg->set($key, $obj);
  }
}
```

Issues

While the *Registry* simplifies access to a number of objects, it still has many of the problems associated with global variables. You have to make sure the requested key is initialized before you access it, and because there's global access to the setter method, your object can still be replaced in another portion of your code unexpectedly. Obviously there are benefits and reasons for global data, but you should remember that any global data is always a bit suspect.

Embedded Registry

Rather than using the *Registry* pattern standalone, as has been shown in this chapter, the *Registry* can be very powerful when combined as a feature of another object. Consider a situation where object creation is somewhat expensive (perhaps due to the number of database calls required to initialize the object) and where the object may be requested one or more times in any given execution of the program, if ever. Could you create a "Finder" class combining aspects of the *Factory* (see *Chapter 3*) and *Registry* patterns to maintain a cache of objects that have already been created instead of creating them again?

Here's a Contact class, where AddressBook is the *Factory*.

```
class AddressBook {
  function &findById($id) {
    return new Contact($id);
  }
}

class Contact {
  function Contact($id) {
    // expensive queries to create object using $id
  }
  // ... other methods
}
```

You could embed the *Registry* within the AddressBook class to seamlessly provide caching. That might look like this:

```
class AddressBook {
  var $registry;

  function AddressBook() {
  $this->registry =& Registry::getInstance();
  }

  function &findById($id) {
    if (!$this->registry->isValid($id)) {
```

```
        $this->registry->set($id, new Contact($id));
        }
        return $this->registry->get($id);
    }
}
```

The AddressBook constructor binds the registry to an instance variable. When a particular ID is created and requested in the findById() method, the *Registry* is checked to see if the object has already been cached. If not, the new object is created and stored in the *Registry*. The requested object is then returned by the function by extracting it from the *Registry*.

6

The MockObject
Pattern

THE RICHNESS OF OBJECT-ORIENTED PROGRAMMING comes in part from the interconnections and interactions between objects. A single object can encapsulate a complex subsystem, making otherwise complicated operations as simple as calling a handful of methods. (The ubiquitous database connection is one such object.)

But often, the interactions between objects are so complex that you become faced with a "chicken and egg"-like conundrum: how to develop and test a new object that depends on the creation of many other objects or on some circumstance that is difficult to realize, such as the recreation of an entire database.

The Problem

How can you easily isolate and test a segment of code that depends on other objects and resources? How can you recreate one or more objects or application states to validate that your code is operating properly?

The Solution

When it's difficult or expensive to test an object *in situ* (or in a facsimile of its production environment), use a *MockObject* to simulate behavior. A *MockObject* has the same interface as the *real* object it's standing in for, but provides pre-programmed responses, tracks method calls, and validates call sequences.

MockObjects are the "special forces" of the testing world. Trained in stealth, they infiltrate targeted code, emulate and monitor communication patterns, and report back results. *MockObjects* can help search for and destroy bugs and can support the more mundane *"peacekeeping"* operations of a normal application test suite.

The ServerStub

The *MockObject* pattern is an extension of another testing pattern called the *ServerStub*. The *ServerStub* pattern stands-in for a resource and returns known values in response to method calls. A *ServerStub* becomes a *MockObject* when you can anticipate the specific sequence of method calls to be made on your *ServerStub*.

Not Really a Design Pattern

This chapter is different from the other chapters in this book because MockObject is a *testing* pattern rather than a design pattern. This may seem like an odd diversion, but the use of this testing pattern can really become foundational and is well worth having in your coding tool set. It differs in another aspect as well while the basics of how to code this pattern is covered, more emphasis is placed on the *usage* of the existing *MockObject* implementation in SimpleTest.

This chapter first presents a very simple example that demonstrates the basic mechanics of SimpleTest *MockObjects*. It then shows how you can use *MockObjects* to help restructure legacy code and test the new solution.

Sample Code

A *MockObject* is a substitute object that makes testing code much simpler. For instance, rather than use a real database connection—which may be impractical for any number of reasons—you can create a *MockObject* to simulate it. Practically, this means a *MockObject* needs to respond to the exact same API as the code that it's standing in for.

Let's create a *MockObject* to stand-in for a simple class called `Accumulator` that sums numeric values. Here's the original `Accumulator`:

```
// PHP4
class Accumulator {
  var $total=0;
  function add($item) {
    $this->total += $item;
  }
  function total() {
    return $this->total;
  }
}
```

add() accumulates values in instance variable $total, and total() returns what's been accumulated so far. A simple use of Accumulator is shown below (the code is written as functions, but could be a class just as well).

```
function calc_total($items, &$sum) {
  foreach($items as $item) {
    $sum->add($item);
  }
}

function calc_tax(&$amount, $rate=0.07) {
  return round($amount->total() * $rate,2);
}
```

The first function, calc_total(), uses an Accumulator to sum the values in a list and is simple enough to test:

```
class MockObjectTestCase extends UnitTestCase {
  function testCalcTotal() {
    $sum =& new Accumulator;

    calc_total(array(1,2,3), $sum);
    $this->assertEqual(6, $sum->total());
  }
}
```

Let's move on to the second case. Assume that instantiating a real Accumulator is very expensive. It'd be ideal if a simple object could stand in for Accumulator and return a set of responses to the surrounding code. Using SimpleTest, you can create a mock Accumulator with this code:

```
Mock::generate('Accumulator');
class MockObjectTestCase extends UnitTestCase {
  // ...

  function testCalcTax() {
      $amount =& new MockAccumulator($this);
      $amount->setReturnValue('total',200);

      $this->assertEqual(
         14, calc_tax($amount));
  }
}
```

To use a *MockObject*, you must typically create a new class for it by hand (more on that momentarily). Luckily, SimpleTest has an easy means of accomplishing this: the `Mock::generate()` method.

In the example above, the method creates a class named `MockAccumulator` that responds to all the `Accumulator` class methods. Additionally, the `MockAccumulator` has other methods to manipulate the *MockObject* instance itself. Once such method is `setReturnValue()`. Given a method name and a value, `setReturnValue()` changes the *MockObject* to return the given value when the named method is called. So, the statement `$amount->setReturnValue('total', 200)` returns 200 whenever the `total()` method is called.

Once initialized, you can pass the `MockAccumulator` class into the `calc_tax()` function to have it act in the place of a real `Accumulator` object.

If you stopped here—with an object returning "canned" responses to method calls—you would have implemented the *ServerStub* pattern. But the *MockObject* goes further to validate which methods were called, how many times, and in what sequence.

Here's an example of validating the "flow" through an object:

```
class MockObjectTestCase extends UnitTestCase {
  // ...

  function testCalcTax() {
      $amount =& new MockAccumulator($this);
      $amount->setReturnValue('total',200);
      $amount->expectOnce('total');

      $this->assertEqual(
         14, calc_tax($amount));

      $amount->tally();
  }
}
```

The expectOnce() method takes a string containing the name of a method that you expect to be called once. The tally() is the actual check to determine if your expectations were met. Here, if MockAccumulator::total() isn't called once and only once, the test fails.

You can use this "tracking" feature of a *MockObject* in many ways. For example, if you pass an array of three values into calc_total(), is Accumulator::add() called three times as is expected?

```
class MockObjectTestCase extends UnitTestCase {
    // ...

    function testCalcTotalAgain() {
        $sum =& new MockAccumulator($this);
        $sum->expectOnce('add');
        calc_total(array(1,2,3), $sum);

        $sum->tally();
    }
}
```

Whoops, what happened here? The test failed instead of passing. The SimpleTest error message states something like:

```
MockObject PHP4 Unit Test
1) Expected call count for [add] was [1] got [3] at line [51]
       in testcalctotalagain
       in mockobjecttestcase
FAILURES!!!
Test cases run: 1/1, Passes: 2, Failures: 1, Exceptions: 0
```

This error message indicates that the add() method was called three times, not the single time the expectOnce() assertion asked for. Instead of expectOnce(), the test should use expectCallCount().

```
class MockObjectTestCase extends UnitTestCase {
    // ...
    function testCalcTotalAgain() {
        $sum =& new MockAccumulator($this);
        $sum->expectCallCount('add', 3);
        calc_total(array(1,2,3), $sum);
        $sum->tally();
    }
}
```

A *MockObject* has the role of an actor—as a *SeverStub* providing reasonable test data in response to method calls—and the role of a critic, validating assumptions about which methods were called.

A Legacy Application

As the next example let's use the MockObject to assist in the restructuring of a legacy application. Consider a simple script that mimics the kind of behaviors you might expect to see in any number of PHP applications: A PHP page generates a login for the user if the user has not yet logged in; the very same page acts as a form handler for the form; it shows different content after a successful login; and it provides logout.

Let's write such a page. First, display a login form if the user hasn't logged in yet:

```html
<html>
<body>
<form method="post">
Name:<input type="text" name="name">
Password:<input type="password" name="passwd">
<input type="submit" value="Login">
</form>
</body>
</html>
```

Next, provide some content if the user is logged in:

```html
<html>
<body>Welcome <?php echo $_SESSION['name']; ?>
<br>Super secret member only content here.
<a href="<?php echo SELF; ?>?clear">Logout</a>
</body>
</html>
```

Adding in the form handling capabilities, session startup, and logout capabilities, and the whole script might look like:

```php
session_start();

define('SELF',
  'http://'.$_SERVER['SERVER_NAME'].$_SERVER['PHP_SELF']);

if (array_key_exists('name', $_REQUEST)
   && array_key_exists('passwd', $_REQUEST)
   && 'admin' == $_REQUEST['name']
```

```
   && 'secret' == $_REQUEST['passwd']) {
   $_SESSION['name'] = 'admin';
   header('Location: '.SELF);
}

if (array_key_exists('clear', $_REQUEST)) {
  unset($_SESSION['name']);
}

if (array_key_exists('name', $_SESSION)
   && $_SESSION['name']) { ?>
   <html>
   <body>Welcome <?=$_SESSION['name']?>
   <br>Super secret member only content here.
   <a href="<?php echo SELF; ?>?clear">Logout</a>
   </body>
   </html> <?php
} else { ?>
   <html>
   <body>
   <form method="post">
   Name:<input type="text" name="name">
   Password:<input type="password" name="passwd">
   <input type="submit" value="Login">
   </form>
   </body>
   </html> <?php
}
```

A goal of restructuring this legacy application should be to create a "testable" application. Immediately, this goal affects the design: if you choose to use some of the convenient features of PHP—such as the superglobals—you sacrifice testing for convenience.

For example, if you use $_SESSION directly, say, then the only way to test such code is to alter $_SESSION. Alas, if you forget to change $_SESSION back to a known state, you could experience interference between tests.

A solution to this problem is to wra

p $_SESSION inside of another class and pass an instance of that wrapper class into any object that needs access to $_SESSION. If you then make a *MockObject* version of the wrapper object for testing, you can have complete control over the object's responses to method calls (acting as a *ServerStub*) and you can verify how it was called (which is the purpose of the *MockObject*).

With this in mind, let's see what a wrapper for the $_SESSION superglobal might look like.

```
class Session {
  function Session() {
    $this->init();
  }
  function init() {
```

```
        if (!isset($_SESSION)) {
          if (headers_sent()) {
            trigger_error(
              'Session not started before creating session object');
          } else {
            session_start();
          }
        }
      }
      function isValid($key) {
        return array_key_exists($key, $_SESSION);
      }
      function get($key) {
        return (array_key_exists($key, $_SESSION))
          ? $_SESSION[$key]
          : null;
      }
      function set($key, $value) {
        $_SESSION[$key] = $value;
      }
      function clear($key) {
        unset($_SESSION[$key]);
      }
    }
```

Session is a wrapper for the $_SESSION superglobal. The tests for Session are similar to the tests developed for the *Registry* class earlier (see *Chapter 5*), but without any intention of getting or setting the values by reference.

You may have noticed the constructor calls a Session::init() method. Why is this method not a part of the constructor itself? It's separate so you can call it statically to make sure the session was started. Here is an example of how the class might be used:

```
Session::init();

$page =& new PageDirector(new Session);
```

Most testing literature devoted to *MockObjects* suggest that you write *MockObjects* by hand. If you want to do that, just flesh out the methods you need far enough to get by testing. For instance, a hand-coded *ServerStub* for the Session class might look like:

```
class MyMockSessionUser1 {
  function isValid($key) {
    return ('user_id' == $key) ? true : false;
  }
```

```
    function get($key) {
      if ('user_id' == $key) {
        return 1;
      }
    }
}
```

Fortunately, you can avoid this error-prone drudgery using SimpleTest. The `Mock::generate()` method allows you to generate a class that you can instantiate and configure dynamically to respond as you need.

MockObject Techniques

SimpleTest's approach is just one of many techniques for using *MockObjects*. Hand-coding *MockObjects* is another (as shown above). With the advent of PHP5, you might see a PHP *MockObject* implementation that makes use of the **__call()** method on objects.

Here's how to recreate `MyMockSessionUser1` (shown above) in a SimpleTest-generated *MockObject* test case:

```
Mock::Generate('Session');

class PageDirectorTestCase extends UnitTestCase {
  function testSomethingWhichUsesSession() {
    $session =& new MockSession($this);

    $session->setReturnValue('isValid', true);
    $session->setReturnValue('get', 1);

    // ...
  }
}
```

Further, you can set expectations about what methods will be called and how many times. You can even verify some methods should not be called at all.

Here's an expanded test to create and validate some mroe compliex expectations.

```
class PageDirectorTestCase extends UnitTestCase {
  function testSomethingWhichUsesSession() {
    $session =& new MockSession($this);

    $session->setReturnValue('isValid', true);
```

```
        $session->setReturnValue('get', 1);

        $session->expectOnce('isValid', array('user_id'));
        $session->expectOnce('get', array('user_id'));
        $session->expectNever('set');

        // the actual code which uses $session

        $session->tally();
    }
}
```

There are many more reasons and ways to use the *MockObject*. Before continuing, let's put together some additional classes to have a context to work from.

Here is the next component in the refactoring of the legacy script, a UserLogin class to check if the user credentials are correct.

```
class UserLogin {
    var $_valid=true;
    var $_id;
    var $_name;
    function UserLogin($name) {
        switch (strtolower($name)) {
        case 'admin':
            $this->_id = 1;
            $this->_name = 'admin';
            break;
        default:
            trigger_error("Bad user name '$name'");
            $this->_valid=false;
        }
    }
    function name() {
        if ($this->_valid) return $this->_name;
    }
    function Validate($user_name, $password) {
        if ('admin' == strtolower($user_name)
            && 'secret' == $password) {
            return true;
        }
        return false;
    }
}
```

(In a real application, you'd likely base this kind of logic on querying a database table. This sort of a small, hard-coded class represents what you might code as a *ServerStub*—a small class that behaves the way you want, but only in a limited set of circumstances.)

The last component to create is the `Response`. It must handle the task of accumulating HTML content for eventual output to the browser, as well as issuing an HTTP redirect if necessary. (You could perform other header manipulation—say for the purposes of caching—in a mature implementation, but this is simpler code meant to serve as a focused, comprehensible example.)

```php
class Response {
  var $_head='';
  var $_body='';
  function addHead($content) {
    $this->_head .= $content;
  }
  function addBody($content) {
    $this->_body .= $content;
  }
  function display() {
    echo $this->fetch();
  }
  function fetch() {
    return '<html>'
      .'<head>'.$this->_head.'</head>'
      .'<body>'.$this->_body.'</body>'
      .'</html>';
  }
  function redirect($url, $exit=true) {
    header('Location: '.$url);
    if ($exit) exit;
  }
}
```

Given these building blocks, it's time to assemble a page built from these newly developed, tested components. Let's put together one final class to coordinate all of the activity for the page, the aptly-named named `PageDirector`. `PageDirector` has a very simple API: you instantiate it and call its `run()` method.

The "bootstrap" file to run the new application would then look like:

```php
<?php
require_once 'classes.inc.php';
define('SELF', 'http://www.example.com/path/to/page.php');

$page =& new PageDirector(new Session, new Response);
$page->run();
?>
```

This file includes the requisite class definitions, defines a constant for itself, creates an instance of the `PageDirector` class (passing dependent instances of the `Session` and `Response` class as part of the constructor), and executes the `PageDirector::run()` method.

Now let's build some test cases to define the expected behavior of the restructured application.

```
require_once 'simpletest/unit_tester.php';
require_once 'simpletest/reporter.php';
require_once 'simpletest/mock_objects.php';
require_once 'simpletest/web_tester.php';

require_once 'classes.inc.php';
Session::init();

class PageWebTestCase extends WebTestCase { /*...*/ }
class ResponseTestCase extends UnitTestCase { /*...*/ }
class UserLoginTestCase extends UnitTestCase { /*...*/ }
class SessionTestCase extends UnitTestCase { /*...*/ }
class PageDirectorTestCase extends UnitTestCase { /*...*/ }

$test = new GroupTest('Application PHP4 Unit Test');
$test->addTestCase(new PageWebTestCase);
$test->addTestCase(new ResponseTestCase);
$test->addTestCase(new UserLoginTestCase);
$test->addTestCase(new SessionTestCase);
$test->addTestCase(new PageDirectorTestCase);
```

This code block shows a bit more of how a typical test file for an application might shape up. It starts by including the SimpleTest files, including the mock_object.php file to test with mock objects. Next, the subject classes are included and the `Session::init()` method is called to start the session.

Following immediately next are all of the test cases, starting with the "safety harness," the `WebTestCase` that ensures the overall application still performs as required, followed by the individual unit tests for the classes used in the new design (though not detailed in this chapter). Last is the `PageDirectorTestCase`, which is discussed next.

The core responsibility of the `PageDirector` class is to coordinate the `Session` and `Response` objects to produce the final output of your page.

```
Mock::Generate('Session');
Mock::Generate('Response');
define('SELF', 'testvalue');

class PageDirectorTestCase extends UnitTestCase {
  // ...
}
```

At the top of the code, Mock::generate() creates *MockObject* class definitions and defines a constant needed later in the tests.

Assuming that tests already exist for Session and Response, the next step is to create tests using MockSession to simulate the desired state of Session. That *MockObject* setup is similar to the example shown at the very start.

Because the PageDirector::run() method is echoing content, you can use output buffering to capture the content and verify it with assertions.

```
class PageDirectorTestCase extends UnitTestCase {
    // ...
    function TestLoggedOutContent() {
        $session =& new MockSession($this);
        $session->setReturnValue('get', null, array('user_name'));
        $session->expectOnce('get', array('user_name'));

        $page =& new PageDirector($session, new Response);

        ob_start();
        $page->run();
        $result = ob_get_clean();

        $this->assertNoUnwantedPattern('/secret.*content/i', $result);
        $this->assertWantedPattern('/<form.*<input[^>]*text[^>]*'
          .'name.*<input[^>]*password[^>]*passwd/ims'
            ,$result);

        $session->tally();
    }
}
```

This code demonstrates the essentials of using a *MockObject* in SimpleTest. The line $session =& new MockSession($this); creates the mock object. You can then use the methods inherited from the SimpleStub class (http://simpletest.sf.net/SimpleTest/MockObjects/SimpleStub.html#sec-method-summary) to create the responses you expect back from this object (as it works in your tested code). Next, instantiate the PageDirector class and use the MockSession in place of the regular class instance the code is expecting.

setReturnValue()

The **setReturnValue()** method lets the *MockObject* participate as an "actor" in the code by specifying what should be returned when a particular method of the *MockObject* is called. There are several variants of this type of method: one speicifes a series of different values to return in sequence and one returns results by reference instead of by value.

expectOnce()

The **expectOnce()** method allows your *MockObject* to act as a "critic" of the tested code by setting up assumptions about which methods will be called and how often. These expectations are reported in the test when you call the *MockObject's* **tally()** method.

```
class PageDirector {
  var $session;
  var $response;
  function PageDirector(&$session, &$response) {
    $this->session =& $session;
    $this->response =& $response;
  }
}
```

Because the `PageDirector` class believes it is participating in a real application rather than a test case, it echoes the resulting page to the browser. Since you don't actually want this behavior during the test, you can use PHP's output buffering (http://php.net/outcontrol) feature to capture what would have been sent to the browser during the execution of the test code.

```
class PageDirector {
  // ...
  function run() {
    if (!$this->isLoggedIn()) {
      $this->showLogin();
    }
    $this->response->display();
  }
  function isLoggedIn() {
    return ($this->session->get('user_name')) ? true : false;
  }
  function showLogin() {
    $this->response->addBody('<form method="post">');
    $this->response->addBody('Name:<input type="text" name="name">');
    $this->response->addBody("\n");
    $this->response->addBody(
      'Password:<input type="password" name="passwd">');
    $this->response->addBody("\n");
    $this->response->addBody('<input type="submit" value="Login">');
    $this->response->addBody('</form>');
  }
}
```

Like application code, tests can also be refactored. In this case, you can see the output buffering trick is going to be required multiple times, so use the "Extract Method" refactoring to simplify the tests. (Recall that methods that begin with the word "test" are the ones that the test suite runs automatically; any other methods can be created to make your testing easier.)

The next code block shows the result of the output buffering being refactored to the `runPage` method, as well as another test for the output generated when the user is logged in.

```php
class PageDirectorTestCase extends UnitTestCase {
  // ...

  function TestLoggedOutContent() {
    $session =& new MockSession($this);
    $session->setReturnValue('get', null, array('user_name'));
    $session->expectOnce('get', array('user_name'));

    $page =& new PageDirector($session, new Response);
    $result = $this->runPage($page);
    $this->assertNoUnwantedPattern('/secret.*content/i', $result);
    $this->assertWantedPattern('/<form.*<input[^>]*text[^>]*'
      .'name.*<input[^>]*password[^>]*passwd/ims'
      ,$result);

    $session->tally();
  }

  function TestLoggedInContent() {
    $session =& new MockSession($this);
    $session->setReturnValue('get', 'admin', array('user_name'));
    $session->expectAtLeastOnce('get');

    $page =& new PageDirector($session, new Response);
    $result = $this->runPage($page);
    $this->assertWantedPattern('/secret.*content/i', $result);
    $this->assertNoUnwantedPattern('/<form.*<input[^>]*text[^>]*'
      .'name.*<input[^>]*password[^>]*passwd/ims'
      ,$result);
    $session->tally();
  }
  function runPage(&$page) {
    ob_start();
    $page->run();
    return ob_get_clean();
  }
}
```

Next, add a conditional check to the `PageDirector::run()` method to see if the user has logged in and decide what template to display based on the result:

```
class PageDirector {
  // ...

  function run() {
    if ($this->isLoggedIn()) {
      $this->showPage(
        new UserLogin($this->session->get('user_name')));
    } else {
      $this->showLogin();
    }
    $this->response->display();
  }

  function showPage(&$user) {
    $vars = array(
      'name' => $user->name()
      ,'self' => SELF
      );
    $this->response->addBodyTemplate('page.tpl', $vars);
  }
}
```

`page.tpl` might look like this:

```
Welcome <?php echo $name; ?>
<br>Super secret member only content here.
<a href="<?php echo $self; ?>?clear">Logout</a>
```

At this point, MockSession is acting as a *ServerStub* to control conditions for determining whether the user is logged in or not. It also functions as a critic, determining if this information was used correctly in two ways: explicitly by defining expectations and verifying them via tally(), and implicitly by generating the correct output based on the values returned by the *ServerStub*.

To continue restructuring of this code, the next step is to move on to form processing. There are two actions to perform: clear the already logged in user and validate the user name and password submitted by the login page to authenticate a user.

Let's start with the logout capability:

```
class PageDirectorTestCase extends UnitTestCase {
  // ...

  function TestClearLoginFunctionality() {
    $_REQUEST['clear'] = null;
```

```
$session =& new MockSession($this);
$session->expectOnce('clear', array('user_name'));
$session->setReturnValue('get', null, array('user_name'));
$session->expectAtLeastOnce('get');

$response = new MockResponse($this);
$response->expectOnce('redirect', array(SELF));

$page =& new PageDirector($session, $response);
$this->assertEqual('', $this->runPage($page));

$response->tally();
$session->tally();
unset($_REQUEST['clear']);
    }
}
```

In the code, the Response object is mocked; otherwise, the script would stop executing once it hit the exit() call in the Response::redirect() method. By mocking the object, you can verify the method was called and what parameters were passed to the method, without actually having the negative side effect—exiting the script—actually taking place.

Here is some code to realize this test:

```
class PageDirector {
  // ...

  function run() {
    $this->processLogin();
    if ($this->isLoggedIn()) {
      $this->showPage(
        new UserLogin($this->session->get('user_name')));
    } else {
      $this->showLogin();
    }
    $this->response->display();
  }

  function processLogin() {
    if (array_key_exists('clear', $_REQUEST)) {
      $this->session->clear('user_name');
      $this->response->redirect(SELF);
    }
  }
}
```

Last is a test for the form handling for login itself.

```php
class PageDirectorTestCase extends UnitTestCase {
  // ...

  function TestLoginFromRequest() {
    $_REQUEST['name'] = 'admin';
    $_REQUEST['passwd'] = 'secret';

    $session =& new MockSession($this);
    $session->expectOnce('set', array('user_name','admin'));

    $response = new MockResponse($this);
    $response->expectOnce('redirect', array(SELF));

    $page =& new PageDirector($session, $response);
    $this->assertEqual('', $this->runPage($page));

    $response->tally();
    $session->tally();

    unset($_REQUEST['name']);
    unset($_REQUEST['passwd']);
  }
}
```

And here's the code required to implement the features specified by the test shown immediately above:

```php
class PageDirector {
  // ...

  function processLogin() {
    if (array_key_exists('clear', $_REQUEST)) {
      $this->session->clear('user_name');
      $this->response->redirect(SELF);
    }
    if (array_key_exists('name', $_REQUEST)
      && array_key_exists('passwd', $_REQUEST)
      && UserLogin::validate(
        $_REQUEST['name'], $_REQUEST['passwd'])) {
      $this->session->set('user_name', $_REQUEST['name']);
      $this->response->redirect(SELF);
    }
  }
}
```

The application is now restructured and has sufficient test coverage so that additional refactoring can clean up oddities like the main script accessing the Session class and looking up the 'user_name' key instead of the UserLogin class knowing about the key and using the session as a resource.

And why does the code access the $_REQUEST superglobal when it could be wrapped in a resource similar to the Session class to facilitate mocking it? There are many more issues with the code: it was after all a somewhat contrived example to lead you gently into these concepts, and hopefully it has served that purpose.

More importantly, you've made use of the *MockObject* testing pattern to isolate the code, decoupling the $_SESSION resource for testing and avoiding the undesirable consequences of a dependent object (the exit() contained in the Response class).

Issues

Testing using *MockObjects* lets you isolate the code you're developing. You can eliminate nasty side effect and latency issues, greatly speeding up the overall time it takes to run your entire test suite. This is good because the longer it takes to run your tests, the less inclined you may be to actually run them, and you want to be able and willing to run your tests often.

There are still gaps in the freshly-refactored application. The $_REQUEST should have been wrapped by a class so it also could be mocked for testing. Recall the showLogin() method, too. It just looks cluttered with all of the addBody() method calls.

Another disadvantage of this kind of coding style is you have no opportunity to use any kind of WYSIWYG HTML editing tools, as all the HTML is embedded inside of the PHP method calls. To get around these limitations, you could add a very simple template mechanism based on PHP. You might introduce a template file like this:

```
<form method="post">
Name:<input type="text" name="name">
Password:<input type="password" name-"passwd">
<input type="submit" value="Login">
</form>
```

It then needs a method to make use of it:

```
class Response {
  // ...

  /**
   * adds a simple template mechanism to the response class
   * @param string  $template  the path and name of the template file
```

```
 * @return  void
 */
function addBodyTemplate($template, $vars=array()) {
  if (file_exists($template)) {
    extract($vars);
    ob_start();
    include $template;
    $this->_body .= ob_get_clean();
  }
}
}
```

Clearly, this is not the fanciest template engine in the world, but it does allow the code in this chapter's example to be tidied up.

The concept of separation of responsibilities is encouraged in GoF:

"Create objects in a separate operation so that subclasses can override the way they are created."

You can get a lot of mileage from this statement if you apply it wholeheartedly to testing: you can have the internal *Factory* method replace the expected instance of the class with a replacement *MockObject*. The traditional testing pattern to follow is subclassing your testing code, and then rewriting the method producing the object. Marcus Baker, the author of SimpleTest, has created the *PartialMock* technique for PHP, which is a shortcut for this testing pattern. You can use a PartialMock to inject other *MockObjects* at the point of creation.

If you have difficulty with understanding how to get your *MockObject* into your code, look over the *Partial MockObject* section of *Appendix B—SimpleTest Testing Practices*.

Resources

There are a few helpful resources to learn more about the *MockObject* pattern. Specific to PHP, you can look at the *MockObject* documentation for SimpleTest (http://simpletest.sf.net/SimpleTest/tutorial_MockObjects.pkg.html). Additionally, Marcus Baker wrote an article titled "Testing Made Easy with Mock Objects" in the January 2004 edition of php|architect.

More generally, the web site http://www.mockobjects.com/ and the c2 wiki page for *MockObjects* (http://www.c2.com/cgi/wiki?MockObject) both make excellent starting points for investigation.

7

The Strategy Pattern

W HEN DEVELOPING OBJECT-ORIENTED CODE, you sometimes need an object to vary its behavior slightly based on circumstance. For example, a Menu might render itself horizontally or vertically depending on a user's "skin" preference, or an Order might calculate sales tax differently based on the customer's shipping address.

A typical implementation of an object like Menu has methods to add(), delete(), and replace() menu items, set() the style, and render() itself. No matter what kind of menu you want to create, Menu offers a consistent interface; only the internal algorithms of one or more methods—at least render(), for example—differ.

But what happens, say, as the number of menu styles expands? Or, in the case of Order, what happens as county, state, and foreign country tax rules are taken into account? If many methods have case statements to implement special cases, an otherwise simple encapsulation soon becomes convoluted, difficult to read and difficult to maintain.

The Problem

How can you change the internal implementation of an object easily, choosing an implementation to use at the time your script is executed, rather than when it was written? How can you code a set of implementations that are easy to maintain and extend?

The Solution

When a class embodies multiple implementations and an instance can dynamically choose any of those implementations, use the *Strategy* pattern to separate the object from its algorithms. Or, put more simply, if a class's methods use `case` statements pervasively, it's a good candidate for refactoring into the *Strategy* pattern.

The *Strategy* design pattern is very powerful because the core idea of the pattern is the OOP principal of *polymorphism*.

There are clear examples of the *Strategy* pattern outside of the domain of programming. If I need to get from home to work in the morning, I can choose among several strategies: I can drive my car, take the bus, walk, ride a bike, or fly in a helicopter. Each strategy has the same result, but uses resources differently, and the choice of the strategy depends on expense, time, the availability of a particular resources (like owning a vehicle), and the convenience of each method. A good strategy on one day may be a poor one the next, so the choice of strategy has to be made dynamically.

You've already seen the start of an example similar to the *Strategy* pattern in the chapter on the *Factory* pattern: the framework for the Monopoly game used a family of similar property classes, because rent calculations for different kinds of properties vary greatly. However, because the calculation of rent was not extracted into it's own class, the rent calculation is actually more representative of the *TemplateMethod* pattern.

An Example

As an example, let's create a cache to store PHP variables. The cache class must write out a representation of a variable to a file, so you can later reload and reuse it. The class should also let you specify an identifier for the cached data and a storage methodology.

Data Caching

A *cache* saves a resource for later reuse. You might create and use a cache if re-creation of the resource from the original source is significantly more expensive than reading it from your cache. Examples of this might be slow aggregate queries from a database or parsing of large XML or configuration files.

Caches are not without issues: your cache can fall out of synch with the data source (becoming *stale*) and some caches require extra memory.

Let's start by developing a cache implementation without the *Strategy* pattern.

Because you might want to cache more than one value, you'll need an identifier to specify which cached item you're interested in. In this example, the identifier is 'application_config'. Here's an example of how a cache might be used:

```php
// PHP4
$config_cache =& new VarCache('application_config');
if ($config_cache->isValid()) {
  $config = $config_cache->get();
} else {
  $config = slow_expensive_function_to_get_config();
  $config_cache->set($config);
}
```

The code creates a new VarCache object stored in the variable $config_cache. The data in the cache is associated with the identifier 'application_config'. If the cache contains a value, isValid() returns true and the cached value is returned; otherwise, the value is computed anew and is saved into the cache for retrieval later on.

As usual, let's start coding by writing a test case. First, an empty cache should always return false in response to the isValid() method.

```php
class VarCacheTestCase extends UnitTestCase {
  function TestUnsetValueIsInvalid() {
    $cache =& new VarCache('foo');
    $this->assertFalse($cache->isValid());
  }
```

Since there's no code for VarCache yet, the simplest implementation is to just stub out the method.

```php
class VarCache {
  function isValid() {}
}
```

That produces a green bar, so it's OK to continue, adding to the test case.

```
class VarCacheTestCase extends UnitTestCase {
    function TestUnsetValueIsInvalid() { /* ... */ }
    function TestIsValidTrueAfterSet() {
        $cache =& new VarCache('foo');
        $cache->set('bar');
        $this->assertTrue($cache->isValid());
    }
```

The test above verifies that a cache is valid when it's non-empty.

Time to start coding the cache class in earnest. VarCache is passed an identifier, so the constructor for an instance must record that. There's also the set() method, which stores a value in the cache and has the side effect of changing the value returned by isValid().

```
class VarCache {
    var $_name;
    function VarCache($name) {
        $this->_name = 'cache/'.$name;
    }
    function isValid() {
        return file_exists($this->_name.'.php');
    }
    function set() {
        $file_handle = fopen($this->_name.'.php', 'w');
        fclose($file_handle);
    }
}
```

The instance variable $_name stores the cache's identifier for the data. In this simple implementation, $_name is used as part of a file name (which would probably be replaced by a database or other store in a real application). set() uses fopen() and fclose() to "touch" a file based on $_name. After calling set(), the file_exists() call in VarCache::isValid() returns true.

Running this test yields a green bar, but running it again provokes a failure! What happened? The first invocation of the tests leaves a file behind, thus interfering with the second run of the tests, a very undesirable condition. Ideally, each test case should be independent.

Fortunately, unit testing frameworks, in general, and SimpleTest specifically, provide facilities to prepare an environment before a test runs and restore the environment to a known state after. UnitTestCase::setUp() performs the former; UnitTestCase::tearDown() performs the latter.

By adding the following to the test case, you can be sure that each test method begins with a fresh start:

```
class VarCacheTestCase extends UnitTestCase {
  function setup() {
    @unlink('cache/foo.php');
  }
  // ...
}
```

Now the cached file is removed prior to the execution of each test method, ensuring isolation for each test method. (In a more realistic use of Test Driven Development, you'd probably write a VarCache::clear() method to handle removal of a cached variable.)

Now that the artifact from the test's been removed, the tests run again, meaning you're ready to continue testing and coding.

```
class VarCacheTestCase extends UnitTestCase {
  function setup() { /* ... */ }
  function TestUnsetValueIsInvalid() { /* ... */ }
  function TestIsValidTrueAfterSet() { /* ... */ }
  function TestCacheRetainsValue() {
    $test_val = 'test'.rand(1,100);
    $cache =& new VarCache('foo');
    $cache->set($test_val);
    $this->assertEqual($test_val, $cache->get());
  }
}
```

The test above validates that VarCache::get() returns the same value that was passed to VarCache::set().

```
class VarCache {
  var $_name;
  function VarCache($name) { /* ... */ }
  function isValid() { /* ... */ }
  function get() {
    if ($this->isValid()) {
      return file_get_contents($this->_name.'.php');
    }
  }
  function set($value) {
    $file_handle = fopen($this->_name.'.php', 'w');
    fwrite($file_handle, $value);
    fclose($file_handle);
  }
}
```

With the additions highlighted in bold, VarCache::set() writes the contents of the $value parameter to the file and VarCache::get() returns the value with file_get_content().

The implementation so far works great for strings and numbers, but fails for more complex variables such as arrays and objects. Expressed as a test case:

```
class VarCacheTestCase extends UnitTestCase {
    // ...
    function TestStringFailsForArray() {
        $test_val = array('one','two');
        $cache =& new VarCache('foo');
        $cache->set($test_val);
        $this->assertError('Array to string conversion');
        $this->assertNotEqual($test_val, $cache->get());
        $this->assertEqual('array',strtolower($cache->get()));
    }
```

For the sake of brevity, let's jump to the end of this implementation, which subsequently serves as a starting point for the *Strategy* refactoring.

Here's a series of additions to complete this variation of VarCache.

```
class VarCache {
    //...
    function get() {
        if ($this->isValid()) {
            include $this->_name.'.php';
            return $cached_content;
        }
    //...
    }
```

The key change here is that the get() method is included (and is therefore expected to be valid PHP). Further, the method returns the variable $cached_content, so whatever the set() method does, it must set that variable!

So, what might this look like for a numeric value?

```
class VarCache {
    //...
    function set($value) {
        $file_handle = fopen($this->_name.'.php', 'w');
        $template = '<?php $cached_content = %s;';
        $content = sprintf($template
```

```
        ,(float)$value);
      fwrite($file_handle, $content);
      fclose($file_handle);
    }
}
```

This works fine for a number, but what about strings? For strings, the PHP cache file template must end in = '%s'; instead of = %s;. This is where a "type" parameter comes in: it will specify a numeric or string (or other type). And in anticipation of adding yet more types, let's add a case statement in the set() method and a _getTemplate() method to make adding new types easier.

```
class VarCache {
  var $_name;
  var $_type;
  function VarCache($name, $type='string') {
    $this->_name = 'cache/'.$name;
    $this->_type = $type;
  }
  // ...
  function _getTemplate() {
    $template = '<?php $cached_content = ';
    switch ($this->_type) {
    case 'string':
      $template .= "'%s';";
      break;
    case 'numeric':
      $template .= '%s;';
      break;
    default:
      trigger_error('invalid cache type');
    }
    return $template;
  }
  function set($value) {
    $file_handle = fopen($this->_name.'.php', 'w');
    switch ($this->_type) {
    case 'string':
      $content = sprintf($this->_getTemplate()
        ,str_replace("'","\\'",$value));
      break;
    case 'numeric':
      $content = sprintf($this->_getTemplate()
        ,(float)$value);
      break;
    default:
      trigger_error('invalid cache type');
    }
    fwrite($file_handle, $content);
    fclose($file_handle);
  }
}
```

At this point, the constructor has an optional second parameter that indicates type, with choices of 'numeric' and 'string'. The final version of the class, shown beow, includes a 'serialize' storage type that stores complex types like arrays or objects.

```php
class VarCache {
  var $_name;
  var $_type;
  function VarCache($name, $type='serialize') {
    $this->_name = 'cache/'.$name;
    $this->_type = $type;
  }
  function isvalid() {
    return file_exists($this->_name.'.php');
  }
  function get() {
    if ($this->isvalid()) {
      include $this->_name.'.php';
      return $cached_content;
    }
  }
  function _getTemplate() {
    $template = '<?php $cached_content = ';
    switch ($this->_type) {
    case 'string':
      $template .= "'%s';";
      break;
    case 'serialize':
      $template .= "unserialize(stripslashes('%s'));";
      break;
    case 'numeric':
      $template .= '%s;';
      break;
    default:
      trigger_error('invalid cache type');
    }
    return $template;
  }
  function set($value) {
    $file_handle = fopen($this->_name.'.php', 'w');
    switch ($this->_type) {
    case 'string':
      $content = sprintf($this->_getTemplate()
        ,str_replace("'","\\'",$value));
      break;
    case 'serialize':
      $content = sprintf($this->_getTemplate()
        ,addslashes(serialize($value)));
      break;
    case 'numeric':
      $content = sprintf($this->_getTemplate()
        ,(float)$value);
      break;
    default:
      trigger_error('invalid cache type');
    }
    fwrite($file_handle, $content);
```

```
        fclose($file_handle);
    }
  }
```

Notice the case statement in both the _getTemplate() and set() methods. Both of these "switch" based on the $_type instance variable. The get() method does not behave differently based on $_type, so it looks like the variability is limited solely to how the information is stored. Multiple case statements are a warning sign that it may be appropriate to refactor to apply the *Strategy* pattern instead.

Sample Code

A change from multiple switch statements to the *Strategy* pattern is a classic example of refactoring. The test cases remain identical; only the internals of the VarCache class change.

The first step in refactoring is to isolate the variations that you want to encapsulate in a separate class. Based on the foregoing example, you have the three "type" variations: 'string', 'numeric', and 'serialize'. The previous example also selects the output format at the time the object is created. Given that "algorithm," you need to create an API that encapsulates it.

You can start with:

```
class CacheWriter {
  function store($file_handle, $var) {
    die('abstract class-implement in concrete CacheWriter');
  }
}
```

This is the PHP4 version of an interface. (You could inherit from this class to guarantee that you correctly wrote the subclass, but that just adds to processing overhead, particularly if you have the definition of the abstract CacheWriter class in a different file from the concrete CacheWriter subclasses.)

The abstract CacheWriter calls for a store() method that accepts a file handle and the variable to store. Each concrete class must implement store(), using whatever algorithm is necessary to output the content of a file that, when included as a PHP script, populates the variable $cached_content with the variable passed as a parameter to the store() method. Each algorithm is implemented as a separate class.

Recall the code that you're replacing:

```php
class VarCache {
  // ...
  function _getTemplate() {
    $template = '<?php $cached_content = ';
    switch ($this->_type) {
    case 'string':
      $template .= "'%s';";
      break;
    }
    // ...
  }
  function set($value) {
    $file_handle = fopen($this->_name.'.php', 'w');
    switch ($this->_type) {
    case 'string':
      $content = sprintf($this->_getTemplate()
        ,str_replace("'","\\'",$value));
      break;
    // ...
    }
    fwrite($file_handle, $content);
    fclose($file_handle);
  }
}
```

For each "type" of caching, you need to extract the relevant portions of the _getTemplate() and
set() methods into each respective class. Here is StringCacheWriter:

```php
class StringCacheWriter /* implements CacheWriter */ {
  function store($file_handle, $string) {
    $content = sprintf(
      "<?php\n\$cached_content = '%s';"
      ,str_replace("'","\\'",$string));
    fwrite($file_handle, $contents);
  }
}
```

(Because PHP 4 does not support the concept of interfaces, simply note the interface in a comment
for documentation.)

Here are the other algorithms—the storage "strategies."

```php
class NumericCacheWriter /* implements CacheWriter */ {
  function store($file_handle, $numeric) {
    $content = sprintf("<?php\n\$cached_content = %s;"
      ,(double)$numeric);
```

```
      fwrite($file_handle, $content);
    }
  }

  class SerializingCacheWriter /* implements CacheWriter */ {
    function store($file_handle, $var) {
      $content = sprintf(
        "<?php\n\$cached_content = unserialize(stripslashes('%s'));"
        ,addslashes(serialize($var)));
      fwrite($file_handle, $content);
    }
  }
```

With the algorithm encapsulated as interchangeable classes (the same API, polymorphism), you can now move back to the VarCache() class to re-implement it using the *Strategy* pattern. The very same test cases should continue to run for the refactored version.

```
  class VarCache {
    var $_name;
    var $_type;
    function VarCache($name, $type='serialize') {
      $this->_name = 'cache/'.$name;
      switch (strtolower($type)) {
      case 'string':     $strategy = 'String';         break;
      case 'numeric':    $strategy = 'Numeric';        break;
      case 'serialize':
      default:           $strategy = 'Serializing';
      }
      $strategy .= 'CacheWriter';
      $this->_type =& new $strategy;
    }
    function isValid() {
      return file_exists($this->_name.'.php');
    }
    function get() {
      if ($this->isValid()) {
        include $this->_name.'.php';
        return $cached_content;
      }
    }
    function set($value) {
      $file_handle = fopen($this->_name.'.php', 'w');
      $this->_type->store($file_handle, $value);
      fclose($file_handle);
    }
  }
```

By creating a concrete instance of the CacheWriter class and binding it to the $_type instance variable, you can use the line $this->_type->store($file_handle, $value) to write the complete cache file, no longer caring which of the algorithms was selected initially.

This shows the defining characteristics of the *Strategy* pattern: a family of algorithms, each encapsulated in an individual class but bound to a container object that only uses the public API in the exact same way independent of the selection of a particular concrete strategy.

Issues

The *Strategy* design pattern is very powerful. While the other patterns introduced so far in this book provide fundamental building blocks for applications, *Strategy* is the first pattern that has the capability to play a truly pivotal part in application design and the transformation of a project.

The ability to swap out the "guts" of an object, altering the behavior or performance of the entire object, is very powerful. Also, a particular strategy is bound to the object once and then forgotten, making the rest of the API easier to implement. Ultimately, which algorithm is in use is completely transparent to the rest of your code.

An unattributed quote seen on the Internet says "Eventually, everything starts to look like the *Strategy* pattern." Why? Because this pattern captures the very spirit of polymorphism, one of the more powerful aspects of OOP.

Related Patterns

The *Strategy* pattern is similar to several other patterns. The main difference between the *Strategy* pattern and the *State* pattern is that *Strategy* binds once, whereas the *State* pattern changes behavior with changes in the values of instance variables (the state of the object). Or, put another way, the *Strategy* pattern changes the behavior of the object during constructon; *State* changes the behavior of the object dynamically over the lifetime of the object.

Design Pattern—State

The *State* pattern allows an object to alter its behavior when its internal state changes. Effectively, the object appears to change its class.

The *Decorator* pattern (see *Chapter 12*) is the conceptual opposite of the *Strategy* pattern. To borrow an analogy from GoF, where the *Strategy* changes the "guts" of an object, the *Decorator* pattern changes its "skin."

One last, related pattern is the *Visitor*. In the *Strategy* pattern, you create a concrete instance of the selected strategy and bind it to an instance variable; in the *Visitor* pattern, the *Strategy* is passed in as a parameter. You could then think of the *Visitor* pattern as the dependency inverse of the *Strategy* pattern.

8

The Iterator Pattern

OBJECT-ORIENTED PROGRAMMING ENCAPSULATES application logic in classes. Classes, in turn, are instantiated as objects, and each individual object has a distinct identity and state. Individual objects are a useful way to organize your code, but often you want to work with a *group of objects*, or a *collection*. A set of rows from a SQL query is a collection, as is the list of Property objects in the Monopoly game examples shown earlier in the book.

A collection need not be homogeneous either. A Window object in a graphical user interface framework could collect any number of control objects — a Menu, a Slider, and a Button, among others. Moreover, the implementation of a collection can vary: a PHP array is a collection, but so is a hash table, a linked list, a stack, and a queue.

The Problem

How can one easily manipulate any collection of objects?

The Solution

Use the *Iterator* pattern to provide uniform access to the contents of a collection.

You may not realize it, but you use the *Iterator* pattern every day—it's embodied in PHP's `array` type and rich set of array manipulation functions. (Indeed, given the combination of the native array type in the language and a host of flexible functions designed to work with this native type, you need a pretty compelling reason not to use arrays as your means of manipulating collections of objects.)

Here's native array iteration in PHP:

```
$test = array('one', 'two', 'three');
$output = '';
reset($test);
do {
    $output .= current($test);
} while (next($test));

echo $output; // produces 'onetwothree'
```

The `reset()` function restarts iteration to the beginning of the array; `current()` returns the value of the current element; and `next()` advances to the next element in the array and returns the new `current()` value. When you advance past the end of the array, `next()` returns `false`. Using these iteration methods, the internal implementation of a PHP array is irrelevant to you.

Iterator couples the object-oriented programming principles of encapsulation and polymorphism. Using *Iterator*, you can manipulate the objects in a collection without explicitly knowing how the collection is implemented or what the collection contains (what kinds of objects). *Iterator* provides a uniform interface to different concrete iteration implementations, which do contain the details of how to manipulate a specific collection, including which items to show (filtering) and in what order (sorting).

Let's create a simple object to manipulate in a collection. (Though this example is in PHP5, *Iterators* are not unique to PHP5 and most of the examples in this chapter work in PHP4 as well, albeit with a healthy amount of reference operators added). The object, `Lendable`, represents media such as movies and albums and is intended to be part of a web site or service to let users review or lend portions of their media collection to other users. (For this example, do not concern yourself with persistence and the like.)

Let's start with the following test as a basis for the design of `Lendable`.

```
// PHP5
class LendableTestCase extends UnitTestCase {
```

```
        function TestCheckout() {
          $item = new Lendable;
          $this->assertFalse($item->borrower);
          $item->checkout('John');
          $this->assertEqual('borrowed', $item->status);
          $this->assertEqual('John', $item->borrower);
        }

        function TestCheckin() {
          $item = new Lendable;
          $item->checkout('John');
          $item->checkin();
          $this->assertEqual('library', $item->status);
          $this->assertFalse($item->borrower);
        }
      }
```

To implement the requirements of this initial test, let's create a class with a few public attributes and some methods to toggle the values of these attributes:

```
class Lendable {
  public $status = 'library';
  public $borrower = '';

  public function checkout($borrower) {
    $this->status = 'borrowed';
    $this->borrower = $borrower;
  }

  public function checkin() {
    $this->status = 'library';
    $this->borrower = '';
  }
}
```

Lendable is a good, generic start. Let's extend it to track items like DVDs or CDs.

Media extends Lendable and tracks details about specific media, including the name of the item, the year it was released, and what type of item it is:

```
class Media extends Lendable {
  public $name;
  public $type;
  public $year;

  public function __construct($name, $year, $type='dvd') {
    $this->name = $name;
```

```
            $this->type = $type;
            $this->year = (int)$year;
        }
    }
```

To keep things simple, Media has three public instance variables, Media::name, Media::year, and Media::type. The constructor takes two arguments and stores the first in $name and the second in $year. The constructor also allows an optional third parameter to specify type (which defaults to "dvd").

Given individual objects to manipulate, you can now create a container to hold them: a Library. Like a regular library, Library should be able to add, remove and count the items in the collection. Eventually, Library should also permit access to individual items (objects) in the collection (which is shown momentarily in the *Sample Code* section of this chapter).

For right now, let's build a test case for Library.

```
class LibraryTestCase extends UnitTestCase {
  function TestCount() {
    $lib = new Library;
    $this->assertEqual(0, $lib->count());
  }
}
```

It's easy enough to write a class that satisfies this test:

```
class Library {
  function count() {
    return 0;
  }
}
```

Let's continue and add some interesting features to the test:

```
class LibraryTestCase extends UnitTestCase {

  function TestCount() { /* ... */ }

  function TestAdd() {
```

```
        $lib = new Library;
        $lib->add('one');
        $this->assertEqual(1, $lib->count());
    }
}
```

An easy way to implement add() is to piggyback on PHP's flexible array functions: you can add items to an array instance variable and use count() to return the number of items in the collection.

```
class Library {
    protected $collection = array();

    function count() {
        return count($this->collection);
    }

    function add($item) {
        $this->collection[] = $item;
    }
}
```

Library is now a collection, but it provides no way to retrieve or manipulate the individual members of the collection.

Let's move on to the purpose of the chapter, implementation of the *Iterator* design pattern.

The following UML class diagram shows the GoF *Iterator* pattern with the Media and Library classes used to make the example concrete.

- Your collection class must provide a *Factory* (see *Chapter* 3) to create an instance of your *Iterator*.

- *Iterator* classes define an interface of first() to go to the beginning of a collection, next() to move to the next item in sequence as you iterate, currentItem() to retrieve the current item from the collection as you iterate, and isDone() to indicate when you have iterated over the entire collection.

In the Sample Code section, the LibraryGofIterator class is an example of a direct implementation of the GoF *Iterator* design pattern.

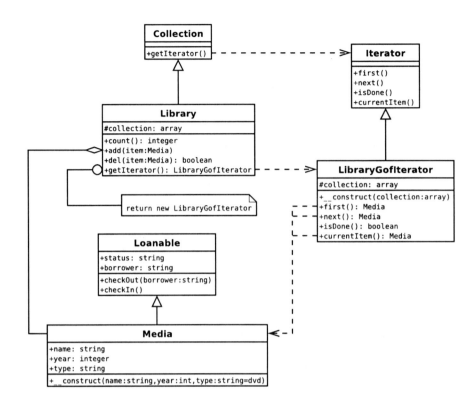

Sample Code

The first step in implementing the GoF *Iterator* pattern within Library is to write a new test case for the new concrete *Iterator*. Since each test method will manipulate a Library filled with Media instances, you can employ the UnitTestCase::setUp() method to populate a variable with a Library in a known state for each test.

Start by adding the Library::getIterator() method as a *Factory* for instances of the LibraryGofIterator class.

```
class IteratorTestCase extends UnitTestCase {
  protected $lib;

  function setup() {
    $this->lib = new Library;
    $this->lib->add(new Media('name1', 2000));
    $this->lib->add(new Media('name2', 2002));
    $this->lib->add(new Media('name3', 2001));
  }

  function TestGetGofIterator() {
```

```
        $this->assertIsA($it = $this->lib->getIterator()
            ,'LibraryGofIterator');
        }
    }
```

Here's the implementation:

```
class Library {
    // ...
    function getIterator() {
        return new LibraryGofIterator($this->collection);
    }
}
```

The getIterator() method passes the Library's $collection to the constructor of the new concrete iterator. This technique has two important implications: each iterator is independent, so multiple iterators can operate at the same time. Additionally, the iterator operates on the collection *as it existed* at the time the iterator was requested. If another item is added to the collection at any time later, you must request another iterator to display it (at least in this implementation).

Let's continue enhancing the test suite by adding assertions to the TestGetGofIterator() method to match the *Iterator* design pattern. The isDone() method should only be true if you've iterated over the entire collection. If the iterator's just been created, isDone() should obviously return false to indicate it's okay to iterate.

```
class IteratorTestCase extends UnitTestCase {
    function setup() { /* ... */ }

    function TestGetGofIterator() {
        $this->assertIsA($it = $this->lib->getIterator()
            ,'LibraryGofIterator');
        $this->assertFalse($it->isdone());
    }
}
```

As usual with TDD, implement the simplest possible code that satisfies your test case:

```
class LibraryGofIterator {
```

```
        function isDone() {
          return false;
        }
    }
```

So, what should happen during the *first* iteration? `currentItem()` should return the first `Media` object added in the `IteratorTestCase::setUp()` method and `isDone()` should continue to be false, since two additional items remain to be iterated over.

```
class IteratorTestCase extends UnitTestCase {
   function setUp() { /* ... */ }
   function TestGetGofIterator() {
     $this->assertIsA($it = $this->lib->getIterator()
       ,'LibraryGofIterator');
     $this->assertFalse($it->isdone());
     $this->assertIsA($first = $it->currentItem(), 'Media');
     $this->assertEqual('name1', $first->name);
     $this->assertFalse($it->isdone());
   }
}
```

It's critical that `LibraryGofIterator` receives the `$collection` in the constructor (see the minimal implementation of `Library` above) and returns the `current()` item of that array from the `currentItem()` method.

```
class LibraryGofIterator {
   protected $collection;
   function __construct($collection) {
     $this->collection = $collection;
   }
   function currentItem() {
     return current($this->collection);
   }
   function isDone() {
     return false;
   }
}
```

What should happen in the next iteration? The `next()` method should change what item is returned by the `currentItem()` method. This next test captures that expected behavior:

```
class IteratorTestCase extends UnitTestCase {
  function setup() { /* ... */ }
  function TestGetGofIterator() {
    $this->assertIsA($it = $this->lib->getIterator(), 'LibraryGofIterator');
    $this->assertFalse($it->isdone());
    $this->assertIsA($first = $it->currentItem(), 'Media');
    $this->assertEqual('name1', $first->name);
    $this->assertFalse($it->isdone());

    $this->assertTrue($it->next());
    $this->assertIsA($second = $it->currentItem(), 'Media');
    $this->assertEqual('name2', $second->name);
    $this->assertFalse($it->isdone());
  }
}
```

Piggybacking again on PHP's array functions, use next() on the array:

```
class LibraryGofIterator {
  protected $collection;
  function __construct($collection) {
    $this->collection = $collection;
  }
  function currentItem() {
    return current($this->collection);
  }
  function next() {
    return next($this->collection);
  }
  function isDone() {
    return false;
  }
}
```

The third iteration looks much like the others, except the isDone() method must return true. You also want next() to indicate success of moving to the next iteration:

```
class IteratorTestCase extends UnitTestCase {
  function setup() { /* ... */ }
  function TestGetGofIterator() {
    $this->assertIsA($it = $this->lib->getIterator(), 'LibraryGofIterator');
    $this->assertFalse($it->isdone());
    $this->assertIsA($first = $it->currentItem(), 'Media');
    $this->assertEqual('name1', $first->name);
    $this->assertFalse($it->isdone());
```

```
        $this->assertTrue($it->next());
        $this->assertIsA($second = $it->currentItem(), 'Media');
        $this->assertEqual('name2', $second->name);
        $this->assertFalse($it->isdone());

        $this->assertTrue($it->next());
        $this->assertIsA($third = $it->currentItem(), 'Media');
        $this->assertEqual('name3', $third->name);
        $this->assertFalse($it->next());
        $this->assertTrue($it->isdone());
    }
}
```

With small modifications to the next() and isDone() methods, all of the tests pass Here's the code so far:

```
class LibraryGofIterator {
    protected $collection;
    function __construct($collection) {
        $this->collection = $collection;
    }

    function first() {
        reset($this->collection);
    }

    function next() {
        return (false !== next($this->collection));
    }

    function isDone() {
        return (false === current($this->collection));
    }

    function currentItem() {
        return current($this->collection);
    }
}
```

There's just one problem with the *Iterator* test case: it doesn't reflect how iterators are typically used. Yes, it tests all of the features of the *Iterator* pattern, but application code uses the *Iterator* in a much simpler way. So, the next step is to write a test using more realistic code.

```
class IteratorTestCase extends UnitTestCase {
    protected $lib;
    function setup() { /* ... */ }
    function TestGetGofIterator() { /* ... */ }
```

```
    function TestGofIteratorUsage() {
      $output = '';
      for ($it=$this->lib->getIterator(); !$it->isDone(); $it->next()){
        $output .= $it->currentItem()->name;
      }
      $this->assertEqual('name1name2name3', $output);
    }
}
```

So far, the implementation of *Iterator* copies an array (the collection) and uses PHP's internal pointer to track the iteration. You can also implement the *Iterator* by keeping track of the collection index by yourself. This requires a new accessor method in Library to fetch an object by key.

```
class Library {
  // ...
  function get($key) {
    if (array_key_exists($key, $this->collection)) {
      return $this->collection[$key];
    }
  }
}
```

Also, you'd pass $this (the library itself) to the constructor instead of $this->collection (the array containing the Media collection) in the Library::getIterator() method.

The "external" iterator would then just track a pointer internally to know which element of the Library collection it's currently referencing, and would use the reference to the Library passed in the constructor to call the get() method to retrieve the current object.

```
class LibraryGofExternalIterator {
  protected $key = 0;
  protected $collection;

  function __construct($collection) {
    $this->collection = $collection;
  }
  function first() {
    $this->key=0;
  }
  function next() {
    return (++$this->key < $this->collection->count());
  }
  function isDone() {
    return ($this->key >= $this->collection->count());
  }
```

```php
    function currentItem() {
      return $this->collection->get($this->key);
    }
  }
```

This implementation assumes your collection array is indexed starting with 0 and is completely sequential.

A Variant Iterator API

While the foregoing code is a complete implementation of the *Iterator* pattern as described by GoF, you may find the four-method API a bit cumbersome. If so, you can collapse next(), currentItem(), and isDone() into just next() by having the latter either advance and return the current item from the collection or return false if the entire collection has been processed.

Here's one way to write a test for this variation of the API:

```php
class IteratorTestCase extends UnitTestCase {
  // ...
  function TestMediaIteratorUsage() {
    $this->assertIsA(
      $it = $this->lib->getIterator('media')
      ,'LibraryIterator');
    $output = '';
    while ($item = $it->next()) {
      $output .= $item->name;
    }
    $this->assertEqual('name1name2name3', $output);
  }
}
```

In the code above, notice the simplified control structure for looping. next() returns an object or false, allowing you to perform the assignment inside the while loop conditional.

The next few examples explore variations of the *Iterator* pattern using the smaller interface. As a convenience, change the Library::getIterator() method to a parameterized *Factory* so you can get either the four-method iterator or the two-method iterator (next() and reset()) from that single method.

```php
class Library {
  // ...
  function getIterator($type=false) {
    switch (strtolower($type)) {
```

```
      case 'media':
        $iterator_class = 'LibraryIterator';
        break;
      default:
        $iterator_class = 'LibraryGofIterator';
      }
      return new $iterator_class($this->collection);
  }
}
```

Here, Library::getIterator() now accepts a parameter to select what kind of iterator to return. The default is LibraryGofIterator (so the existing tests still pass). Passing the string media to the method creates and returns a LibraryIterator instead.

This is some code to implement LibraryIterator:

```
class LibraryIterator {
  protected $collection;
  function __construct($collection) {
    $this->collection = $collection;
  }
  function next() {
    return next($this->collection);
  }
}
```

Oops! The dreaded red bar! What happened to get the error "Equal expectation fails at character 4 with name1name2name3 and name2name3"? Somehow, the first iteration was skipped—that's a bug. To fix the error, return current() for the first call of the next() method.

```
class LibraryIterator {
  protected $collection;
  protected $first=true;
  function __construct($collection) {
    $this->collection = $collection;
  }
  function next() {
    if ($this->first) {
      $this->first = false;
      return current($this->collection);
    }
    return next($this->collection);
  }
}
```

Presto! A green bar and a streamlined `while` loop iterator.

Filtering Iterator

With *Iterators,* you can do more than just present each item of the collection. You can also select what items are presented. Let's modify the `Library::getIterator()` to allow two additional iterator types.

```
class Library {
  // ...
    function getIterator($type=false) {
      switch (strtolower($type)) {
      case 'media':
        $iterator_class = 'LibraryIterator';
        break;
      case 'available':
        $iterator_class = 'LibraryAvailableIterator';
        break;
      case 'released':
        $iterator_class = 'LibraryReleasedIterator';
        break;
      default:
        $iterator_class = 'LibraryGofIterator';
      }
      return new $iterator_class($this->collection);
  }
}
```

The class `LibraryAvailableIterator` should only iterate over items that have a status of "library" (recall that the `checkOut()` method changes the status to "borrowed").

```
class IteratorTestCase extends UnitTestCase {
  // ...
    function TestAvailableIteratorUsage() {
      $this->lib->add($dvd = new Media('test', 1999));
      $this->lib->add(new Media('name4', 1999));
      $this->assertIsA(
        $it = $this->lib->getIterator('available')
        ,'LibraryAvailableIterator');
      $output = '';

      while ($item = $it->next()) {
        $output .= $item->name;
      }
      $this->assertEqual('name1name2name3testname4', $output);

      $dvd->checkOut('Jason');
      $it = $this->lib->getIterator('available');
      $output = '';
```

```
        while ($item = $it->next()) {
          $output .= $item->name;
        }
        $this->assertEqual('name1name2name3name4', $output);
    }
  }
```

This test creates a new `Media` instance and stores it in the variable `$dvd`. The first highlighted `assertEqual()` assertion verifies that the new item is present when iterating with `LibraryAvailableIterator`. Next, the test uses the `checkOut()` method and verifies that the new item is missing from the display.

The code to implement filtering is very similar to `LibraryIterator::next()`, except filtering is done prior to returning the item. If the current item does not match the filter criteria, the code returns `$this->next()` instead.

```
class LibraryAvailableIterator {
  protected $collection = array();
  protected $first=true;
  function __construct($collection) {
    $this->collection = $collection;
  }
  function next() {
    if ($this->first) {
      $this->first = false;
      $ret = current($this->collection);
    } else {
      $ret = next($this->collection);
    }
    if ($ret && 'library' != $ret->status) {
      return $this->next();
    }
    return $ret;
  }
}
```

Sorting Iterator

An iterator can do more than show all or a portion of the collection. An iterator can also show the collection in a specific order. Let's create an iterator that sorts the `Media` in the collection by release date.

For a test, add some `Media` instances with dates older that those of the items added in the `setUp()` method. If the iterator works, these older items should be sorted to the beginning of the iteration.

```
class IteratorTestCase extends UnitTestCase {
  // ...
  function TestReleasedIteratorUsage() {
    $this->lib->add(new Media('second', 1999));
    $this->lib->add(new Media('first', 1989));
    $this->assertIsA(
      $it = $this->lib->getIterator('released')
      ,'LibraryReleasedIterator');
    $output = array();
    while ($item = $it->next()) {
      $output[] = $item->name .'-'. $item->year;
    }
    $this->assertEqual(
      'first-1989 second-1999 name1-2000 name3-2001 name2-2002'
      ,implode(' ',$output));
  }
}
```

This test uses the items in each iteration slightly differently: instead of just appending the $name values in a string, a string is formed from both the $name and $year properties, which is then appended to an $output array.

The implementation of LibraryReleasedIterator is nearly identical to LibraryIterator, except for one additional line in the constuctor:

```
class LibraryReleasedIterator extends LibraryIterator {
  function __construct($collection) {
    usort($collection, create_function('$a,$b','return ($a->year - $b->year);'));
    $this->collection = $collection;
  }
}
```

The line in bold sorts the $collection array prior to iteration. You can avoid copying all of the other code for the class by simply inheriting from the LibraryIterator class itself.

Is it possible to use an external iterator to accomplish this same sorted iteration? Yes, but you must pull a few tricks to accomplish it.

```
class LibraryReleasedExternalIterator {
  protected $collection;
  protected $sorted_keys;
  protected $key=-1;

  function __construct($collection) {
```

```
    $this->collection = $collection;
    $sort_funct = create_function(
      '$a,$b,$c=false',
      'static $collection;
      if ($c) {
        $collection = $c;
        return;
      }
      return ($collection->get($a)->year -
        $collection->get($b)->year);');
    $sort_funct(null,null,$this->collection);
    $this->sorted_keys = $this->collection->keys();
    usort($this->sorted_keys, $sort_funct);
  }

  function next() {
    if (++$this->key >= $this->collection->count()) {
      return false;
    } else {
      return $this->collection->get($this->sorted_keys[$this->key]);
    }
  }
}
}
```

Key here is the creation of a utility function for performing the sort. The sorting function needs to have access to the collection so it can fetch members for comparison. However, because the generated function is used in a usort(), you don't have the option of passing the collection as an additional parameter. Instead, you can use the trick shown in the code block above to store a reference to the collection inside the function prior to calling it with usort().

What you're sorting is the list of keys for the collection. When usort() is complete, the keys will be sorted in order by the year attribute of each object in the collection.

In the next() method, an object in the collection is accessed via the get() method, but indirectly through the $sorted_keys mapping. If you recall the external version of the GoF-style iterator, arrays with gaps or strings in the keys could be problematic. This same trick could be used for a simple external iterator to alleviate the problem of gaps in the sequence of keys.

SPL Iterator

No chapter on the *Iterator* design pattern and PHP would be complete without discussing the "Standard PHP Library" (SPL) iterator.

The while loop structure used so far is very compact and usable, but PHP coders may be more comfortable with the foreach structure for array iteration. Wouldn't it be nice to use a collection directly in a foreach loop? That's exactly what the SPL iterator is for.

(Even though this chapter has been written entirely for PHP5, the following SPL code is the only code that works solely in PHP5, and then only if you've compiled PHP 5 with SPL enabled.) Harry

Fuecks wrote a nice article introducing the SPL and covering the SPL iterator; see http://www.site-point.com/article/php5-standard-library.

Using SPL is essentially a completely different way to implement iteration, so let's start over with a new unit test case and a new class, the ForeachableLibrary.

```php
class SplIteratorTestCase extends UnitTestCase {
  protected $lib;

  function setup() {
    $this->lib = new ForeachableLibrary;
    $this->lib->add(new Media('name1', 2000));
    $this->lib->add(new Media('name2', 2002));
    $this->lib->add(new Media('name3', 2001));
  }

  function TestForeach() {
    $output = '';
    foreach($this->lib as $item) {
      $output .= $item->name;
    }
    $this->assertEqual('name1name2name3', $output);
  }
}
```

ForeachableLibrary is the collection that implements the SPL Iterator interface. You have to implement five functions to create an SPL iterator: current(), next(), key(), valid(), and rewind(). key() returns the current index of your collection. rewind() is like reset(): iteration restarts at the start of your collection.

```php
class ForeachableLibrary
    extends Library
    implements Iterator {
  protected $valid;

  function current() {
    return current($this->collection);
  }

  function next() {
    $this->valid = (false !== next($this->collection));
  }

  function key() {
    return key($this->collection);
  }

  function valid() {
```

```
      return $this->valid;
    }

    function rewind() {
      $this->valid = (false !== reset($this->collection));
    }
  }
```

Here, the code we just implements the required functions working on the $collection attribute. (If you don't implement all five functions and you add the implements Iterator to your class definition, PHP will generate a fatal error.) The tests are "green," so everything is happy.

There's just one problem: the implementation is limited to one style of iteration — sorting or filtering is impossible.

Can anything be done to rectify this? Yes! Apply what you learned from the *Strategy* pattern (see *Chapter 7*) and delegate the SPL iterator's five functions to another object.

This is a test for PolymorphicForeachableLibrary.

```
class PolySplIteratorTestCase extends UnitTestCase {
  protected $lib;
  function setup() {
    $this->lib = new PolymorphicForeachableLibrary;
    $this->lib->add(new Media('name1', 2000));
    $this->lib->add(new Media('name2', 2002));
    $this->lib->add(new Media('name3', 2001));
  }

  function TestForeach() {
    $output = '';
    foreach($this->lib as $item) {
      $output .= $item->name;
    }
    $this->assertEqual('name1name2name3', $output);
  }
}
```

The only difference between this case and the test for SplIteratorTestCase is the class of the $this->lib attribute created in the setUp() method. That makes sense: the two classes must behave identically.

Here's PolymorphicForeachableLibrary.

```
class PolymorphicForeachableLibrary
  extends Library
```

```
    implements Iterator {
  protected $iterator;
  function current() {
    return $this->iterator->current();
  }
  function next() {
    return $this->iterator->next();
  }
  function key() {
    return $this->iterator->key();
  }
  function valid() {
    return $this->iterator->valid();
  }
  function rewind() {
    $this->iterator =
      new StandardLibraryIterator($this->collection);
    $this->iterator->rewind();
  }
}
```

Library is extended to get the collection manipulation methods. The SPL methods are added, too, all delegating to the $iterator attribute, which is created in rewind(). Below is the code for the StandardLibraryIterator.

```
class StandardLibraryIterator {
  protected $valid;
  protected $collection;
  function __construct($collection) {
    $this->collection = $collection;
  }
  function current() {
    return current($this->collection);
  }
  function next() {
    $this->valid = (false !== next($this->collection));
  }
  function key() {
    return key($this->collection);
  }
  function valid() {
    return $this->valid;
  }
  function rewind() {
    $this->valid = (false !== reset($this->collection));
  }
}
```

This code should look familiar: essentially, it's a copy of the five SPL functions from the

ForeachableLibrary class. The tests pass.

OK, the code is more complex now, but how does it support additional iterator types? Let's add a test for a "released" version of the iterator to see how additional iterator types work in this design.

```
class PolySplIteratorTestCase extends UnitTestCase {
  // ...
  function TestReleasedForeach() {
    $this->lib->add(new Media('second', 1999));
    $this->lib->add(new Media('first', 1989));
    $output = array();
    $this->lib->iteratorType('Released');
    foreach($this->lib as $item) {
      $output[] = $item->name .'-'. $item->year;
    }
    $this->assertEqual(
      'first-1989 second-1999 name1-2000 name3-2001 name2-2002'
      ,implode(' ',$output));
  }
}
```

This test case above should look familiar, too, as it's very similar to the previous "release" iterator, but using the foreach control structure to loop.

```
class PolymorphicForeachableLibrary
  extends Library
  implements Iterator {
  protected $iterator_type;
  protected $iterator;
  function __construct() {
    $this->iteratorType();
  }
  function iteratorType($type=false) {
    switch(strtolower($type)) {
    case 'released':
      $this->iterator_type = 'ReleasedLibraryIterator';
      break;
    default:
      $this->iterator_type = 'StandardLibraryIterator';
    }
    $this->rewind();
  }
  // ...
  function rewind() {
    $type = $this->iterator_type;
    $this->iterator = new $type($this->collection);
    $this->iterator->rewind();
  }
}
```

The new iteratorType() method lets you switch which style of iterator you want to use. (Since the iterator type isn't chosen during the instantiation of the object and because you can choose a different iterator type on-the-fly by calling the iteratorType() method again, the code is actually implementing the *State* pattern, rather than the *Strategy* pattern.)

```
class ReleasedLibraryIterator
  extends StandardLibraryIterator {
  function __construct($collection) {
    usort($collection
      ,create_function('$a,$b','return ($a->year - $b->year);'));
    $this->collection = $collection;
  }
}
```

You can easily implement ReleasedLibraryIterator by extending StandardLibraryIterator and overriding the constructor to add the sorting of the incoming array. And with that you have a working PolymorphicForeachableLibrary.

Issues

Iterators are a nice way to standardize working with collections of objects in your applications. The examples here have been based on arrays, but the ability to work on non-array based collections with an identical interface is powerful.

The ability to use collections in the foreach control structure is indeed cool. The only unfortunate issue with the SPL implementation is the significant potential for name space clashing with "Iterator". How much PHP4 object-oriented code has some sort of an Iterator class as a base class for the libraries' iterators? Of those, how many define the five required methods in the same capacity? Perhaps implements Foreachable would have been a less intrusive name.

If you choose to use the SPL, you should investigate the other supported iterators, like RecursiveArrayIterator and numerous other flavors.

9

The Observer Pattern

P ART OF THE EXPRESSIVENESS OF OBJECT-ORIENTED PROGRAMMING is the ability to build
complex networks of interconnections between objects. Linked together, objects can exchange
services and information.

Often, you want objects to "chatter" when the state of an object changes. But for many reasons,
you may prefer to not "hard code" the lines of communications. Perhaps you want to form and reform
connections to respond to conditions in your application or perhaps you simply want to refactor the
communication code to avoid interdependencies between classes.

The Problem

How can you alert (potentially) many objects when a certain object's state changes? Is there a scheme
that's dynamic—one that allows interconnections to come and go as a script executes?

The Solution

The *Observer* pattern allows objects to express interest in the state of another object and provides a mechanism for the "observed," or the *subject,* to contact all of its "observers," the *clients,* when its state changes.

The *Observer* is a collaboration between an `Observable` class (the subject) and one or more `Observer` classes (the clients). The `Observable` class allows `Observers` to register with it. Then, whenever the state of the `Observable` object changes, all registered `Observers` are notified.

The *Observer* pattern separates the subject from the client, leaving it up to each `Observer` to take its own action in response to the change. (The *Observer* pattern is also known as *Publish/Subscribe,* which is an equally valid metaphor for the interaction between the objects in the pattern.)

The *Observer* pattern is flexible and extensible. The burden of knowing what classes want to follow the `Observable`'s state information and how each of those classes intends to use the information is removed from the `Observable` class itself. Additionally, an `Observer` can register or unregister at any time, as appropriate. You can also define multiple concrete `Observer` classes, allowing for varied behavior in your application.

Sample Code

As an example, you can use the *Observer* pattern to create a much more flexible error handler for your PHP scripts. The default error handler might dump information to the screen, but additional handlers could write to a log file, write to *syslog,* send email, or transmit a page to your beeper. You might even conceive of a tiered scheme that only alerts those `Observers` that have registered for certain kinds of errors, say, from warnings to something severe like a database server crash.

In fact, let's create a set of classes to implement just such an error handler for PHP using *Observer.* A new class, `ErrorHandler`, is the subject of the *Observer* design pattern. Two other classes, `FileErrorLogger` and `EmailErrorLogger`, are *Observer* clients that log errors in a file and via email, respectively. Expressed in UML, this is what you're after:

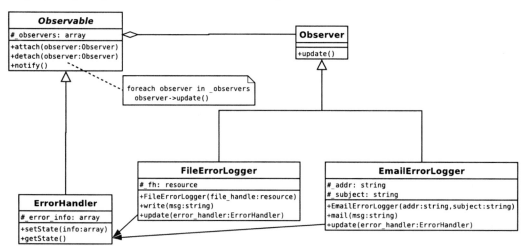

To implement an error handler based on the *Observer* pattern, start by looking at the complexities and commonalities of `FileErrorLogger` and `EmailErrorLogger` that have nothing to do with being observers. How does the `FileErrorLogger` write to a file and how does the `EmailErrorLogger` send an email? Next, look at the mechanics required to implement the *Observer* pattern and then focus on the details of `ErrorHandler`, the subject of the pattern. Finally, write the error handler function to use the `ErrorHandler` class.

The end game is expressed in this code snippet:

```
// PHP4
$eh =& getErrorHandlerInstance();
$eh->attach(new EmailErrorLogger('jsweat_php@yahoo.com'));
$eh->attach(new FileErrorLogger(fopen('error.log','w')));

set_error_handler('observer_error_handler');

// ... later
trigger_error('this is an error');
```

`ErrorHandler` is a *Singleton* (see *Chapter 4: The Singleton Pattern*) that various error logging observers can register with using `attach()`. `set_error_handler()` points to a function that uses `ErrorHandler`. Later, when an error is triggered, all of the observers are notified.

To validate the operation of this *Observer*, your tests have to verify that all of the actions of the observers (logging to a file, emailing the error) have taken place and worked properly. To be brief, let's look at an abbreviated set of tests. (More complete test cases for this example are available in the source code download for this book.)

Here's a portion of the `FileErrorLogger` unit test case that validates: that the class has the capability to log to a file handle passed into the object at the time it is instantiated:

```
class FileErrorLoggerTestCase extends UnitTestCase {
  var $_fh;
  var $_test_file = 'test.log';

  function setup() {
    @unlink($this->_test_file);
    $this->_fh = fopen($this->_test_file, 'w');
  }

  function TestRequiresFileHandleToInstantiate() { /* ... */ }

  function TestWrite() {
    $content = 'test'.rand(10,100);
    $log =& new FileErrorLogger($this->_fh);
```

```
      $log->write($content);
      $file_contents = file_get_contents($this->_test_file);
      $this->assertWantedPattern('/'.$content.'$/', $file_contents);
    }

    function TestWriteIsTimeStamped() { /* ... */ }
  }
```

The `setup()` method in this test case creates a file handle pointing to a new file called test.log and stores the handle in the $_fh attribute. This writable file handle is then passed as an argument to the constructor of the `FileErrorLogger` object being tested. The value of $content is passed to the `write()` method and the file is checked to see that $content has indeed written to the test.log file. (This test is predicated on the ability of PHP to write to the directory where the test.log file is being created.)

Some code to allow `FileErrorLogger` to pass the test might be:

```
class FileErrorLogger {
  var $_fh;
  function FileErrorLogger($file_handle) {
    $this->_fh = $file_handle;
  }
  function write($msg) {
    fwrite($this->_fh, date('Y-m-d H:i:s: ').$msg);
  }
}
```

A similar test validates the `EmailErrorLogger` class.

```
class EmailErrorLoggerTestCase extends UnitTestCase {
  function TestEmailAddressFirstConstructorParameter() {
    $log =& new EmailErrorLogger;
    $this->assertErrorPattern('/missing.*1/i');
  }
  function TestMail() {
    $log =& new EmailErrorLogger('jsweat_php@yahoo.com');
    $log->mail('test message');
  }
}
```

And the following `EmailErrorLogger` code passes the tests:

```
class EmailErrorLogger {
  var $_addr;
  var $_subject;

  function EmailErrorLogger($addr,
    $subject='Application Error Message') {
    $this->_addr = $addr;
    $this->_subject = $subject;
  }

  function mail($msg) {
    mail($this->_addr
      ,$this->_subject
      ,date('Y-m-d H:i:s: ').$msg);
  }
}
```

How do you validate that EmailErrorLogger actually sent email? Yes, you can open your mailbox and look for the message, but that's not an automated test. Instead, this test looks like an ideal candidate for *MockObject*. (Creating one to handle the mail side of the interaction is left as an exercise for you, the reader. See *Chapter 6: The MockObject Pattern* for more information and look over the FakeMail project at http://sf.net/projects/fakemail/.)

With the concrete observers in place, let's move on and implement the *Observer* pattern in the ErrorHandler class, starting with the attach() method.

```
class Observer {
  function update() {
    die('abstract method');
  }
}
Mock::Generate('Observer');

class ErrorHandlerTestCase extends UnitTestCase {
  function TestAttach() {
    $eh =& new ErrorHandler;
    $observer =& new MockObserver($this);
    $observer->expectOnce(
      'update'
      ,array('*'));  // array(&$eh)

    $eh->attach($observer);
    $eh->notify();

    $observer->tally();
  }
  function TestDetach() { /* ... */ }
}
```

For this test, a simple `Observer` class is created to represent the interface of all the concrete observers. To test the `attach()` method, a *MockObject* based on `Observer` is created and attached to the `ErrorHandler` test instance. Then, when the public `notify()` method is called, the *MockObject* verifies that `update()` was called.

Notice the commented `array(&$eh)` in the creation of the mock `Observer` expectations. Ideally, this is what the test should validate; however, due to a limitation of the PHP language, this generates a `Fatal error: Nesting level too deep - recursive dependency?`. To avoid that problem, the code uses the "wild card" capability of SimpleTest expectations to allow for any argument to allow the expectation to pass.

Nesting Level Too Deep

Because **ErrorHandler** contains a reference to the mock Observer in the **$_observers** array that's then passed to the mock Observer as part of the expectation, PHP generates a "Nesting level too deep" error. Recursive dependencies like this one are a fundamental PHP issue that can be found in even simple conditions . See http://bugs.php.net/bug.php?id=31449.

The `ErrorHandler` would start to shape up like this:

```
class ErrorHandler {
    var $_observers=array();

    function attach(&$observer) {
        $this->_observers[] =& $observer;
    }

    function notify() {
        foreach(array_keys($this->_observers) as $key) {
            $observer =& $this->_observers[$key];
            $observer->update($this);
        }
    }
}
```

Based on the code above, you need to add an `update()` method to each of the concrete observers. In each case, the `update()` method needs to know how to get information from the `ErrorHandler` class being observed to perform its function. Here is the added code:

```
class FileErrorLogger {
    var $_fh;
    function FileErrorLogger($file_handle) {
```

```
      $this->_fh = $file_handle;
    }
    function write($msg) {
      fwrite($this->_fh, date('Y-m-d H:i:s: ').$msg);
    }
    function update(&$error_handler) {
      $error = $error_handler->getState();
      $this->write($error['msg']);
    }
}


class EmailErrorLogger {
  var $_addr;
  var $_subject;
  function EmailErrorLogger($addr,
    $subject='Application Error Message') {
    $this->_addr = $addr;
    $this->_subject = $subject;
  }
  function mail($msg) {
    mail($this->_addr
      ,$this->_subject
      ,date('Y-m-d H:i:s: ').$msg);
  }
  function update(&$error_handler) {
    $error = $error_handler->getState();
    $this->mail($error['msg']);
  }
}
```

Each of the two update() methods takes the ErrorHandler as an argument, extracts the error information from that object, and calls an internal instance method to process the error. Each of the update() methods extracts the error information from the getState() method of ErrorHandler. The method is named getState() to keep with the pattern outlined in GoF, but may be more appropriately named getError() or getErrorInfo(), which are more meaningful to the domain.

Optionally, if you dislike the coupling between the objects in this pattern, you can change update() to send a message (the error array in this case or perhaps some messenger object) instead of a reference to itself.

Here is a new version of ErrorHandler that implements the latter variation, and includes the detach() code:

```
class ErrorHandler {
  var $_observers=array();
  var $_error_info;
  function attach(&$observer) {
    $this->_observers[] =& $observer;
  }
  function detach(&$observer) {
```

```
        foreach(array_keys($this->_observers) as $key) {
          if ($this->_observers[$key] === $observer) {
            unset($this->_observers[$key]);
            return;
          }
        }
      }
    }
    function notify() {
      foreach(array_keys($this->_observers) as $key) {
        $observer =& $this->_observers[$key];
        $observer->update($this);
      }
    }
    function getState() {
      return $this->_error_info;
    }
    function setState($info) {
      $this->_error_info = $info;
      $this->notify();
    }
  }
```

You now have a complete implementation of the *Observer* pattern.

Now, returning to the original goal of this chapter, let's see how to use ErrorHandler in a real PHP script. To include the *Observer* in a PHP application, you must setup the instance of ErrorHandler and make sure the function bound to the set_error_handler() method uses the exact same reference. This sounds like a problem from the recent past: a *Singleton*.

Lets make a *Factory* method that's a simple PHP function to return the *Singleton* instance of ErrorHandler:

```
function &getErrorHandlerInstance() {
  static $instance = array();
  if (!$instance) $instance[0] =& new ErrorHandler();
  return $instance[0];
}
```

Now, let's write the error handler function that gets the *Singleton* ErrorHandler, changes its state to reflect the error, and triggers the *Observer* notifications:

```
function observer_error_handler(
  $errno, $errstr, $errfile, $errline, $errcontext) {
  $eh =& getErrorHandlerInstance();
  $eh->setState(array(
    'number'  => $errno
```

```
      ,'msg'     => $errstr
      ,'file'    => $errfile
      ,'line'    => $errline
      ,'context' => $errcontext
      ));
}
```

You may notice that there's no call to `ErrorHandler::notify()`. Why? Because `ErrorHandler` automatically sends notifications whenever the state is changed:

```
class ErrorHandler {
  // ...
  function setState($info) {
    $this->_error_info = $info;
    $this->notify();
  }
}
```

There are obviously pros and cons to this "notify on set" approach. The advantage is the client code doesn't have to remember to trigger the notification.

However, if you had several changes to make to the state of the subject object, all of which were performed in different methods, you might choose instead to force the client code to explicitly call `notify()`.

Since you have all of this scaffolding in place, how easy is it to add another type of logging into the mix? Say you now want the capability to log to the system log. A quick check of the PHP manual (http://www.php.net/syslog) reveals a few helpful functions to set up logging. These can easily be wrapped into a new class, ready to attach to `ErrorHandler`:

```
class SyslogErrorLogger {
  function SyslogErrorLogger($msg) {
    define_syslog_variables();
    openlog($msg, LOG_ODELAY, LOG_USER);
  }
  function log($msg) {
    syslog(LOG_WARNING, $msg);
  }
  function update(&$error_handler) {
    $error = $error_handler->getState();
    $this->log($error['msg']);
  }
}
```

> ⓘ **The Utility of Error Logs**
>
> Logs are very useful—*if* someone reads them. On the other hand, if no one makes user of the logs, then logging is just clutter in your code.
>
> For a more eloquent treatment of this subject, take a look at :
>
> http://www.lastcraft.com/blog/index.php?p=4

Issues

The *Observer* pattern is very useful. The example shown here was a fairly static—the observers would be configured during the initialization of the script and left static after that. Where the *Observer* pattern really shows its flexibility is in a more dynamic application where you add and remove observers based on other events in your script. Given the usually brief "lifetime" or execution time of PHP scripts, this is more likely to be different configurations of observers during different executions of a script, rather than dynamically changing over the course of a script. This would likely be much different in an environment like PHP-GTK, which does have protracted script execution.

10

The Specification Pattern

A S AN APPLICATION TAKES SHAPE, bits of business logic sprout up everywhere, seemingly of their own volition. One object must limit items based on price; another object must choose the right rate for sales tax; and yet another must determine if any special conditions apply to the current order. Some business rules are simple, requiring little more than one or two boolean comparisons, while other rules can require protracted computations, needing database queries and user input to guide them.

Writing code transforms the abstract (a business rule) into something concrete. But abstractions (such as shopping styles, tax rates, and shipping fee calculations) have a way of evolving and multiplying and such changes can easily overwhelm a hapless developer. To stay safe—as you've seen so far in this book—it's ideal to encapsulate and isolate what readily changes whenever possible. And indeed, that's also a wise strategy for business rules, too.

The Problem

Is there a clean way to encapsulate business logic? Is there a technique that facilitates adaptation and reuse?

The Solution

The *Specification* pattern is designed to *validate* and *select*.

- Validation determines if a particular object satisfies a certain criteria.
- Selection identifies those elements of a collection that satisfy the given criteria.

The *Specification* pattern allows you to structure these criteria for flexible use in your application.

Refactoring already encourages you to capture decisions in methods to promote clarity and reuse. The *Specification* pattern takes this one step further by systematizing this structure into separate objects that can then be plugged back into your application where appropriate. In many cases, *Specification* objects are parameterized and can often be combined to easily build complex logical expressions in your application's domain.

Additional Reading

Eric Evans and Martin Fowler published an article about the *Specification* pattern available at:
`http://www.martinfowler.com/apsupp/spec.pdf`.

This pattern is also covered in detail in Eric Evans's book "Domain Driven Design" on pages 224 and 273.

To provide reasonable coverage of this pattern, this chapter is organized into three logical steps. The first is a "pure" example that shows the basic concepts of the pattern applied to an object. (Evans and Fowler refer to this as a *"Hard Coded Specification."*) The next step demonstrates how to build parameterized specifications, which provide a more dynamic and flexible framework for reusing the *Specification* pattern (a so-called *"Parameterized Specification"*). Finally, the last step develops a "Policy Factory" as an easy means of assembling many *Specification* objects together into an easily used package (a *"Composite Specification"*).

Traveling to Warm Destinations

My family and I recently planned a vacation and my wife wanted to go "somewhere warm." While there are umpteen travel-related sites, none that we visited provided a temperature for each destination. Instead, we had to constantly flip over to weather.com and do searches. That's terribly inconvenient. Let's remedy the situation and add a temperature search feature to a hypothetical travel web site. Let's use the *Specification* pattern as a guide to show what you might code to compare a traveler's desired minimum temperature to the average temperature of a number of destinations.

Let's start by creating some very simple domain objects. First is a `Traveler`, which stores a preferred minimum temperature.

```php
// PHP5
class Traveler {
    public $min_temp;
}
```

Next, let's create a class to represent destinations. Since average temperature is a key criterion, the constructor for `Destination` should expect an array with twelve values, where each value is the average temperature for each month of the year.

```php
class Destination {

    protected $avg_temps;

    public function __construct($avg_temps) {
        $this->avg_temps = $avg_temps;
    }
}
```

`Destination` also needs a means of retrieving the average temperature of the destination for any given month:

```php
class Destination {
    //...

    public function getAvgTempByMonth($month) {
        $key = (int)$month - 1;
        if (array_key_exists($key, $this->avg_temps)) {
            return $this->avg_temps[$key];
        }
    }
}
```

Finally, the `Trip` class combines a `Traveler` and a `Destination` with a date.

```
class Trip {
  public $date;
  public $traveler;
  public $destination;
}
```

Given these objects, you can extract the month of travel from `Trip::date` and compare the average temperature of the `Destination` for that month with the minimum temperature desired by the `Traveler`. (This comparison may not be very complicated, but it gives you something to work with.)

Let's look at how to implement the "warm destination" business logic as a *Specification* pattern and see how to apply the pattern to validate each destination and select all suitable destinations.

Sample Code

The heart of the *Specification* pattern is an object with an `IsSatisfiedBy()` method that accepts a parameter to evaluate and returns a boolean value based on the *Specification's* criteria.

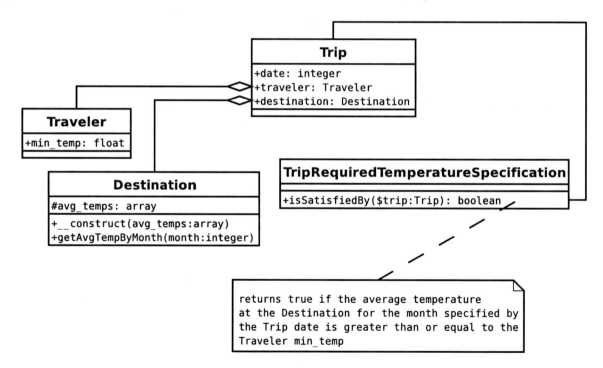

The "destination is warm enough" criteria might look like:

```
class TripRequiredTemperatureSpecification {
  public function isSatisfiedBy($trip) {
    $trip_temp = $trip->destination->getAvgTempByMonth(
      date('m', $trip->date));
    return ($trip_temp >= $trip->traveler->min_temp);
  }
}
```

Here are some tests to verify how this *Specification* works.

An initial unit test case provides some Destinations to work with:

```
class TripSpecificationTestCase extends UnitTestCase {
  protected $destinations = array();
  function setup() {
    $this->destinations = array(
      'Toronto' => new Destination(
        array(24, 25, 33, 43, 54, 63, 69, 69, 61, 50, 41, 29))
      ,'Cancun' => new Destination(
        array(74, 75, 78, 80, 82, 84, 84, 84, 83, 81, 78, 76))
    );
  }
}
```

(Recall that Destination requires an array of monthly average temperatures to be passed to each instance at creation. Being an American author, I have selected degrees Fahrenheit for these examples. For reference, Vicki's desired 70 degrees Fahrenheit is equivalent to 21 degrees Celsius.)

The next test builds a Traveler, setting its preferred minimum temperature and travel date and selecting a Destination. The first combination, 70 degrees in Toronto in mid-February, should fail, as expected:

```
class TripSpecificationTestCase extends UnitTestCase {
  // ...
  function TestTripTooCold() {
    $vicki = new Traveler;
    $vicki->min_temp = 70;

    $toronto = $this->destinations['Toronto'];

    $trip = new Trip;
    $trip->traveler = $vicki;
    $trip->destination = $toronto;
    $trip->date = mktime(0,0,0,2,11,2005);
```

```
        $warm_enough_check = new TripRequiredTemperatureSpecification;
        $this->assertFalse($warm_enough_check->isSatisfiedBy($trip));
    }
}
```

However, the next combination, at least 70 degrees in mid-February in Cancun, passes as expected:

```
class TripSpecificationTestCase extends UnitTestCase {
    // ...
    function TestTripWarmEnough() {
        $vicki = new Traveler;
        $vicki->min_temp = 70;

        $cancun = $this->destinations['Cancun'];

        $trip = new Trip;
        $trip->traveler = $vicki;
        $trip->destination = $cancun;
        $trip->date = mktime(0,0,0,2,11,2005);

        $warm_enough_check = new TripRequiredTemperatureSpecification;
        $this->assertTrue($warm_enough_check->isSatisfiedBy($trip));
    }
}
```

Parameterized Specification

TripRequiredTemperatureSpecification knows quite a bit about the structure of a Trip object, digging into all three public attributes. This isn't bad per se; in fact, when I've used the *Specification* pattern, I've found there are usually a few *Specifications* that benefit from this detailed knowledge of specific expected parameter objects. However, that kind of intimacy tends to make reusing the *Specification* in other contexts much harder.

Fortunately, reuse has been addressed in variants of the *Specification* pattern. In particular, the *Parameterized Specification* pattern changes the constructor to accept a parameter (hence the name), which is then used in the criteria evaluation in isSatisfiedBy().

Let's look at a *Parameterized Specification* using the same travel site domain objects. Assume that you want to scan a list of destinations and present a list of cities that meet the "warm enough" criteria.

To use the existing TripRequiredTemperatureSpecification, you'd have to create a Trip object for each evaluation. But because (in this specific problem) the Traveler and the date of travel are constant, only the Destination need change as you iterate over the list of possible destinations.

Using the *Parameterized Specification,* you remember the traveler's preferred temperature and travel date and compare against a `Destination` passed as a parameter to the `isSatisfiedBy()` method.

The constructor for `DestinationRequiredTemperatureSpecification`, *Parameterized Specification* object, requires a `Traveler` and a date to instantiate the *Specification*:

```
class DestinationRequiredTemperatureSpecification {
  protected $temp;
  protected $month;
  public function __construct($traveler, $date) {
    $this->temp = $traveler->min_temp;
    $this->month = date('m', $date);
  }
}
```

With the consistent data of temperature and date stored in instance variables, `DestinationRequiredTemperatureSpecification`'s `isSatisfiedBy()` method takes a `Destination` as a parameter and evaluates the criterion:

```
class DestinationRequiredTemperatureSpecification {
  // ...
  function isSatisfiedBy($destination) {
    return
      ($destination->getAvgTempByMonth($this->month) >= $this->temp);
  }
}
```

You can now write a test case to filter a list of destinations:

```
class DestinationSpecificationTestCase extends UnitTestCase {
  // similar setup to TripSpecificationTestCase

  function TestFindingDestinations() {
    $this->assertEqual(2, count($this->destinations));

    $valid_destinations = array();
    $vicki = new Traveler;
    $vicki->min_temp = 70;
    $travel_date = mktime(0,0,0,2,11,2005);

    $warm_enough = new DestinationRequiredTemperatureSpecification(
    vicki, $travel_date);
```

```
    foreach($this->destinations as $dest) {
      if ($warm_enough->isSatisfiedBy($dest)) {
        $valid_destinations[] = $dest;
      }
    }

    $this->assertEqual(1, count($valid_destinations));
    $this->assertIdentical(
      $this->destinations['Cancun'],
      $valid_destinations[0]);
  }
}
```

You can see how a *Parameterized Specification* gives you an extra degree of freedom.

Let's look at another example where the data type and the *Specification* are extremely flexible by necessity.

One of the most common and most maddening problems to solve in a web application is validating form input. Forms tend to change during development (and even beyond) and the number of forms in a rich application can grow rather quickly. You could create a unique object to encapsulate each and every form and use the *Specification* pattern to validate each object, but that's a maintenance nightmare.

Is there a convenient data type that can adapt readily to any form? If so, is there a way to validate such a dynamic data type?

The answer to each of those questions is an emphatic yes.

The Web Application Component Toolkit's (WACT) DataSource interface can get, set, and dynamically create object properties (something akin to PHP4's __get() and __set() methods), which are a handy encapsulation of a form. (Readers familiar with Java can think of a DataSource as a HashMap.) Meanwhile, the *Parameterized Specification* pattern provides a model to validate a DataSource against a set of criteria.

WACT

WACT, the Web Application Component Toolkit, available on SourceForge at http://wact.sf.net/, is a library of PHP code for solving common web application problems. WACT focuses heavily on techniques of refactoring, unit testing, and design pattern use. Information related to the WACT concept of a **DataSource** is located at http://wact.sf.net/index.php/DataSource.

The include file for the WACT DataSource class is included in this book's source code download so you can test the policy code.

For this example, the DataSource class can be thought of as the following code, which is nearly identical to the Registry class developed in *Chapter 5*:

```
class DataSource {
  protected $store = array();

  function get($key) {
    if (array_key_exists($key, $this->store))
      return $this->store[$key];
  }

  function set($key, $val) {
    $this->store[$key] = $val;
  }
}
```

DataSource accesses an object's properties indirectly using string identifiers. set() alters existing properties or dynamically creates new properties; get() retrieves properties by name.

When your application must process a form, load the DataSource with $_POST values and then use the *Parameterized Specification* to perform the validation. (The same technique can also be applied to configuration files. Load the DataSource from your configuration file and then validate it with *Specifications*.)

Let's construct some simple *Parameterized Specification* classes to use as building blocks. First, let's make a *Specification* that passes if a certain field is equal to a specified value.

```
class FieldEqualSpecification {
  protected $field;
  protected $value;

  public function __construct($field, $value) {
    $this->field = $field;
    $this->value = $value;
  }

  public function isSatisfiedBy($datasource) {
    return ($datasource->get($this->field) == $this->value);
  }
}
```

The idea here is very simple: store a field and its desired value during construction, fetch the desired field from the DataSource passed to isSatisfiedBy(), and compare it to the desired value.

To test this *Specification*, write a test case to instantiate a DataSource:

```
class SpecificationsTestCase extends UnitTestCase {
  protected $ds;
  function setup() {
    $this->ds = new DataSource;
    $this->ds->set('name', 'Jason');
    $this->ds->set('age', 34);
    $this->ds->set('email', 'jsweat_php@yahoo.com');
    $this->ds->set('sex', 'male');
    }
  }
}
```

Above, `setup()` creates a `DataSource` object with a known set of properties. This test method includes one assertion that should pass and another that should fail.

```
class SpecificationsTestCase extends UnitTestCase {
  // ...
  function TestFieldEqualSpecification() {
    $name_jason = new FieldEqualSpecification('name', 'Jason');
    $this->assertTrue($name_jason->isSatisfiedBy($this->ds));

    $sex_other = new FieldEqualSpecification('sex', 'other');
    $this->assertFalse($sex_other->isSatisfiedBy($this->ds));
  }
}
```

Often when evaluating strings, a *regular expression* can help you define what you're looking for far better than a series of exact comparisons. Let's add the power of regular expression matching to our *Specification* tool set with `FieldMatchSpecification`:

```
class FieldMatchSpecification {
  protected $field;
  protected $regex;
  public function __construct($field, $regex) {
    $this->field = $field;
    $this->regex = $regex;
  }
  public function isSatisfiedBy($datasource) {
    return preg_match($this->regex, $datasource->get($this->field));
  }
}
```

Here, the name of the field to evaluate and a PCRE expression are saved during construction. isSatisfiedBy() then extracts the named field from the passed DataSource and compares its value to the regular expression using preg_match().

Here's how you might write a test for FieldMatchSpecification:

```
class SpecificationsTestCase extends UnitTestCase {
  // ...

  function TestFieldMatchSpecification() {
    $valid_email = new FieldMatchSpecification(
      'email',
      '/^[^\s@]+@[^\s.]+(?:\.[^\s.]+)+/');
    $this->assertTrue($valid_email->isSatisfiedBy($this->ds));

    $name_ten_letters = new FieldMatchSpecification(
      'name',
      '/^\w{10}$/');
    $this->assertFalse($name_ten_letters->isSatisfiedBy($this->ds));
  }
}
```

The email regex looks for "a bunch of non-space, non-@ characters, followed by an @ character, followed by two or more groups of non-space, non-period characters separated by periods." The assertion for the $name_ten_letters *Specification* says the value should consist of exactly ten "word" characters.

Regular Expressions

Many books devote entire chapters to regular expressions and entire books are devoted to the topic, so please realize this is a simplistic example rather than a complete example of what an email address regex should look like.

Let's make one last concrete *Specification* to verify if a field is greater than or equal to a value. Not surprisingly, its name is FieldGreaterThanOrEqualSpecification.

```
class FieldGreaterThanOrEqualSpecification {
  protected $field;
  protected $value;

  public function __construct($field, $value) {
    $this->field = $field;
    $this->value = $value;
  }
```

```
public function isSatisfiedBy($datasource) {
  return ($datasource->get($this->field) >= $this->value);
}
}
```

There's not much magic here: store the relevant field and value to be compared in the constructor and verify the extracted field in the isSatisfiedBy() method.

Here's a test case showing the FieldGreaterThanOrEqualSpecification in action.

```
class SpecificationsTestCase extends UnitTestCase {
  // ...
  function TestFieldGreaterThanOrEqualSpecification() {
    $adult =
      new FieldGreaterThanOrEqualSpecification('age', 18);
    $presidential_age =
      new FieldGreaterThanOrEqualSpecification('age', 35);

    $this->assertTrue($adult->isSatisfiedBy($this->ds));
    $this->assertFalse($presidential_age->isSatisfiedBy($this->ds));
  }
}
```

Have you noticed how the code begins to document itself when *Specification* objects are labeled with reasonable names? $adult->isSatisfiedBy($something) can be understood at a glance, without really having to dig into the details of the code. This is one of the "bonuses" of the *Specification* pattern.

It should be clear by now that the *Specification* pattern represents an interface. To explicitly express this in PHP5:

```
interface Specification {
  public function isSatisfiedBy($datasource);
}
```

Armed with some basic building blocks, let's assemble them into a format with even greater utility. Because the net result from a *Specification*'s isSatisfiedBy() method is a boolean, it would be nice to be able to apply boolean logic to the different concrete specifications.

To implement logical And, create a class that combines two concrete specification instances and returns true if a given `DataSource` parameter satisfies *both*.

```php
class AndSpecification implements Specification {
  protected $spec;
  protected $andSpec;
  public function __construct($spec, $andSpec) {
    $this->spec = $spec;
    $this->andSpec = $andSpec;
  }
  function isSatisfiedBy($datasource) {
    return ($this->spec->isSatisfiedBy($datasource)
      && $this->andSpec->isSatisfiedBy($datasource));
  }
}
```

You can achieve Logical Or with a similar structure:

```php
class OrSpecification implements Specification {
  protected $spec;
  protected $orSpec;
  public function __construct($spec, $orSpec) {
    $this->spec = $spec;
    $this->orSpec = $orSpec;
  }
  function isSatisfiedBy($datasource) {
    return ($this->spec->isSatisfiedBy($datasource)
      || $this->orSpec->isSatisfiedBy($datasource));
  }
}
```

Given these "logical" *Specifications* and the earlier set of *Specifications,* you can perform some complex validations:

```php
class PolicyFactory {
  public function createJasonPolicy() {
    $name_jason = new FieldEqualSpecification('name', 'Jason');
    $age_at_least_thirty =
      new FieldGreaterThanOrEqualSpecification('age', 30);
    $male = new FieldEqualSpecification('sex', 'male');
    $jasons_email = new OrSpecification(
      new FieldEqualSpecification('email', 'jsweat_php@yahoo.com')
      ,new FieldEqualSpecification('email',
        'jsweat@users.sourceforge.net'));
    return new AndSpecification(
      $name_jason, new AndSpecification(
```

```
            $age_at_least_thirty,
            new AndSpecification($male, $jasons_email)
        ));
    }
}
```

`PolicyFactory` looks a bit messy at first, primarily due to the number of temporary variables holding instances of the individual concrete specifications. However, the interesting part of the code is the use of `OrSpecification` and `AndSpecification` classes (highlighted above). The two concrete instances of `FieldEqualSpecification` for email are passed as parameters to the constructor method of the `OrSpecification`. Because the `OrSpecification` implements the `Specification` interface, the `$jasons_email` object can be treated just like any other concrete Specification instance. Indeed, it's used just that way four lines later in new `AndSpecification($male, $jasons_email)`.

Given `PolicyFactor`, it's now possible to do:

```
$jason = PolicyFactory::createJasonPolicy();
$jason->isSatisfiedBy($datasource);
```

These two lines of code verify that $datasource's name field is "Jason", its age field is at least 30, and its email field is either "jsweat_php@yahoo.com" or "jsweat@users.sourceforge.net".

All of those intermediate variables to hold the concrete specifications are not aesthetically pleasing. Can the generation of the policy be cleaned up to make the code easier to read and maintain? Yes! Simply take advantage of a new feature in PHP5 to *chain* method calls from objects returned by methods.

A first step might be to allow individual concrete *Specifications* to know how to "And" and "Or" themselves. This could be done by introducing *Factory* methods (see *Chapter 3 - The Factory Method Pattern*) to create `AndSpecification` and `OrSpecification` classes. Since these features would be common to all `Specifications`, it would be a good idea to move them into an abstract base class.

```
abstract class BaseSpecification implements Specification {
    protected $field;
    public function and_($spec) { return new AndSpecification($this, $spec); }
    public function or_($spec) { return new OrSpecification($this, $spec); }
}
```

The funny method names and_() and or_() are needed because "and" and "or" are keywords in PHP.

By introducing this base class, the concrete classes written so far must be modified to inherit from BaseSpecification:

```
class FieldEqualSpecification extends BaseSpecification {
  // ...
}
```

The next step is to introduce *Factory* methods to create the individual concrete specifications more easily. This might be done in a separate factory class, but for convenience, you can add the methods to the PolicyFactory class.

```
class PolicyFactory {
  protected function equal($field, $value) {
    return new FieldEqualSpecification($field, $value);
  }
  protected function gTorEq($field, $value) {
    return new FieldGreaterThanOrEqualSpecification($field, $value);
  }
}
```

Now, let's combine both of these *Factory* methods to create a statement like the following:

```
class PolicyFactory {
  // ..
  public function createJasonPolicy() {
    return $this->equal('name', 'Jason')->and_(
      $this->gTorEq('age', 30)->and_(
      $this->equal('sex', 'male')->and_(
      $this->equal('email', 'jsweat_php@yahoo.com')->or_(
      $this->equal('email', 'jsweat@users.sourceforge.net')
    ))));
  }
}
```

createJasonPolicy() creates a policy just as before, but the code is far more readable.

After all of this refactoring, the class diagram looks like this:

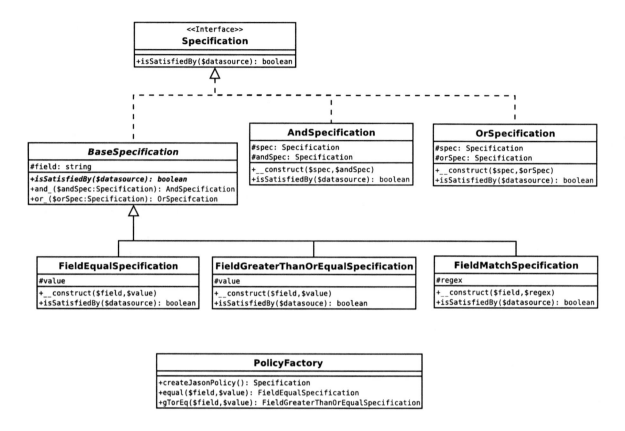

The *Specification* pattern facilitates better structure and organizes business logic in your application's domain model. One of the reasons I wanted to include this pattern in the book is because it begins to show how patterns are modified and combined in real world applications.

11

The Proxy Pattern

HAVE YOU EVER WANTED to delay the creation of an object because it uses expensive resources and not every path through your code requires the object? Have you ever wanted to restrict access to an object, say, to provide one set of methods to a user and additional, privileged methods to an administrator? Both needs are fairly common and are representative of a larger problem: how do you provide a consistent interface to an object that may vary in nature—or not even exist yet?

The Problem

How can you provide access to an object without providing the object directly?

The Solution

The *Proxy* pattern provides a surrogate—a placeholder—for another object, effectively placing code in between a *client* object and a *subject* object. A *Proxy* might provide lazy instantiation, access control, or just about anything else, including just passing through the calls. A *Proxy* for purely local resources is sometimes referred to as a *virtual proxy*. A *Proxy* for remote services is often called a *remote proxy*. A *Proxy* that enforces access control is called a *protection proxy*.

Here is a diagram of (one method in) a remote proxy. SoapClient is a go-between for local objects (the clients) that want to call SoapServer (the subject) to acquire weather information. The entire task of constructing, transmitting, and receiving via HTTP, and parsing complex XML documents to effectuate the remote communications is handled within the SoapClient class. The net result is a replication of the remote SoapServer objects API, thus having the SoapClient acting as a local surrogate—a proxy—for the remote SoapServer resource.

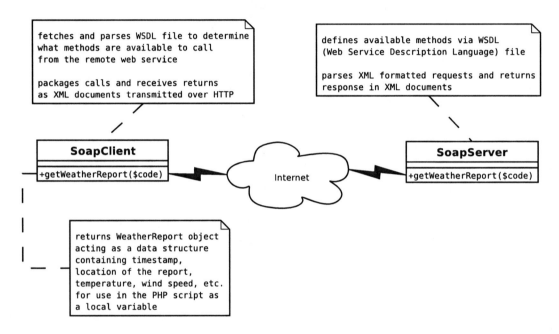

There is another variant of the *Proxy* pattern called a s*mart proxy*. This term is a sort of a catch-all for additional logic added before allowing access to the subject object.

Handle-Body Patterns
The *Proxy Pattern*, the *Decorator Pattern*, and the *Adapter Pattern* (the latter two patterns are covered in the next two chapters) have a similar structure when programmed. The essential difference between the three patterns is how they're used.

Other variations of this structure can be found at **http://www.c2.com/cgi/wiki?HandleBodyPattern**.

The essence of the *Proxy* is to hold a reference to the subject object in an instance variable and to pass method calls on the *Proxy* class down to the subject.

Let's look at the *Proxy* pattern in it's simplest form. First, you need a subject class to proxy.

```
// PHP4
class Subject {
  function someMethod() {
    sleep(1); //do something
  }
}
```

Next, you need the *Proxy* class. This class needs to have an instance of the subject to proxy to.

```
class ProxySubject {
  var $subject;
  function ProxySubject() {
    $this->subject =& new Subject;
  }
}
```

In the `ProxySubject` above, the subject is created in the constructor (but other alternatives, such as passing in as a parameter to the constructor or creating the subject from a *Factory*, are equally viable).

Lastly, your *Proxy* class must provide *all* of the public methods your subject class supports. In this case, that's just the `someMethod()` method.

```
class ProxySubject {
  var $subject;
  function ProxySubject() {
    $this->subject =& new Subject;
  }
  function someMethod() {
    $this->subject->someMethod();
  }
}
```

`ProxySubject` calls the real `Subject` using `$this->subject->someMethod()`.

A *Proxy* might have some methods that pass straight through, and others where additional logic (lazy loading, guarding) is applied before for-warding the call.

Here's `ProxySubject` expressed as a UML class diagram:

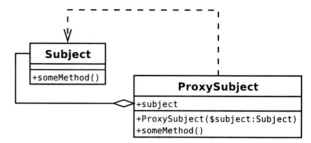

Sample Code

The simple example above shows the basic structure of the *Proxy* pattern, but let's move on to a more interesting and realistic example.

Web services have become very popular and PHP5 includes a good deal of support for protocols like SOAP that make it very easy to consume a remote service. Part of the construction of a SOAP client is the processing of the WSDL file. However, you may wish to delay processing the WSDL file until you're sure you need to use the object. This next example of a *Proxy* shows both a remote proxy—accessing a SOAP service—and lazy instantiation.

RemoteProxy

First, some quick basics on the new PHP5 `SoapClient` code. You must have compiled PHP5 with the –enable-soap option to use the `SoapClient` class. Once you do that, you can create a `SoapClient` instance by passing the URL to the service's WSDL file in the constructor:

```
// PHP5
$client = new SoapClient(
  'http://live.capescience.com/wsdl/GlobalWeather.wsdl');
```

PHP4 SoapClients

If you have coded PHP4 SOAP clients before, PHP5's technique may seem almost like cheating. PHP5's **SoapClient** is an extension, so it's native PHP code and fast, since the actually parsing and formatting of XML messages is done in C.

Some PHP4 SOAP Libraries include:
- phpsoaptoolkit (http://phpsoaptoolkit.sf.net/phpsoap/),
- PEAR::SOAP (http://pear.php.net/package/SOAP)
- ez SOAP (http://ez.no/ez_publish/documentation/development/libraries/ez_soap)
- nusoap (http://sf.net/projects/nusoap/).

All of these PHP4 libraries handle the remote message formatting and transmission in PHP code and are examples of a *remote proxy*.

The first question you might have is what methods does the `SoapClient` respond to? You can easily enumerate the methods at runtime by doing `var_dump(get_class_methods(get_class($client)));`. To be more precise, you could express this as a test case:

```
class ProxyTestCase extends UnitTestCase {
  const WSDL = 'http://live.capescience.com/wsdl/GlobalWeather.wsdl';
  private $client;
  function setUp() {
    $this->client = new SoapClient(ProxyTestCase::WSDL);
  }
  function TestMethodsOfSoapClient() {
    $soap_client_methods = array(
      '__construct',
      '__call',
      '__soapCall',
      '__getLastRequest',
      '__getLastResponse',
      '__getLastRequestHeaders',
      '__getLastResponseHeaders',
      '__getFunctions',
      '__getTypes',
      '__doRequest');
    $this->assertEqual(
      $soap_client_methods,
      get_class_methods(get_class($this->client)));
  }
}
```

At first, it might seem useless to write a test like this—couldn't you just dump this information any time you wanted to? Perhaps, but this test could be useful to have in your application test suite to protect yourself during PHP upgrades, to understand if any methods have been added, or to discover if any methods you rely on have been removed, and to verify PHP was compiled with the SOAP option. That being said, this test *is* extremely fragile: it's vulnerable to changes caused by refactoring and is highly dependent on the ordering of the listed functions. For now, though, the test describes how `SoapClient` looks. If you want to put in a similar test in your test suite, it's best to refactor it to do `in_array` lookups and only target the functions you are explicitly using in your code.

You can use the `SoapClient::__getFunctions()` method to understand what facilities the targeted SOAP service provides. In the case of GlobalWeather.wsdl, you have:

```
class ProxyTestCase extends UnitTestCase {
  function TestSoapFunctions() {
    $globalweather_functions = array(
```

```
             'Station getStation(string $code)',
             'boolean isValidCode(string $code)',
             'ArrayOfstring listCountries()',
             'ArrayOfStation searchByCode(string $code)',
             'ArrayOfStation searchByCountry(string $country)',
             'ArrayOfStation searchByName(string $name)',
             'ArrayOfStation searchByRegion(string $region)',
             'WeatherReport getWeatherReport(string $code)'
             );

        $this->assertEqual(
            $globalweather_functions,
            $this->client->__getFunctions());
    }
}
```

SoapClient::__getFunctions() returns an array of strings that represent the API for the web service. For each method, the expected return type, the name of the method, and the expected parameter types are listed.

(Again this kind of test is useful in an application suite to immediately alert you to changes in the published web service. You can easily envision a bug hunt ensuing if weather information suddenly stopped appearing on your page due to a subtle change in the API that you were unaware of. With this kind of a check in place, you'd be alerted to the change as soon as you ran the unit test case.)

The last thing to look at in this brief introduction to the PHP5 SoapClient is actually consuming the service. As an example, let's look up the weather for Moline, Illinois. The airport code for Moline is "KMLI." To get the current weather status at the Moline airport, call the getWeatherReport() method and pass the string 'KMLI' as an argument. The call returns a WeatherReport object:

```
class ProxyTestCase extends UnitTestCase {
    function TestGetWeatherReport() {
        $moline_weather = $this->client->getWeatherReport('KMLI');
        $this->assertIsA($moline_weather, 'stdClass');
    }
}
```

Because WeatherReport is not actually a class defined in your application, the SoapClient returns all objects as instances of stdClass. You can then move on to evaluate the attributes of the returned object:

```
class ProxyTestCase extends UnitTestCase {
  function TestGetWeatherReport() {
    $moline_weather = $this->client->getWeatherReport('KMLI');
    $this->assertIsA($moline_weather, 'stdClass');
    $weather_tests = array(
       'timestamp' => 'String'
      ,'station' => 'stdClass'
      ,'phenomena' => 'Array'
      ,'precipitation' => 'Array'
      ,'extremes' => 'Array'
      ,'pressure' => 'stdClass'
      ,'sky' => 'stdClass'
      ,'temperature' => 'stdClass'
      ,'visibility' => 'stdClass'
      ,'wind' => 'stdClass'
      );
    foreach($weather_tests as $key => $isa) {
      $this->assertIsA($moline_weather->$key,
        $isa,
        "$key should be $isa, actually [%s]");
    }
  }
}
```

This code creates a mapping between attribute and the expected type. You can then iterate over this list of expectations and use assertIsA() to verify the correct type. You can verify other aggregated objects as well:

```
class ProxyTestCase extends UnitTestCase {
  function TestGetWeatherReport() {
    // continued ...
    $temp = $moline_weather->temperature;
    $temperature_tests = array(
       'ambient' => 'Float'
      ,'dewpoint' => 'Float'
      ,'relative_humidity' => 'Integer'
      ,'string' => 'String'
      );
    foreach($temperature_tests as $key => $isa) {
      $this->assertIsA($temp->$key,
        $isa,
        "$key should be $isa, actually [%s]");
    }
  }
}
```

Some abbreviated actual output from this method might look like:

```
stdClass Object
(
  [timestamp] => 2005-02-27T13:52:00Z
  [station] => stdClass Object
    (
      [icao] => KMLI
      [wmo] => 72544
      [iata] =>
      [elevation] => 179
      [latitude] => 41.451
      [longitude] => -90.515
      [name] => Moline, Quad-City Airport
      [region] => IL
      [country] => United States
      [string] => KMLI - Moline, Quad-City Airport, IL, United States @ 41.451'N -90.515'W 179m
    )
  // ...
  [temperature] => stdClass Object
    (
      [ambient] => 0.6
      [dewpoint] => -2.8
      [relative_humidity] => 78
      [string] => 0.6c (78% RH)
    )
  // ...
)
```

Lazy Proxy

Now that you have a basic understanding of the PHP5 SoapClient—which is itself a *remote proxy*—how can you write a *Lazy Instantiating Proxy* for SoapClient?

```
class GlobalWeather {
  private $client;

  // 'Station getStation(string $code)',
  public function getStation($code) {
    return $this->client->getStation($code);
  }
}
```

getStation() should proxy to the $client instance variable's getStation() method. However, at this point, the SoapClient instance hasn't been created and stored it in the $client variable, because, as mentioned earlier, processing of the WSDL file involves remote processing that should be delayed until absolutely needed.

You can delay instantiation of SoapClient by interposing some lazy loading code prior to making the client call:

```
class GlobalWeather {
  private $client;

  private function lazyLoad() {
    if (! $this->client instanceof SoapClient) {
      $this->client = new SoapClient(
        'http://live.capescience.com/wsdl/GlobalWeather.wsdl');
    }
  }

  // 'Station getStation(string $code)',
  public function getStation($code) {
    $this->lazyLoad();
    return $this->client->getStation($code);
  }
}
```

lazyLoad() creates the SoapClient on demand. There's just one problem: I'm a lazy coder and I'm already disappointed that I have to create all of the proxied methods and add the $this->lazyLoad(); line to each one. Is there something more succinct? Yes. Once again, take advantage of the new PHP5 ability to chain method calls of returned objects.

Rename lazyLoad() to client() and return the $client instance from the method. Now all of the proxied methods can access the client() method rather than the $client attribute. Lazy instantiation made easy!

```
class GlobalWeather {
  private function client() {
    if (! $this->client instanceof SoapClient) {
      $this->client = new SoapClient(
        'http://live.capescience.com/wsdl/GlobalWeather.wsdl');
    }
    return $this->client;
  }

  // ...

  // 'boolean isValidCode(string $code)
  public function isValidCode($code) {
    return $this->client()->isValidCode($code);
  }

  // and so on for other SOAP service methods ...

  // 'WeatherReport getWeatherReport(string $code)
```

```
    public function getWeatherReport($code) {
      return $this->client()->getWeatherReport($code);
    }
  }
```

So what does the *Lazy Instantiation Proxy* class for the GlobalWeather service buy you? You have a local class that you can create in your program at any time and the remote resources aren't parsed until you actually need them. And there is yet another advantage of using this *Proxy* class: with the supported methods of the SOAP service enumerated in the *Proxy*, you can now mock this class for testing.

LazyProxy Delayed Exceptions

In PHP5, creation of an object can generate an exception. By using a *Lazy Instantiation Proxy*, you delay this potential exception until the first time you use a method that creates the object. (This might even be what you are trying to accomplish with the *Proxy*.) This is obviously not a central part of the pattern, but is something you should keep in mind.

Dynamic Proxy

PHP5 provides some nice features to quickly assemble a *Proxy* class without writing out each method explicitly.

```
class GenericProxy {
  protected $subject;
  public function __construct($subject) {
    $this->subject = $subject;
  }
  public function __call($method, $args) {
      return call_user_func_array(
        array($this->subject, $method),
        $args);
  }
}
```

The key here is the __call() method (also available in PHP4 via the EXPERIMENTAL overload extension). The method __call() allows you to redirect every call to the *Proxy* class to the $subject instead.

Since __call() has lower precedence than actual methods, you can define a real method of the *Proxy* class and it executes instead of the __call() proxy. You can use this structure as scaffolding for your *Proxy* class, and then add in the specific features required for your use of the *Proxy* pattern.

Issues

The *Proxy* pattern is useful in many circumstances where you want to hold an object "at arms distance" for some reason: lazy loading, guarding state changing methods, and so on. As demonstrated by the GlobalWeather class developed in this chapter, you can also use the *Proxy* pattern to make remote resources appear to be available on your local computer.

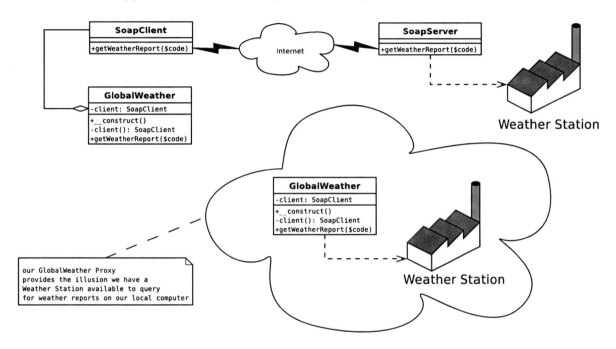

Dynamic proxies are trivial to code and therefore quick and easy for you to implement in your application. However, (as with any implementation relying on __call()), reflection cannot provide visibility into such an object. In particular, if you want to have a *Proxy* that adheres to an interface, you cannot rely on the __call(), but must code at least all of the interface methods explicitly in your *Proxy* class.

12

The Decorator Pattern

IF YOU'VE DEVELOPED OBJECT-ORIENTED PHP code for even a short time or have come this far in this book, you know that you can change or augment the capabilities of a class via *inheritance,* an essential feature of any object-oriented programming language. If an existing PHP class is missing a method or if an existing method needs a little more "oomph," you simply extends the class into a new class and bolt on the extra code.

But subclassing is not always possible or appropriate. What if you want to change the behavior of an object *after* it's been instantiated? Or, what if you want to slightly extend the behavior of many classes? The former can only be done at run-time; the latter is obviously possible, but may lead to a proliferation of subtly-different classes—a maintenance nightmare.

The Problem
How can you structure your code to easily add conditional or rarely used features without putting the extra code directly in your class?

The Solution

The *Decorator Pattern* provides a flexible alternative to subclassing. *Decorator* allows you to modify objects dynamically, adding capabilities without causing an explosion of subclasses.

Decorator is especially useful when used with families of subclasses. If you have a set of subclasses (derived from the same superclass) and you need to add additional capabilities that can be applied independent of the subclass, you can use *Decorator* to avoid both duplicating code and increasing the number of concrete subclasses.

This idea is easiest to understand with some example class diagrams. Consider a simple form library based on the "widget" concept, where you have a class for each type of form control you want to represent. Such as class diagram might look like:

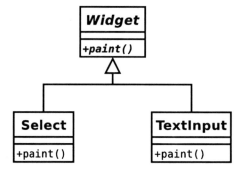

Select and TextInput are subclasses of Widget. Say that you want to add a "labeled" widget, a form input that tells you what the input is for. Since any given form control might be labeled, you might subclass each concrete widget like this:

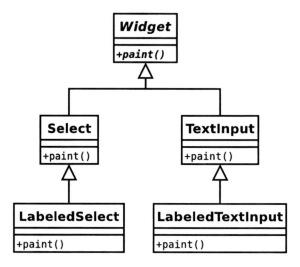

That class diagram doesn't look too bad, so let's add another feature. During form validation you want to be able to indicate if a form control is invalid. The code you need to apply for an "invalid" control again applies to any widget, so it's off to the races to make even more subclasses:

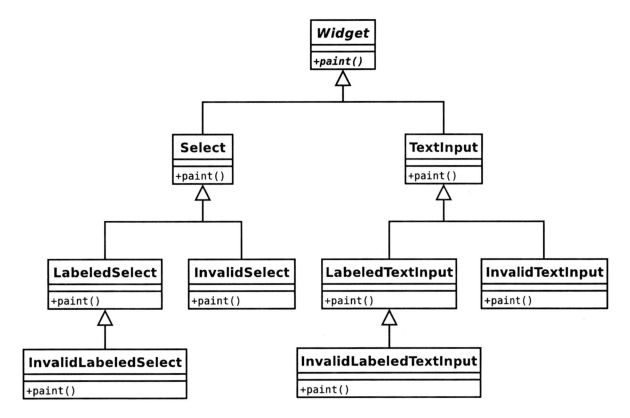

Here the explosion of subclasses isn't the only problem. Think about all of the duplicated code you'd now have spread throughout your entire class hierarchy. There has to be a better way! Indeed, the *Decorator* pattern is the way out of this mess.

The *Decorator* pattern is structurally very similar to the *Proxy* pattern (see *Chapter 11*). A *Decorator* object holds a reference to an object and faithfully recreates the public interface to the decorated object. The *Decorator* can also add methods, extending the interface of the decorated object or can override methods at will, even overriding methods conditionally during the execution of a script.

To explore the *Decorator* pattern, let's take the notion of the form widget library discussed earlier and implement the label and invalidation features using the *Decorator* pattern instead of inheritance.

Sample Code

What should the widget library do?

- Easily create form elements;
- Output form elements as an HTML form; and
- Perform some simple validation on each element.

For this example, let's create a form with inputs for a first name, a last name, and an email address. All of the fields should be required and the email address should vaguely resemble a valid email address. As HTML, the form might look something like this:

```
<form action="formpage.php" method="post">
<b>First Name:</b> <input type="text" name="fname" value=""><br>
<b>Last Name:</b> <input type="text" name="lname" value=""><br>
<b>Email:</b> <input type="text" name="email" value=""><br>
<input type="submit" value="Submit">
</form>
```

And with a little bit of CSS styling might render like this:

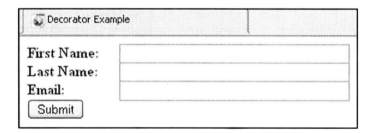

To establish a uniform API, let's create a `Widget` base class (if this was a PHP5 example, this might be an interface). Since all widgets (form elements) must render at least some output, `Widget` holds only a `paint()` method.

```
class Widget {
  function paint() {
    return $this->_asHtml();
  }
}
```

Let's start with a basic text input widget. It must include the name of the input field and the value of the input and must be able to render as HTML.

```
class TextInput extends Widget {
  var $name;
  var $value;
  function TextInput($name, $value='') {
    $this->name = $name;
    $this->value = $value;
  }
  function _asHtml() {
    return '<input type="text" name="'.$this->name.'" value="'
      .$this->value.'">';
  }
}
```

A basic test can verify that the HTML is correct and the name and value passed in as parameters to the constructor carry through to the rendered output:

```
class WidgetTestCase extends UnitTestCase {
  function testTextInput() {
    $text =& new TextInput('foo', 'bar');

    $output = $text->paint();

    $this->assertWantedPattern(
      '~^<input type="text"[^>]*>$~i', $output);
    $this->assertWantedPattern('~name="foo"~i', $output);
    $this->assertWantedPattern('~value="bar"~i', $output);
  }
}
```

The TextInput widget works, but its user interface is horrible, as it lacks a friendly description, such as "First Name" or "Email Address." So, the next logical feature to add to a Widget is a description. Enter the Decorator pattern, which can add a capability uniformly to any Widget.

To start, let's make a generic WidgetDecorator class that can be extended to create specific concrete decorators. At a minimum, the WidgetDecorator class must accept a Widget in its constructor and replicate the public paint() method.

```
class WidgetDecorator {
  var $widget;
```

```
function WidgetDecorator(&$widget) {
  $this->widget =& $widget;
}
function paint() {
  return $this->widget->paint();
}
}
```

To construct a label, pass the content of the label and an original widget:

```
class Labeled extends WidgetDecorator {
  var $label;
  function Labeled($label, &$widget) {
    $this->label = $label;
    $this->WidgetDecorator($widget);
  }
}
```

Labeled also needs to intercept the paint() call and add the label information to the output:

```
class Labeled extends WidgetDecorator {
  var $label;

  function Labeled($label, &$widget) {
    $this->label = $label;
    $this->WidgetDecorator($widget);
  }

  function paint() {
    return '<b>'.$this->label.':</b> '.$this->widget->paint();
  }
}
```

You can verify this works with a test like this:

```
class WidgetTestCase extends UnitTestCase {
  function testLabeled() {
    $text =& new Labeled(
      'Email'
      ,new TextInput('email'));

    $output = $text->paint();
```

```
        $this->assertWantedPattern('~^<b>Email:</b> <input~i', $output);
    }
}
```

With the basic capabilities of `TextInput` and `Labeled`, you can start to assemble a class to manage the form in aggregate.

`FormHandler` has a static `build()` method to create an array of `Widget` form elements:

```
class FormHandlerTestCase extends UnitTestCase {
    function testBuild() {
        $this->assertISA($form = FormHandler::build(new Post), 'Array');
        $this->assertEqual(3, count($form));
        $this->assertISA($form[1], 'Labeled');
        $this->assertWantedPattern('~email~i', $form[2]->paint());
    }
}
```

Some code to realize `FormHandler` might be:

```
class FormHandler {
    function build() {
        return array(
            new Labeled('First Name', new TextInput('fname'))
            ,new Labeled('Last Name', new TextInput('lname'))
            ,new Labeled('Email', new TextInput('email'))
        );
    }
}
```

Now, this code doesn't do you much good without the corresponding `$_POST` values. Because this code must be tested using a *MockObject* (see *Chapter 6*), let's wrap the `$_POST` values in a hash-like object similar to a `Registry` (see *Chapter 5*) or the simulated WACT `DataSource` from the *Specification* pattern (see *Chapter 10*):

```
class Post {
    var $store = array();
    function get($key) {
        if (array_key_exists($key, $this->store))
            return $this->store[$key];
```

```
    }
    function set($key, $val) {
      $this->store[$key] = $val;
    }
}
```

A convenience method can act as both a *Factory* and a means of automatically filling the hash with the keys from $_POST.

```
class Post {
  // ...
    function &autoFill() {
      $ret =& new Post;
      foreach($_POST as $key => $value) {
        $ret->set($key, $value);
      }
      return $ret;
    }
}
```

Using Post class, you can modify FormHandler::build() to use the existing $_POST values for defaults:

```
class FormHandler {
    function build(&$post) {
      return array(
        new Labeled('First Name'
          , new TextInput('fname', $post->get('fname')))
        ,new Labeled('Last Name'
          , new TextInput('lname', $post->get('lname')))
        ,new Labeled('Email'
          , new TextInput('email', $post->get('email')))
        );
    }
}
```

You can now create a PHP script to use this FormHandler to generate the HTML form:

```
<form action="formpage.php" method="post">
<?php
```

```
$post =& Post::autoFill();
$form = FormHandler::build($post);

foreach($form as $widget) {
  echo $widget->paint(), "<br>\n";
}

?>
<input type="submit" value="Submit">
</form>
```

You now have a form handler that posts back to itself and retains the posted values.

Let's move on to adding some validation for the form. The approach is to write another Widget *Decorator* to represent an "invalid" state and to extend the FormHandler class to add a validate() method to process the array of Widget instances. If a Widget is "invalid," let's make it stand out by wrapping it in a <span> element with a class of "invalid". Here's a test that demonstrates that goal:

```
class WidgetTestCase extends UnitTestCase {
  // ...
  function testInvalid() {
    $text =& new Invalid(
      new TextInput('email'));

    $output = $text->paint();

    $this->assertWantedPattern(
      '~^<span class="invalid"><input[^>]+></span>$~i', $output);
  }
}
```

Here's the Invalid WidgetDecorator subclass:

```
class Invalid extends WidgetDecorator {
  function paint() {
    return '<span class="invalid">'.$this->widget->paint().'</span>';
  }
}
```

One nice thing about *Decorators* is that you can chain them together. The Invalid *Decorator* just knows that it is wrapping a widget: it doesn't care if the widget is a TextInput, a Select, or a Labeled-decorated version of any Widget.

This leads to the next logical test case:

```php
class WidgetTestCase extends UnitTestCase {
  // ...
  function testInvalidLabeled() {
    $text =& new Invalid(
      new Labeled(
        'Email'
        ,new TextInput('email')));
    $output = $text->paint();

    $this->assertWantedPattern('~<b>Email:</b> <input~i', $output);
    $this->assertWantedPattern(
      '~^<span class="invalid">.*</span>$~i', $output);
  }
}
```

With the `Invalid` *Decorator* in hand, let's tackle the `FormHandler::validate()` method:

```php
class FormHandlerTestCase extends UnitTestCase {
  // ...

  function testValidateMissingName() {
    $post =& new Post;
    $post->set('fname', 'Jason');
    $post->set('email', 'jsweat_php@yahoo.com');

    $form = FormHandler::build($post);
    $this->assertFalse(FormHandler::validate($form, $post));

    $this->assertNoUnwantedPattern('/invalid/i', $form[0]->paint());
    $this->assertWantedPattern('/invalid/i', $form[1]->paint());
    $this->assertNoUnwantedPattern('/invalid/i', $form[2]->paint());
  }
}
```

This test captures all of the basics: set up a stub `Post` instance, use it to build a `Widget` collection, and then pass that collection to the validate method.

```php
class FormHandler {
  function validate(&$form, &$post) {
    // first name required
    if (!strlen($post->get('fname'))) {
      $form[0] =& new Invalid($form[0]);
    }
```

```
      // last name required
      if (!strlen($post->get('lname'))) {
        $form[1] =& new Invalid($form[1]);
      }
    }
  }
```

Ugly Code

Two "uglies" stare back at me when I look at this code: accessing the form element by a numeric index and having to pass the **$_Post** array into the validation. In later refactoring, it'd probably be better to make a **Widget** collection as an associative array indexed by the form element name, or perhaps a *Registry* as a next logical step. You could also add a method to the **Widget** class to return it's current value, removing the need to pass around the **$_Post** instance past the construction of the **Widget** collection. Both of these are out of scope for the purpose of this example.

With the names validating, let's move on to adding a simple regex to validate the email address:

```
class FormHandlerTestCase extends UnitTestCase {
  // ...

  function testValidateBadEmail() {
    $post =& new Post;
    $post->set('fname', 'Jason');
    $post->set('lname', 'Sweat');
    $post->set('email', 'jsweat_php AT yahoo DOT com');

    $form = FormHandler::build($post);
    $this->assertFalse(FormHandler::validate($form, $post));

    $this->assertNoUnwantedPattern('/invalid/i', $form[0]->paint());
    $this->assertNoUnwantedPattern('/invalid/i', $form[1]->paint());
    $this->assertWantedPattern('/invalid/i', $form[2]->paint());
  }
}
```

Code to implement this simple email validation might look like:

```
class FormHandler {
  function validate(&$form, &$post) {
    // first name required
    if (!strlen($post->get('fname'))) {
      $form[0] =& new Invalid($form[0]);
    }
    // last name required
```

```
      if (!strlen($post->get('lname'))) {
        $form[1] =& new Invalid($form[1]);
      }
      // email has to look real
      if (!preg_match('~\w+@(\w+\.)+\w+~'
          ,$post->get('email'))) {
        $form[2] =& new Invalid($form[2]);
      }
    }
  }
}
```

You can also create a test case for when the form does validate:

```
class FormHandlerTestCase extends UnitTestCase {
  // ...

  function testValidate() {
    $post =& new Post;
    $post->set('fname', 'Jason');
    $post->set('lname', 'Sweat');
    $post->set('email', 'jsweat_php@yahoo.com');

    $form = FormHandler::build($post);
    $this->assertTrue(FormHandler::validate($form, $post));

    $this->assertNoUnwantedPattern('/invalid/i', $form[0]->paint());
    $this->assertNoUnwantedPattern('/invalid/i', $form[1]->paint());
    $this->assertNoUnwantedPattern('/invalid/i', $form[2]->paint());
  }
}
```

This creates the need to track any validation failures inside the method so it can return true if everything checks out.

```
class FormHandler {
  // ...
  function validate(&$form, &$post) {
    $valid = true;
    // first name required
    if (!strlen($post->get('fname'))) {
      $form[0] =& new Invalid($form[0]);
      $valid = false;
    }
    // last name required
    if (!strlen($post->get('lname'))) {
      $form[1] =& new Invalid($form[1]);
      $valid = false;
    }
```

```
        // email has to look real
        if (!preg_match('~\w+@(\w+\.)+\w+~'
            ,$post->get('email'))) {
          $form[2] =& new Invalid($form[2]);
          $valid = false;
        }
        return $valid;
    }
}
```

Those are all the building blocks required to add validation to the page. Here's a screen shot of the end game.

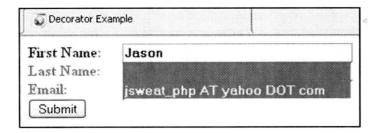

And the page to generate it:

```
<html>
<head>
<title>Decorator Example</title>
<style type="text/css">
.invalid {color: red; }
.invalid input { background-color: red; color: yellow; }
#myform input { position: absolute; left: 110px; width: 250px;  font-weight: bold;}
</style>
</head>
<body>
<form action="<?php echo $_SERVER['PHP_SELF']; ?>" method="post">
<div id="myform">
<?php
error_reporting(E_ALL);
require_once 'widgets.inc.php';

$post =& Post::autoFill();
$form = FormHandler::build($post);
if ($_POST) {
  FormHandler::validate($form, $post);
}

foreach($form as $widget) {
  echo $widget->paint(), "<br>\n";
```

```
        }

    ?>
    </div>
    <input type="submit" value="Submit">
    </form>
    </body>
    </html>
```

Issues

Decorators are another one of those design patterns that grow on you after you've worked with them a bit. The *Decorator* pattern allows you to easily bypass rigid inheritance problems. You can think of a *Decorator* as effectively changing the class of an object at run-time or perhaps even several times as you use the object in different contexts throughout your scripts.

Perhaps the most important aspect of the *Decorator* pattern is it's ability to "trump" inheritance. The "Problem" section showed a subclass explosion using inheritance. With a *Decorator*-based solution, the UML class diagram now resembles this more succinct and flexible solution:

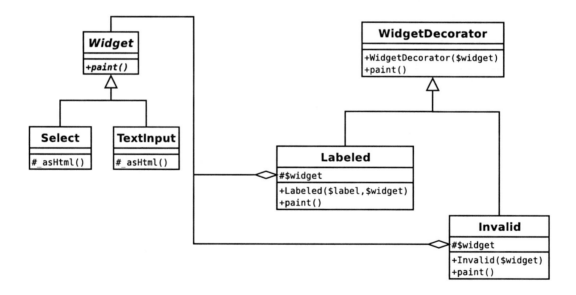

13

The Adapter Pattern

INTERFACES CHANGE. It's a simple and perennial fact that programmers have to (albeit grudgingly) accept and contend with. Vendors change their code; system libraries are revised; and programming languages and their incumbent libraries evolve. One of my son's countless toys succinctly describes the dilemma: you can't fit a square peg in a round hole.

The Problem

How can you protect yourself from changes in the API of external libraries you use? If you write a library, can you provide a means to allow existing users of your software to seamlessly upgrade, even if you've changed your API? How can you change the interface of an object to better suit your needs?

The Solution

The *Adapter* pattern provides a different interface to an object. You can use an *Adapter* to realize a familiar interface to a different object, avoiding the hassle of updating or refactoring your client code.

Consider what happens when (not if!) the API of a third-party library changes. You could just bite the bullet and change all of your client code, but it's often not that simple. You might be working on a new project that requires the features of the newer version of the library, but already have dozens of older legacy applications that work fine with the previsou version of the library. You probably could- n't justify the use of the new feature if the upgrade meant touching the client code for all of the other applications as well.

Handle-Body Pattern

The *Adapter* pattern is the last example of a *Handle-Body* style pattern. The structure of an *Adapter* is similar to a *Proxy* and a *Decorator*, but the intent of an *Adapter* is to change the API of the wrapped object, where both the *Proxy* and the *Decorator* keep the same interface.

Sample Code

Let's see how to protect an existing application from API changes.

Assume that you've searched high and low for exactly the right library and finally discovered HwLib, a (hypothetical) set of code designed to send messages.

This is the source code for the HwLib class:

```
// PHP4
/**
 * the HwLib helps programmers everywhere write their first program
 * @package HelloWorld
 * @version 1
 */
class HwLib {
  /**
   * Say "Hello"
   * @deprec  this function is going away in the future
   * @return  string
   */
  function hello() {
    return 'Hello ';
  }
  /**
   * target audience
   * @return  string
   */
  function world() {
    return 'World!';
  }
}
```

And here's an example of the library in action:

```
$hw =& new HwLib;
echo $hw->hello(), $hw->world();
```

HwLib is well-documented. The authors have even commented explicitly that the hello() method will be deprecated (obsoleted) in a future version.

Next, assume the future has arrived and HwLib version 2 has just been released. A brand new greet() method replaces hello().

Here's the new version of the library (with comments stripped):

```
// version 2
class HwLib {
  function greet() {
    return 'Greetings and Salutations ';
  }
  function world() {
    return 'World!';
  }
}
```

To start coding against both versions of HwLib, first create some tests based on the HwLib version 1 interface:

```
class AdapterTestCase extends UnitTestCase {
  function TestOriginalApp() {
    $lib =& new HwLib;
    $this->assertEqual(
      'Hello World!'
      ,$lib->hello().$lib->world());
  }
}
```

You can also show that simply upgrading the library causes the application to fail.

```
class AdapterTestCase extends UnitTestCase {
```

```
function TestOriginalAppWouldFail() {
    $lib =& new HwLib; // now using HwLib version 2
    $this->assertFalse(method_exists($lib, 'hello'));
  }
}
```

(The test uses method_exists() as an illustration. If you simply switch to version 2 of the library and rerun the AdapterTestCase with the TestOriginalApp() test, PHP fails with the message Fatal error: Call to undefined function: hello().)

The solution to the API "upgrade" is to build an *Adapter*.

The first item of business is to get a reference to an instance of the HwLib version 2 class into your Adapter class.

```
class HwLibV2ToV1Adapter {
  var $libv2;
  function HwLibV2ToV1Adapter (&$libv2) {
    $this->libv2 =& $libv2;
  }
}
```

This example shows the instance passed into the constructor, but you might just create a new instance, use a *Factory* or a *Singleton,* or use some other creational pattern that's appropriate for your requirements. (The use of composition in HwLibV2ToV1Adapter should seem familiar after the past two chapters.)

Given the HwLib version 2 object, how can you make it appear to be an instance of the HwLib version 1?

```
class HwLibV2ToV1Adapter {
  var $libv2;
  function HwLibV2ToV1Adapter (&$libv2) {
    $this->libv2 =& $libv2;
  }
  function hello() {
    return $this->libv2->greet();
  }
  function world() {
    return $this->libv2->world();
  }
}
```

The `HwLibV2ToV1Adapter::hello()` method delegates to the `$libv2` objects `greet()` method. So, how do you use this in your application?

```
class AdapterTestCase extends UnitTestCase {
  function TestOriginalAppWithAdapter() {
    $lib =& new HwLibV2ToV1Adapter(new HwLib);
    $this->assertEqual(
      'Greetings and Salutations World!'
      ,$lib->hello().$lib->world());
  }
}
```

But now the application test and the application code are somewhat brittle. Is there a way to make both of these easier to maintain in the long run? Yes!

Recall (from *Chapter 3)* how a *Factory* provides a more flexible means of creating instances of objects. To better "future proof" the code, start with a simple *Factory* function:

```
function &HwLibInstance() {
  return new HwLib;
}
```

To test the *Factory,* call it instead of creating the instance directly:

```
class AdapterTestCase extends UnitTestCase {
  function TestAppWithFactory() {
    $lib =& HwLibInstance();
    $this->assertWantedPattern(
      '/\w+ World!$/'
      ,$lib->hello().$lib->world());
  }
}
```

There are two things to notice: the *Factory* creates the object and the `assertEqual()` validation has been changed to the more flexible `assertWantedPattern()`. You can now use a regular expression to capture the "core" of what you're looking for from the library, perhaps making the test itself less brittle.

Next, upgrade the HwLib library. As you install HwLib version2, you can modify the

HwLibInstance() function to accommodate the new version:

```
function &HwLibInstance($ver=false) {
  switch ($ver) {
  case 'V2':
    return new HwLib;
  default:
    return new HwLibV2ToV1Adapter(new HwLib);
  }
}
```

Now re-run the AdapterTestCase. The tests continue to pass! (Green bars are great.) Because the original application call didn't pass a parameter, the HwLibInstance() Factory defaults to returning an instance of the HwLib wrapped in the HwLibV2toV1Adapter class. However, if you're writing new code, you can pass in a parameter of 'V2' to let the function know you want the HwLib newer version directly without adapting it.

In the future, if you choose to upgrade to version 3 of the HwLib library, the *Factory* might change to look like:

```
function &HwLibInstance($ver=false) {
  switch ($ver) {
  case 'V3':
    return new HwLib;
  case 'V2':
    return new HwLibV3ToV2Adapter(new HwLib);
  default:
    return new HwLibV2ToV1Adapter(
      new HwLibV3ToV2Adapter(new HwLib));
  }
}
```

Issues

As the sample code showed, you can use the *Adapter* pattern to protect yourself from a changing external library — providing forwards compatibility. As a developer of a library, you could write the adapter yourself to give users of your library an easier path to use the newer version without changing all of their existing code.

The *Adapter* pattern as presented in the GoF book uses inheritance rather than composition. This is advantageous in a strongly-typed language, because the *Adapter* is actually a subclass of the target class, and therefore integrates better with typed methods.

Here's an example of the HwLib adapter using inheritance:

```
class HwLibGofAdapter extends HwLib { // extending version 2.0
  function hello() {
    return parent::greet();
  }
}
```

A world() method isn't provided because it's already a part of the subclass due to inheritance.

```
class AdapterTestCase extends UnitTestCase {
  function TestHwLibGofAdapter() {
    $lib =& new HwLibGofAdapter;
    $this->assertEqual(
      'Greetings and Salutations World!'
        ,$lib->hello().$lib->world());
  }
}
```

I personally favor the composition method for greater flexibility (particularly in combination with *Dependency Inversion*); however, the inheritance method does provide both versions of the interface, which might be a point of flexibility for you to consider in your own implementation.

Dependency Inversion Principle

The *Dependency Inversion Principle* (first defined at http://www.objectmentor.com/resources/articles/dip.pdf by Robert C. Martin) is an OOP design guideline that states: higher level modules should not depend on lower levels and details should depend on abstractions. A very simple example of the *Dependency Inversion Principle* in combination with an *Adapter* pattern is available at http://www.phplondon.org/wiki/DependencyInversion.

The *Adapter* pattern focus alters the API for a single object. A related design pattern (not covered in this book) is the *Facade* pattern. The purpose of the *Facade* is to present a simpler interface to an entire sub-system composed of many objects—in contrast to wrapping a single object—and may be a pattern worth investigating if you are trying to isolate your code from third-party libraries.

14

The Active Record Pattern

The design patterns you've seen so far greatly improve the readability and maintainability of script internals; however, none have confronted a fundamental requirement and challenge of architecting and developing web applications: connecting to a database. This chapter and the next two chapters—*Table Data Gateway* and *Data Mapper*—provide three design patterns that better organize how your application interacts with a database.

The Problem

Most web applications persist information in a database. Is there a way to abstract database connectivity to simplify table access and integrate persistence with business logic?

The Solution

Conceptually, the *Active Record* pattern is the simplest of the database-related design patterns. The *Active Record* pattern embeds the knowledge of how to interact with the database directly into the class performing the interaction.

While *Active Record* leads to a high degree of coupling between application code and database structure, in relatively simple circumstances the issues inherent in coupling may be far easier to manage than adopting a more complex solution. *Active Record* is also sufficient for many first-time database projects. Only if complications arise that cannot be easily addressed with the *Active Record* pattern should you refactor to a *Table Data Gateway* (see *Chapter 15*), a *Data Mapper* (see *Chapter 16*), or another database design pattern.

Patterns of Enterprise Application Architecture

According to Martin Fowler's book, *Patterns of Enterprise Application Architecture,* an *enterprise application* is integrated with other applications, contains significant business logic (or illogic, as application requirements often reveal), and includes lots of concurrently accessed, persistent data that's accessed from a variety of interfaces. Interestingly, web applications share many of those very characteristics, which may explain why Fowler's book resonates strongly with PHP programmers.

PHP Data Objects

One project to watch is *PDO.* PDO is a PHP extension for high-performance database access (*not* database abstraction). PDO is a C—language wrapper of the native drivers and is therefore very fast. PDO provides prepared statements for all PDO drivers, enhancing the security of scripts using the library.

Sample Code

Any discussion of database connectivity depends on choosing both a database and an access layer. This and the following two chapters use the popular open source database MySQL (http://www.mysql.com/) and the ADOdb (http://adodb.sf.net/) access layer. I established ADOdb as a standard in my workplace because it has excellent performance and it abstracts the Oracle OCI interface and interfaces to PostgreSQL, Sybase, MySQL, and other databases in a uniform, simple-to-use PHP API, allowing you to focus on your programming and business logic.

Feel free to substitute you own database and access layer, as most of the concepts presented here readily port to other solutions.

Before looking at the *Active Record* pattern, let's start with basic database connectivity. It's ideal to have a central, simple way to specify connection parameters (the hostname, username, password, and database) and to create a database connection object. A *Singleton* (see *Chapter 4*) typically suffices.

Here's a DB class with a conn() method that returns the *Singleton* instance of the ADOConnection class.

```
// PHP5
require_once 'adodb/adodb.inc.php';

class DB {
  //static class, we do not need a constructor
  private function __construct() {}

  public static function conn() {
    static $conn;

    if (!$conn) {
      $conn = adoNewConnection('mysql');
      $conn->connect('localhost', 'username', 'passwd', 'database');
      $conn->setFetchMode(ADODB_FETCH_ASSOC);
    }

    return $conn;
  }

}
```

The DB class allows you to control the type of database and the connection parameters used in connecting to the database. At the top, the code includes the ADOdb library (you may need to adjust the include path to suit your environment); The DB constructor is private since there's no need to ever create an instance of DB; And the line $conn->setFetchMode(ADODB_FETCH_ASSOC) instructs the result set object to return rows as associative arrays of field_name => value. Using an associative array is an important best practice to adopt in working with databases, so your code remains unaffected (less brittle) by the ordering of fields in SELECT clauses of your SQL statements.

As an example application, let's create an *Active Record* object to maintain a table of hyperlinks. Here's the SQL to create the hyperlinks table in a MySQL database:

```
define('BOOKMARK_TABLE_DDL', <<<EOS
CREATE TABLE `bookmark` (
  `id` INT NOT NULL AUTO_INCREMENT ,
  `url` VARCHAR( 255 ) NOT NULL ,
  `name` VARCHAR( 255 ) NOT NULL ,
  `description` MEDIUMTEXT,
  `tag` VARCHAR( 50 ) ,
  `created` DATETIME NOT NULL ,
  `updated` DATETIME NOT NULL ,
PRIMARY KEY ( `id` )
)
EOS
);
```

Test Independence

Tests should be independent of each other; otherwise, the mere running of a certain test could interfere with the results of latter tests.

To avoid interference between tests that rely on a database, it's best to drop and recreate the database (or just specific tables) between each test method. SimpleTest provides the standard xUnit `setup()` method to prepare for each test.

Here's how you might "reset" the database between each test:

```
class ActiveRecordTestCase extends UnitTestCase {
  protected $conn;
  function __construct($name='') {
    $this->UnitTestCase($name);
    $this->conn = DB::conn();
  }

  function setup() {
    $this->conn->execute('drop table bookmark');
    $this->conn->execute(BOOKMARK_TABLE_DDL);
  }
}
```

The code populates the $conn attribute with a standard `ADOConnection` object and then uses the connection's `execute()` method to perform SQL statements dropping and recreating the table. Because this is in the `setup()` method, each test method starts out with a fresh copy of the database table to work with.

Going a little further, you can do some basic sanity checks of the `setup()` method (and learn a little bit about the `ADOConnection` API along the way):

```
class ActiveRecordTestCase extends UnitTestCase {
  // ...

  function testSetupLeavesTableEmptyWithCorrectStructure() {
    $rs = $this->conn->execute('select * from bookmark');
    $this->assertIsA($rs, 'ADORecordSet');
    $this->assertEqual(0,$rs->recordCount());
    foreach(array(
      'id',
      'url',
      'name',
      'description',
      'tag',
      'created',
      'updated') as $i => $name) {
      $this->assertEqual($name, $rs->fetchField($i)->name);
```

```
      }
    }
  }
```

Even if you're unfamiliar with ADOdb, you can probably still discern that the `execute()` method returns an `ADORecordSet` object if successful. The object has a `recordCount()` method, which is used here to verify the table is empty. The record set object also has some methods to explore result set metadata and the `fetchField()` is used to verify the structure of the table.

Record Creation

After connecting to the database, your "Create, Read, Update, and Delete" (CRUD) application must be able to create rows in the database.

CRUD

The acronym *CRUD* stands for Create, Read, Update and Delete. These are the basic foundations of any application that interacts with a database.

Many   PHP   web   applications   are   examples   of   CrudScreen   applications (http://c2.com/cgi/wiki?CrudScreen).

The sample application saves bookmarks to a database, so let's name the *Active Record* class `Bookmark`. To create a new bookmark, use `new` to create a `Bookmark` and set the instance's properties. When all of the (mandatory) properties are set, use the `save()` method to store the bookmark in the database.

This test captures that intent:

```
class ActiveRecordTestCase extends UnitTestCase {
  // ...
  function testNew() {
    $link = new Bookmark;

    $link->url = 'http://simpletest.org/';
    $link->name = 'SimpleTest';
    $link->description = 'SimpleTest project homepage';
    $link->tag = 'testing';

    $link->save();
    $this->assertEqual(1, $link->getId());
  }
}
```

According to this test, the class Bookmark has a few public attributes and a save() method. After the instance is saved in the database, getId() should return the database row ID assigned to this Bookmark.

Here are the Bookmark class attributes:

```
class Bookmark {
    public $url;
    public $name;
    public $description;
    public $tag;
}
```

Let's turn to the save() method. It requires a database connection, so let's use the DB::conn() connection factory in the constructor:

```
class Bookmark {
    protected $id;
    protected $conn;
    // ...

    public function __construct() {
        $this->conn = DB::conn();
    }
}
```

$conn is now a database connection suitable for save() to use.

```
class Bookmark {
    // ...

    const INSERT_SQL = "
        insert into bookmark (url, name, description,
            tag, created, updated)
        values (?, ?, ?, ?, now(), now())
        ";
    protected function save() {
        $rs = $this->conn->execute(
            self::INSERT_SQL
            ,array($this->url, $this->name,
                $this->description, $this->tag));
        if ($rs) {
            $this->id = (int)$this->conn->Insert_ID();
        } else {
```

```
        trigger_error('DB Error: '.$this->conn->errorMsg());
      }
    }
  }
```

The ADOdb MySQL driver supports positional parameter substitution and also properly quotes the parameters. SQL parameters are indicated in a query by question marks (?) and you pass the substitution values in an array as a second parameter to the execute() method.

The Insert_ID() method should catch your eye: it returns the value of the AUTO_INCREMENT field from the last executed insert statement.

So far, the tests have proven that attributes can be set, that save() is functional, and that the $id attribute has been set to 1. Let's dig a little more into the database table and verify that the other bookmark attributes have been set properly, too.

```
class ActiveRecordTestCase extends UnitTestCase {
  // ...
  function testNew() {
    $link = new Bookmark;

    $link->url = 'http://simpletest.org/';
    $link->name = 'SimpleTest';
    $link->description = 'SimpleTest project homepage';
    $link->tag = 'testing';

    $link->save();
    $this->assertEqual(1, $link->getId());

    // fetch the table as an array of hashes
    $rs = $this->conn->getAll('select * from bookmark');
    $this->assertEqual(1, count($rs), 'returned 1 row');
    foreach(array('url', 'name', 'description', 'tag') as $key) {
      $this->assertEqual($link->$key, $rs[0][$key]);
    }
  }
}
```

The highlighted code fetches the entire bookmark table. The getAll() method executes the passed query and returns the resultset as an array of row hashes. The assertEqual() line validates that only a single row is present in the result test. The foreach loop compares the attributes of the object $link to fields in the row returned.

The code works, but adding bookmarks this way—setting each attribute by hand—can get a bit tedious. Instead, let's add a convenience method to the test case to facilitate adding bookmark objects.

The `ActiveRecordTestCase::add()` method takes four parameters and creates and inserts a new *Active Record* `Bookmark` object. And just in case you want to use the new object in tests later, `add()` returns the created `Bookmark` object as well.

```
class ActiveRecordTestCase extends UnitTestCase {
  // ...

  function add($url, $name, $description, $tag) {
    $link = new Bookmark;

    $link->url = $url;
    $link->name = $name;
    $link->description = $description;
    $link->tag = $tag;

    $link->save();
    return $link;
  }
}
```

You can actually write a test method inside the test case to prove this works:

```
class ActiveRecordTestCase extends UnitTestCase {
  // ...

  function testAdd() {
    $this->add('http://php.net', 'PHP',
      'PHP Language Homepage', 'php');
    $this->add('http://phparch.com', 'php|architect',
      'php|arch site', 'php');
    $rs = $this->conn->execute('select * from bookmark');
    $this->assertEqual(2,$rs->recordCount());
    $this->assertEqual(2,$this->conn->Insert_ID());
  }
}
```

Now that bookmarks can be created and saved to the database, let's add a way for an *Active Record* `Bookmark` object to easily retrieve data from the database and store the values as instance attributes. A common technique to create an *Active Record* object is to pass an identifier such as the bookmark ID (or some set of criteria) to its constructor and load the row associated with that ID from the database. Here is a test that demonstrates that:

```
class ActiveRecordTestCase extends UnitTestCase {
  // ...

  function testCreateById() {
    $link = $this->add(
      'http://blog.casey-sweat.us/',
      'My Blog',
      'Where I write about stuff',
      'php');
    $this->assertEqual(1, $link->getId());

    $link2 = new Bookmark(1);
    $this->assertIsA($link2, 'Bookmark');
    $this->assertEqual($link, $link2);
  }
}
```

This test passes an ID to the constructor, something the existing tests do not do. Passing an ID has to be optional, because existing tests that create new, empty Bookmark instances must continue to work.

Here's some code to realize the requirements of the test(s):

```
class Bookmark {
  // ...

  const SELECT_BY_ID = 'select * from bookmark where id = ?';
  public function __construct($id=false) {
    $this->conn DB::conn();

    if ($id) {
      $rs = $this->conn->execute(
        self::SELECT_BY_ID
        ,array((int)$id));

      if ($rs) {
        $row = $rs->fetchRow();
        foreach($row as $field => $value) {
          $this->$field = $value;
        }
      } else {
        trigger_error('DB Error: '.$this->conn->errorMsg());
      }
    }
  }

  // ...
}
```

This constructor allows an $id parameter, which is false by default. If a non-false $id parameter is passed, then Bookmark queries the database for a row in the bookmark table with the corresponding ID. If such a row exists, all of the attributes of the object are set to the values recovered by the database query.

Testing Database Failure

Databases usually just work, but failure is not unheard of. To make sure your code operates correctly under failure conditions, let's simulate a failure using a *Mock Object* (see *Chapter 6 — The Mock Object Pattern*), which stands in for the connection object.

```
Mock::generate('ADOConnection');

class ActiveRecordTestCase extends UnitTestCase {
  //...
  function testDbFailure() {
    $conn = new MockADOConnection($this);
    $conn->expectOnce('execute', array('*','*'));
    $conn->setReturnValue('execute',false);
    $conn->expectOnce('errorMsg');
    $conn->setReturnValue('errorMsg',
      'The database has exploded!!!!');
  }
}
```

This code calls Mock::generate() to create a MockADOConnection class, creates an instance of the mock connection, sets up some basic return values to indicate failure, and defines some expectations about what's to be called in these circumstances.

However, because the Bookmark constructor makes a call to the static DB:conn() method to retrieve the database connection, it's difficult to inject the mock connection into that code. There are several possible workarounds: add a method to change $this->conn, add an optional parameter to each method, or add a parameter to the constructor. Let's opt for the latter: add an optional connection class parameter to the Bookmark constructor:

```
class Bookmark {
  // ...
  public function __construct($id=false, $conn=false) {
    $this->conn = ($conn) ? $conn : DB::conn();
    // ...
  }
}
```

Now new `Bookmark` works as normal, but new `Bookmark(1, $connection)` uses the `$connection` object instead of the normal `ADOConnection` object.

With that code in place, you can now easily replace the "normal" database connection object with a `MockADOconnection` and verify the results of a "database failure."

```
class ActiveRecordTestCase extends UnitTestCase {
  // ...

  function testDbFailure() {
    $conn = new MockADOConnection($this);
    $conn->expectOnce('execute', array('*','*'));
    $conn->setReturnValue('execute',false);
    $conn->expectOnce('errorMsg');
    $conn->setReturnValue('errorMsg',
      'The database has exploded!!!!');

    $link = new Bookmark(1,$conn);
    $this->assertErrorPattern('/exploded/i');

    $conn->tally();
  }
}
```

Active Record Instance ID

In the previous example, most of the attributes are public; however, the ID of the bookmark is protected to avoid accidents changing its value (this would be problematic when you wanted to later update the bookmark). Since `$id` is protected, add an accessor method to retrieve it from the `Bookmark`.

```
class Bookmark {
  protected $id;
  //...
  public function getId() {
    return $this->id;
  }
}
```

How do you test this?

```
class ActiveRecordTestCase extends UnitTestCase {
  // ...
```

```
        function testGetId() {
          $this->add('http://php.net', 'PHP',
            'PHP Language Homepage', 'php');
          // second bookmark, id=2
          $link = $this->add('http://phparch.com',
            'php|architect', 'php|arch site', 'php');

          $this->assertEqual(2, $link->getId());
        }
      }
```

Immediately above, add() persists several bookmarks and verifies that the latter of the two matches.

So far, so good, but what if you want to verify the database entry based on a different criteria than the bookmark ID? How can you make sure the correct ID from the database is being returned? A good technique is to SELECT from the database using a known attribute and verify the ID from the returned row. Here's a test using this methodology:

```
    class ActiveRecordTestCase extends UnitTestCase {
      // ...
      function testGetId() {
        $this->add('http://php.net', 'PHP',
          'PHP Language Homepage', 'php');
        // second bookmark, id=2
        $link = $this->add('http://phparch.com',
          'php|architect', 'php|arch site', 'php');

        $this->assertEqual(2, $link->getId());

        $alt_test = $this->conn->getOne(
          "select id from bookmark where url = 'http://phparch.com'");
        $this->assertEqual(2, $alt_test);
        //alternatively
        $this->assertEqual($link->getId(), $alt_test);
      }
    }
```

Notice that this test resembles the SQL you might execute manually to verify the insertion of the data into the bookmark table. By coding this as a test, rather than simply performing it once by hand, you can continue to verify it is taking place each time you run the tests.

Searching for Records

At the moment, a Bookmark can be stored in a database and can be (re)created by retrieving the database row that matches the bookmark's ID. But what happens—as is usually the case—when the ID is not known or you want to search the database for a more pertinent value, such as a partial name or a URL. A common solution is to add "finder" methods.

For example, you might want a findByUrl() method to find Bookmarks similar to the parameter passed to the method. Here's that intention expressed as a test:

```php
class ActiveRecordTestCase extends UnitTestCase {
  // ...

  function testFindByUrl() {
    $this->add('http://blog.casey-sweat.us/', 'My Blog',
      'Where I write about stuff', 'php');
    $this->add('http://php.net', 'PHP',
      'PHP Language Homepage', 'php');
    $this->add('http://phparch.com', 'php|architect',
      'php|arch site', 'php');

    $result = Bookmark::findByUrl('php');

    $this->assertIsA($result, 'array');
    $this->assertEqual(2, count($result));
    $this->assertEqual(2, $result[0]->getId());
    $this->assertEqual('php|architect', $result[1]->name);
  }
}
```

The test creates some data, searches for rows that contain "php" somewhere in the URL, and then verifies characteristics of the returned array of Bookmark objects. FindByUrl() is a static method, because you want Bookmark objects, but do not yet have an instance of the Bookmark class to work with. (Alternatively, you could move these "finder" methods to an object of their own, but for now the finder methods are a part of the *Active Record* Bookmark class.)

Here's some code to realize the requirements expressed by the test:

```php
class Bookmark {
  // ...

  const SELECT_BY_URL = "
    select id
    from bookmark
    where url like ?";
  public static function findByUrl($url) {
    $rs = DB::conn()->execute(
      self::SELECT_BY_URL
      ,array("%$url%"));
    $ret = array();
    if ($rs) {
      foreach ($rs->getArray() as $row) {
        $ret[] = new Bookmark($row['id']);
      }
```

```
    }
    return $ret;
  }
}
```

Updating Records

The Create and Read portions of CRUD are complete; what about Update? It makes sense to use save() to update an *Active Record* object, but as it is now, save() only handles INSERT statements. To recap, save() looks like this:

```
class Bookmark{
  // ...

  const INSERT_SQL = "
    insert into bookmark (url, name, description,
      tag, created, updated)
    values (?, ?, ?, ?, now(), now())
    ";
  protected function save() {
    $rs = $this->conn->execute(
      self::INSERT_SQL
      ,array($this->url, $this->name,
        $this->description, $this->tag));
    if ($rs) {
      $this->id = (int)$this->conn->Insert_ID();
    } else {
      trigger_error('DB Error: '.$this->conn->errorMsg());
    }
  }
}
```

However, after you already have a valid instance, you would rather see something like:

```
class Bookmark {
  // ...

  const UPDATE_SQL = "
    update bookmark set
      url = ?,
      name = ?,
      description = ?,
      tag = ?,
      updated = now()
    where id = ?
    ";
```

```
      public function save() {
        $this->conn->execute(
          self::UPDATE_SQL
          ,array(
            $this->url,
            $this->name,
            $this->description,
            $this->tag,
            $this->id));
      }
    }
```

To differentiate between INSERT and UPDATE, you need to detect if a bookmark is new or if it's been loaded from the database.

First, refactor the two "versions" of save() into individual protected methods with the descriptive names insert() and update().

```
class Bookmark {
  // ...

  protected function insert() {
    $rs = $this->conn->execute(
      self::INSERT_SQL
      ,array($this->url, $this->name,
        $this->description, $this->tag));
    if ($rs) {
      $this->id = (int)$this->conn->Insert_ID();
    }
  }
  protected function update() {
      $this->conn->execute(
        self::UPDATE_SQL
        ,array(
          $this->url,
          $this->name,
          $this->description,
          $this->tag,
          $this->id));
  }
}
```

Now you can change save() to look at this info:

```
class Bookmark {
  const NEW_BOOKMARK = -1;
  protected $id = Bookmark::NEW_BOOKMARK;
  // ...
```

```
        public function save() {
          if ($this->id == Bookmark::NEW_BOOKMARK) {
            $this->insert();
          } else {
            $this->update();
          }
        }
      }
```

Just one last issue: timestamps change in the database whenever you insert or update a record. There is no other way to keep an accurate timestamp in the Bookmark other than making another trip to the database to retrieve it. Since this applies to either inserts or updates, change the *Active Record* class to always update the timestamp before leaving the save() method in order to prevent the latter from getting out of sync.

```
class Bookmark {
  // ...
  public function save() {
    if ($this->id == self::NEW_BOOKMARK) {
      $this->insert();
    } else {
      $this->update();
    }
    $this->setTimeStamps();
  }
  protected function setTimeStamps() {
    $rs = $this->conn->execute(
      self::SELECT_BY_ID
      ,array($this->id));
    if ($rs) {
      $row = $rs->fetchRow();
      $this->created = $row['created'];
      $this->updated = $row['updated'];
    }
  }
}
```

Bookmark gets to the heart of the *ActiveRecord* pattern: save() knows the SQL statement required to update or insert into the database table, knows the object's current state, and can assemble the needed parameter substitution array from the object's own attributes. Let's test it:

```
class ActiveRecordTestCase extends UnitTestCase {
  // ...
```

```
function testSave() {
  $link = Bookmark::add(
    'http://blog.casey-sweat.us/',
    'My Blog',
    'Where I write about stuff',
    'php');

  $link->description =
    'Where I write about PHP, Linux and other stuff';
  $link->save();

  $link2 = Bookmark($link->getId());
  $this->assertEqual($link->getId(), $link2->getId());
  $this->assertEqual($link->created, $link2->updated);
}
}
```

For now, let's skip how to implement DELETE. There is an example in *Chapter 16—The Data Mapper Pattern*, but you can easily derive it from the insert() and update() methods.

Issues

The *Active Record* pattern is simple in both concept and execution and probably represents what most initial attempts to refactor from procedural coding to object-oriented programming would look like. It's nice to have all of your SQL code grouped into a single location and the *Active Record* pattern gives you a nice way to couple business logic with database access to persist the object.

The example in this chapter used an actual database to develop and test the code. Another way to test simple database code is to use *Mock Objects* (see *Chapter 6*) to completely simulate the database connection. Unfortunately though, this approach does not scale. SQL is a complex language and mocking individual statements tightly couples tests with database specifics. Using freshly-created, actual tables provide a higher degree of comfort, without the brittle effects of Mocking SQL.

If there's a downside to the *Active Record* pattern, it's complexity. An *Active Record* class can grow quite quickly—it attracts features like a magnet. For example, the Bookmark classes only included a findById() method, but you'd likely also want findByUrl(), findByDescription(), findByGroup(), findRecentlyCreated(), and so on.

Another issue, which is possible to see in the testing of the save() method, is that objects can become "duplicated." For example, $link and $link2 in the test case aren't the same objects, though they both refer to the same bookmark ID. You could test this explicitly also:

```
class ActiveRecordTestCase extends UnitTestCase {
  // ...
  function testSave() {
```

```
// ...

    $this->assertNotIdentical($link, $link2);
  }
}
```

If it's important to work around this issue, you might want to add an internal *Registry* (see *Chapter 5*) to make sure all instances of the object returned by Bookmark(1) are in fact the same object. Because you're actually using the new operator to create the objects instead of a *Factory* method, you might have to restructure the Bookmark class as a *Proxy* (see *Chapter 11*) to the actual *Active Record* class to really pull this off.

Another aspect of the *Active Record* pattern is that it is designed to work with data one row at a time. This is fairly typical of "admin" screens for applications where you might be editing an article, a link, a comment or any other row from a database, but a good deal of web pages deal with result sets or combinations of rows, which is more the domain of our next chapter—*The Table Data Gateway Pattern*.

15

The Table Data Gateway Pattern

THE PREVIOUS CHAPTER USED the *Active Record* pattern to create, retrieve, update, (and by extension, delete) individual rows in a database table. *Active Record* is one of the simplest ways to abstract database connectivity, but its simplicity is also its Achilles heel. An *Active Record* class manages only a single row, making it inefficient for web applications that present information en masse, such as travel booking or online shopping. In those kinds of applications—likely the majority of all web applications—result sets are the more common currency.

The Problem

How can you easily manipulate a database table and all of the rows in that table?

The Solution

The *Table Data Gateway* pattern resembles the *Active Record* pattern. In fact, much of the code for this new pattern is borrowed from the code in *Chapter 14—The Active Record Pattern* (it reuses the exact same DB class and BOOKMARK_TABLE_DDL constant, and as before, ADOdb serves as the database access library). However, the *Table Data Gateway* pattern focuses on *tables*—collections of rows—instead of individual rows.

Sample Code

Let's start with the create operation, which adds new records to a table.

The test case function TableDataGatewayTestCase::testAdd() captures the steps required to add two URLs to the bookmark table. It largely mirrors *Chapter 14*'s ActiveRecordTestCase::testAdd(), but is distinct because it introduces the new BookmarkGateway *Table Data Gateway* class.

```php
class TableDataGatewayTestCase extends UnitTestCase {

    function testAdd() {
        $gateway = new BookmarkGateway($conn = DB::conn());
        $gateway->add(
          'http://simpletest.org/',
          'SimpleTest',
          'The SimpleTest homepage',
          'testing');
        $gateway->add(
          'http://blog.casey-sweat.us/',
          'My Blog',
          'Where I write about stuff',
          'php');

        $rs = $this->conn->execute('select * from bookmark');
        $this->assertEqual(2,$rs->recordCount());
        $this->assertEqual(2,$conn->Insert_ID());

    }
}
```

Similar to *Active Record*, TableDataGatewayTestCase instantiates the pattern class and adds some records to the database. However, because the *Table Data Gateway* pattern works on an entire table, you need only create one pattern object and re-use that object to add any number of new records to its table.

Here's one possible implementation of BookmarkGateway:

```php
class BookmarkGateway {
    protected $conn;
    public function __construct($conn) {
```

```
        $this->conn = $conn;
    }

    const INSERT_SQL = "
      insert into bookmark (url, name, description,
        tag, created, updated)
      values (?, ?, ?, ?, now(), now())
      ";
    public function add($url, $name, $description, $group) {
      $rs = $this->conn->execute(
        self::INSERT_SQL
        ,array($url, $name, $description, $group));
      if (!$rs) {
        trigger_error('DB Error: '.$this->conn->errorMsg());
      }
    }
  }
}
```

Much of this is likely to look familiar, as the "scaffolding" of the *Active Record* and *Table Data Gateway* pattern is similar: the INSERT_SQL statement, the mapping of function parameters, and the management of database errors are the same as *Active Record*. add() creates one record at a time, too.

With the "create" of CRUD implemented, it's time to move on to "retrieve."

Test Case Structure

Since the point of the *Table Data Gateway* is to work with a database table populated with records, you'll likely need a convenient way to initialize the table to a known state before running each test. One quick solution is to create a base class for all of your tests, including two helper functions, setup() and addSeveralBookmarks, to recreate the table from scratch and load some data, respectively.

Here's such a BaseTestCase class:

```
class BaseTestCase extends UnitTestCase {
  protected $conn;
  function __construct($name='') {
    $this->UnitTestCase($name);
    $this->conn = DB::conn();
  }

  function setup() {
    $this->conn->execute('drop table bookmark');
    $this->conn->execute(BOOKMARK_TABLE_DDL);
  }

  function addSeveralBookmarks($gateway) {
    // add(url, name, desc, tag)
    $gateway->add('http://blog.casey-sweat.us/'
```

```
        ,'Jason\'s Blog'
        ,'PHP related thoughts'
        ,'php');
    $gateway->add('http://www.php.net/'
        ,'PHP homepage'
        ,'The main page for PHP'
        ,'php');
    $gateway->add('http://slashdot.org/'
        ,'/.'
        ,'News for Nerds'
        ,'new');
    $gateway->add('http://google.com/'
        ,'Google'
        ,'Google Search Engine'
        ,'web');
    $gateway->add('http://www.phparch.com/'
        ,'php|architect'
        ,'The home page of php|architect,
            an outstanding monthly PHP publication'
        ,'php');
    }
  }
```

Now every test case derived from `BaseTestCase` inherits its constructor, a `setup()` method, and `addSeveralBookmarks()`, which pre-loads some data.

Returning Recordsets as Arrays

Whenever you realize a *Table Data Gateway* class, you must choose a data structure to represent result sets returned from access methods. A very common idiom in PHP is to return a vector (a 0-indexed array) of row hashes, which are associative arrays of field => value pairs.

Getting such a structure from the `ADOConnection` in `BookmarkGateway` is nearly trivial, since the `ADOResultSet::getArray()` method follows the exact same idiom.

For example, here's a `findAll()` method that returns the entire contents of the *Table Data Gateway* class's table:

```
class BookmarkGateway {
  // ...
  public function findAll() {
    $rs = $this->conn->execute('select * from bookmark');
    if ($rs) {
      return $rs->getArray();
    } else {
      trigger_error('DB Error: '.$this->conn->errorMsg());
    }
  }
}
```

Trivial or not, it needs a test:

```
class TableDataGatewayTestCase extends BaseTestCase {
  // ...
  function testFindAll() {
    $gateway = new BookmarkGateway(DB::conn());
    $this->addSeveralBookmarks($gateway);

    $result = $gateway->findAll();
    $this->assertIsA($result, 'Array');
    $this->assertEqual(5, count($result));
  }
}
```

If you want to go further, you can check some of the individual returned rows:

```
class TableDataGatewayTestCase extends BaseTestCase {
  // ...
  function testFindAll() {
    $gateway = new BookmarkGateway(DB::conn());
    $this->addSeveralBookmarks($gateway);

    $result = $gateway->findAll();
    $this->assertIsA($result, 'Array');
    $this->assertEqual(5, count($result));

    $this->assertIsA($result[0], 'Array');
    $this->assertEqual(7, count($result[1]));

    $expected_keys = array(
       'id'
      ,'url'
      ,'name'
      ,'description'
      ,'tag'
      ,'created'
      ,'updated');
    $this->assertEqual(
      $expected_keys
      ,array_keys($result[3]));
  }
}
```

(Indexes 0, 1, and 3 were selected at random, and could have been any of the five returned rows.) Because the values in the returned set are (supposed to be the) values you initially stored, you can also create tests to compare values directly:

```
class TableDataGatewayTestCase extends BaseTestCase {
  // ...

  function testFindAll() {
    $gateway = new BookmarkGateway(DB::conn());
    $this->addSeveralBookmarks($gateway);

    $result = $gateway->findAll();

    // ...

    $this->assertEqual('PHP homepage', $result[1]['name']);
    $this->assertEqual('http://google.com/', $result[3]['url']);
  }
}
```

Returning Iterable Object Collections

Arrays are a native PHP type, and the large number of PHP array functions makes them easy to use in your application. However, you may want to return result sets as a collection of objects instead. Indeed, it's fairly common to return collections of data transfer objects (basic containers for values, with little additional logic)—there's even an ADOResultSet() method provided just for that purpose. Let's create a finder method to lookup records based on the value of the table's 'tag' field. And since this example is in PHP5, let's also require that the returned result set be iterable (see *Chapter 8—The Iterator Pattern*), usable with using the PHP foreach construct.

(Returning an array of row hashes is the default for the ADOdb iterator. I intentionally made the requirements for this example a bit more complicated to force the return of data transfer objects instead, which makes for more interesting code. And as you'll see, the sample solution applies some of the design patterns you learned earlier in this book.)

Here are those requirements (perhaps) more succinctly expressed as a test case:

```
class TableDataGatewayTestCase extends BaseTestCase {
  // ...
  function testFindByTag() {
    $gateway = new BookmarkGateway(DB::conn());
    $this->addSeveralBookmarks($gateway);

    $result = $gateway->findByTag('php');
    $this->assertIsA($result, 'AdoResultSetIteratorDecorator');

    $count=0;
    foreach($result as $bookmark) {
      ++$count;
      $this->assertIsA($bookmark, 'ADOFetchObj');
```

```
      }
      $this->assertEqual(3, $count);
   }
}
```

What's the code look like?

```
class BookmarkGateway{
  // ...
  public function findByTag($tag) {
    $rs = $this->conn->execute(
      'select * from bookmark
       where tag like ?'
      ,array($tag.'%'));
    return new AdoResultSetIteratorDecorator($rs);
  }
}
```

As is typical, findByTag() first calls execute() to collect a result set. The ADOdb execute() method takes a SQL statement to execute and an optional array of bind variables as parameters. Because findByTag() requires a wild-carded LIKE operator and because ADOdb automatically quotes the query string, it's necessary to append the wild card % to the variable inside of the bind array.

The method execute() yields a result set, which is then wrapped by AdoResultSetIteratorDecorator(), the next bit of code to write. The purpose of AdoResultSetIteratorDecorator() is to "transform" a result set into an iterable collection of objects, hence its name.

ADOdb provides iterator support by including the adodb-iterator.inc.php file. This defines an ADODB_Iterator class that essentially decorates an ADOResultSet in the PHP5 SPL Iterator interface. This quickly allows you to provide a foreach-able result set. However, the default behavior of the iterator is to return *an associative array*, as you can see from this new test case:

```
class AdoResultSetIteratorDecoratorTestCase extends BaseTestCase {
  function testADOdbDecorator() {
    $gateway = new BookmarkGateway($this->conn);
    $this->addSeveralBookmarks($gateway);

    $rs = $this->conn->execute('select * from bookmark');
    foreach($rs as $row) {
      $this->assertIsA($row, 'array');
      $this->assertIsA($rs->fetchObj(), 'ADOFetchObj');
    }
```

```
    }
  }
```

Here, the table is created, populated, and iterated over using the ADOdb iterator.

The highlighted line is effectively a cheat to be avoided. Yes, you can extract an object for each row, but then you have to repeat this awkward code everywhere in your production to iterate over the collection.

A far better solution—and one that meets the requirement of an iterable collection of objects more directly—is to *decorate* the ADOdb iterator.

Testing External Libraries

Writing small test cases can help you explore a third-party library to gain a better understanding of its features. A batch of test cases can also capture dependencies, or how your code specifically uses the library, which allows you to find and resolve problems quickly if the library changes during an upgrade.

If you're worried about such external dependencies, it might be appropriate to introduce an *Adapter* (see *Chapter 13—The Adapter Pattern*) to isolate your code from the dependency.

Let's write a test case to demonstrate how the iterator should behave:

```
class AdoResultSetIteratorDecoratorTestCase extends BaseTestCase {
  // ...
  function testRsDecorator() {
    $gateway = new BookmarkGateway($this->conn);
    $this->addSeveralBookmarks($gateway);
    $rs = $this->conn->execute('select * from bookmark');
    $count=0;
    foreach(new AdoResultSetIteratorDecorator($rs) as $bookmark) {
      ++$count;
      $this->assertIsA($bookmark, 'ADOFetchObj');
      $this->assertTrue($bookmark->id > 0);
      $this->assertTrue(strlen($bookmark->url) > 10);
    }
    $this->assertEqual(5,$count);
  }
}
```

And here's how to decorate the ADODB_Iterator to meet the expectations of the test case:

```
require_once 'adodb/adodb-iterator.inc.php';

class AdoResultSetIteratorDecorator implements Iterator {
  protected $rs;
  public function __construct($rs) {
    $this->rs = new ADODB_Iterator($rs);
  }

  public function current() {
    return $this->rs->fetchObj();
  }

  public function next() {
    return $this->rs->next();
  }
  public function key() {
    return $this->rs->key();
  }
  public function valid() {
    return $this->rs->valid();
  }
  public function rewind() {
    return $this->rs->rewind();
  }
}
```

Here, most of the *Iterator* interface method is proxied to the decorated result set, but the current() method is overridden to return the result of the fetchObj() method.

Back to the *Table Data Gateway*, you should now understand how findByTag() works.

```
class BookmarkGateway {
  // ...
  public function findByTag($tag) {
    $rs = $this->conn->execute(
      'select * from bookmark
       where tag like ?'
      ,array($tag.'%'));
    return new AdoResultSetIteratorDecorator($rs);
  }
}
```

Updating Rows

Next, let's tackle the "update" of CRUD. Conceptually, you need to populate the table, find an object, change it, store it, and then find it again to verify that the change has been persisted.

Returning to the TableDataGatewayTestCase, here's the code to find a record...

```
class TableDataGatewayTestCase extends BaseTestCase {
  // ...
  function testUpdate() {
    $gateway = new BookmarkGateway(DB::conn());
    $this->addSeveralBookmarks($gateway);

    $result = $gateway->findByTag('php');
    $bookmark = $result->current();
    $this->assertIsA($bookmark, 'ADOFetchObj');
    $this->assertEqual(
      'http://blog.casey-sweat.us/'
      ,$bookmark->url);
    $this->assertEqual(
      'PHP related thoughts'
      ,$bookmark->description);
  }
}
```

... and the code to change it:

```
class TableDataGatewayTestCase extends BaseTestCase {
  // ...
  function testUpdate() {
    $gateway = new BookmarkGateway(DB::conn());
    $this->addSeveralBookmarks($gateway);

    $result = $gateway->findByTag('php');
    $bookmark = $result->current();
    $this->assertIsA($bookmark, 'ADOFetchObj');
    $this->assertEqual(
      'http://blog.casey-sweat.us/'
      ,$bookmark->url);
    $this->assertEqual(
      'PHP related thoughts'
      ,$bookmark->description);

    $new_desc = 'A change to see it is updated!';
    $bookmark->description = $new_desc;
    $gateway->update($bookmark);
  }
}
```

Having changed the record, find it again to verify the change:

```
class TableDataGatewayTestCase extends BaseTestCase {
  // ...
  function testUpdate() {
```

```
$gateway = new BookmarkGateway(DB::conn());
$this->addSeveralBookmarks($gateway);

$result = $gateway->findByTag('php');
$bookmark = $result->current();
$this->assertISA($bookmark, 'ADOFetchObj');
$this->assertEqual(
  'http://blog.casey-sweat.us/'
  ,$bookmark->url);
$this->assertEqual(
  'PHP related thoughts'
  ,$bookmark->description);

$new_desc = 'A change to see it is updated!';
$bookmark->description = $new_desc;
$gateway->update($bookmark);

$result = $gateway->findByTag('php');
$bookmark = $result->current();
$this->assertEqual(
  'http://blog.casey-sweat.us/'
  ,$bookmark->url);
$this->assertEqual(
  $new_desc
  ,$bookmark->description);
  }
}
```

With that test case in hand, it's time to add the update() method to BookmarkGateway:

```
class BookmarkGateway{
  // ...

  const UPDATE_SQL = 'update bookmark set
       url = ?
      ,name = ?
      ,description = ?
      ,tag = ?
      ,updated = now()
    where id = ?';

  public function update($bookmark) {
    $this->conn->execute(
      self::UPDATE_SQL
      ,array(
         $bookmark->url
        ,$bookmark->name
        ,$bookmark->description
        ,$bookmark->tag
        ,$bookmark->id
        ));
  }
```

BookmarkGateway knows both the SQL to perform the update, and the mapping of the data transfer object attributes to the parameter substitution in the SQL statement.

Issues

The *Table Data Gateway* operates on tables, which is likely to better correlate to the work performed in web applications. Yet the *Table Data Gateway* is still strongly-coupled with the structure of the database table. Decoupling code from the structure of the database is the subject of the next chapter, *The Data Mapper Pattern.*

16

The Data Mapper Pattern

The two previous chapters—*The Active Record Pattern* and *The Table Data Gateway Pattern*—showed strategies that abstract a table row and an individual table, respectively. While both patterns are useful, each pattern's implementation is closely coupled with the structure of the underlying database, so solutions based on those patterns tend to be brittle. For instance, if your code uses field names as keys in row arrays or attributes in row data objects, you're application is tied to the structure of the database and you may have to make extensive changes in PHP for every (relatively) minor change in a table.

Because code and databases often change during development and evolve after they're deployed, there are real benefits to separating domain code and its database(s) as much as possible, insulating each other from interdependencies and reducing the work required to realize a change in either.

The Problem

How can you minimize the coupling between your application's classes and its database? For example, how can you minimize the rework required if one or more fields in a table change names?

The Solution

The *Data Mapper* pattern decouples the attributes of objects from the table fields that persist them. The essence of the *Data Mapper* pattern is a class that *maps* or translates domain object attributes and/or methods to database table fields and vice versa. It is the job of the *Data Mapper* to understand both representations of the information and be able to route information back and forth, creating new domain objects based on information in the database and updating or deleting information in the database using the information from the domain objects.

The mapping between object-oriented code and the database tables and fields can be stored in a variety of forms. One possibility would be hand-coding the correlation in the *Data Mapper* class. Another option is a PHP array coded into the class itself. The class can also draw the information from an external source, such as INI files or XML files.

The figure below shows a class diagram of the *Data Mapper* pattern applied to the problem domain—storing URL bookmarks—used in the previous two chapters. In the figure, the Bookmark object is the domain object and the BookmarkMapper is an implementation of the *Data Mapper* pattern. Bookmark should contain business logic such as the validation of URLs. BookmarkMapper acts as a complete cross-reference between Bookmark getter and setter methods and the bookmark table field structure.

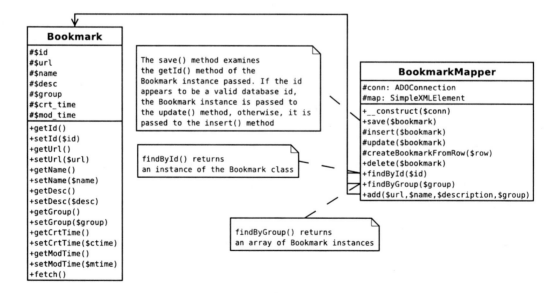

The two classes are closely related: BookmarkMapper acts as a *Factory* for Bookmark instances and accepts instances of the `Bookmark` class as a parameter for many of the `BookmarkMapper` operations.

Sample Code

Using the UML diagram as a roadmap, let's develop the two classes `Bookmark` and `BookmarkMapper`.

First, as mentioned above, some kind of configuration is required to handle the mapping between table columns and object methods. In this example, let's use an XML configuration file.

The goal of this configuration is to list the bookmark table's fields and to specify which methods populate and extract the respective information in the `Bookmark` object. A very simple XML format suffices, consisting of a `<bookmark>` root element and a series of `<field>` elements that look like this:

```
<field>
  <name>url</name>
  <accessor>getUrl</accessor>
  <mutator>setUrl</mutator>
</field>
```

The `<name>` element holds the actual physical database field name. The `<accessor>` element names the method to extract attributes and is optional, as some of the fields, such as timestamps, need not be mapped. The `<mutator>` element holds the `Bookmark` method to use when populating object values.

(Other information could be added to this mapping. For example, you could also declare the type and size of each field and use that information to dynamically construct the SQL necessary to create the database table from scratch. This might be of particular interest to you if your application has some kind of a packaged installation script written in PHP, where you could create the table structures using this mapping. You might also automatically type cast numeric and date fields when setting the PHP object attributes based on such information.)

The complete XML file looks like this:

```
<bookmark>
  <field>
    <name>id</name>
    <accessor>getId</accessor>
    <mutator>setId</mutator>
  </field>
  <field>
    <name>url</name>
    <accessor>getUrl</accessor>
    <mutator>setUrl</mutator>
  </field>
```

```
        <field>
          <name>name</name>
          <accessor>getName</accessor>
          <mutator>setName</mutator>
        </field>
        <field>
          <name>description</name>
          <accessor>getDesc</accessor>
          <mutator>setDesc</mutator>
        </field>
        <field>
          <name>tag</name>
          <accessor>getGroup</accessor>
          <mutator>setGroup</mutator>
        </field>
        <field>
          <name>created</name>
          <mutator>setCrtTime</mutator>
        </field>
        <field>
          <name>updated</name>
          <mutator>setModTime</mutator>
        </field>
      </bookmark>
```

We can use PHP5's aptly-named SimpleXML features to read and parse this file. All you do is call `sim-plexml_load_file('bookmark.xml')` and you have a ready made composite `SimpleXMLElement` object with all of the information from the XML file. Here, the result looks like:

```
object(SimpleXMLElement)#21 (1) {
  ["field"]=>
  array(7) {
  [0]=>
  object(SimpleXMLElement)#15 (3) {
    ["name"]=>
    string(2) "id"
    ["accessor"]=>
    string(5) "getId"
    ["mutator"]=>
    string(5) "setId"
  }
  [1]=>
  object(SimpleXMLElement)#19 (3) {
    ["name"]=>
    string(3) "url"
    ["accessor"]=>
    string(6) "getUrl"
    ["mutator"]=>
    string(6) "setUrl"
  }
  //...<snip>...
  [4]=>
  object(SimpleXMLElement)#23 (3) {
```

```
      ["name"]=>
      string(3) "tag"
      ["accessor"]=>
      string(8) "getGroup"
      ["mutator"]=>
      string(8) "setGroup"
    }
  //...<snip>...
}
```

Since the XML file maps the domain space to the database space, `BookmarkMapper` will read this XML configuration file when it's constructed.

Before diving into `BookmarkMapper`, lets delve into the `Bookmark` class a bit. Assuming that `Bookmark` has been used quite a bit in existing projects, it's best to affect it as little as possible. Moreover, `Bookmark` shouldn't change simply to accommodate `BookmarkMapper`. Indeed, the *Data Mapper* pattern is intended to be unobtrusive. The domain object itself remains completely oblivious to the existence of the *Data Mapper*.

This brings up another important requirement for implementing the *Data Mapper* pattern: since each domain object remains unaware of the *Data Mapper*, all pertinent domain objects *must* provide public access of some kind to all relevant attributes so that the *DataMapper* can properly initialize the domain object during creation and read the properties while saving the domain object. `Bookmark` has all protected attributes, but provides getter and setter methods for each, so it meets the requirement.

Let's start with code for setting and retrieving the "url" attribute of our `Bookmark` class.

```
class Bookmark {
  protected $url;
  // ...

  public function getUrl() {
    return $this->url;
  }
  public function setUrl($url) {
    $this->url = $url;
  }
}
```

You can avoid the monotony of writing umpteen simple getter and setter methods using *reflection*. By having the object "peer" into itself, you can have the object determine if a particular property should have getters and setters or not and what those methods should be named.

Let's start with some tests:

```
class BookmarkTestCase extends BaseTestCase {
  //...
  function testAccessorsAndMutators() {
    $bookmark = new Bookmark(false);

    $props = array('Url', 'Name', 'Desc',
      'Group', 'CrtTime', 'ModTime');
    foreach($props as $prop) {
      $getprop = "get$prop";
      $setprop = "set$prop";
      $this->assertNull($bookmark->$getprop());

      $val1 = 'some_val';
      $bookmark->$setprop($val1);
      $this->assertEqual($val1,
        $bookmark->$getprop());

      $val2 = 'other_val';
      $bookmark->$setprop($val2);
      $this->assertNotEqual($val1,
        $bookmark->$getprop());
      $this->assertEqual($val2,
        $bookmark->$getprop());
    }
  }
}
```

For each of the Bookmark attributes, the test sets a value using the mutator method and then validates that the accessor method returns the same value. The value is then changed again and verified again.

This code relies on convention rather than some explicit mapping. Access and mutator method names begin with get and set, respectively, and are then named after the attribute (which is in lowercase). For example, the name of the access method for "url" is getUrl(); the mutator method for "url" is setUrl().

Here's some code to implement the dynamic access and mutator methods.

```
class Bookmark {
  protected $url;
  protected $name;
  protected $desc;
  protected $group;
  protected $crttime;
  protected $modtime;

  //...

  public function __call($name, $args) {
    if (preg_match('/^(get|set)(\w+)/', strtolower($name), $match)
```

```
        && $attribute = $this->validateAttribute($match[2])) {
        if ('get' == $match[1]) {
          return $this->$attribute;
        } else {
          $this->$attribute = $args[0];
        }
      }
    }
    protected function validateAttribute($name) {
      if (in_array(strtolower($name),
        array_keys(get_class_vars(get_class($this))))) {
        return strtolower($name);
      }
    }
  }
```

This code relies on the PHP5 "magic" method __call(), which is called whenever an *undefined* (not explicitly defined in the class) instance method is called. __call() is essentially a fallback method. The name of the (missing) method called is passed to __call() as the first parameter and any methods arguments are passed in an array as the second parameter.

To achieve dynamically-created getter and setter methods, the name of the method called is extracted to see if it starts with "get" or "set" and correctly names one of the object's attributes. If so, the attribute is modified or returned as appropriate. This dynamic approach replaces the hand-coded getUrl() and setUrl(), so those can be safely elided from the code.

There is one side effect to be concerned about, though: this code silently fails for *any* other methods called. To prevent that, let's throw an exception if the called method is improper.

```
class Bookmark {
  //...

  public function __call($name, $args) {
    if (preg_match('/^(get|set)(\w+)/', strtolower($name), $match)
      && $attribute = $this->validateAttribute($match[2])) {
      if ('get' == $match[1]) {
        return $this->$attribute;
      } else {
        $this->$attribute = $args[0];
      }
    } else {
      throw new Exception(
        'Call to undefined method Bookmark::'.$name.'()');
    }
  }
}
```

You can also test for this exception:

```
class BookmarkTestCase extends BaseTestCase {
  //...

  function testBadGetSetExceptions() {
    $mapper = new BookmarkMapper($this->conn);
    $this->addSeveralBookmarks($mapper);
    $bookmark = $mapper->findById(1);

    try {
      $this->assertNull($bookmark->getFoo());
      $this->fail('no exception thrown');
    }
    catch (Exception $e) {
      $this->assertWantedPattern('/undefined.*getfoo/i',
        $e->getMessage());
    }

    try {
      $this->assertNull($bookmark->setFoo('bar'));
      $this->fail('no exception thrown');
    }
    catch (Exception $e) {
      $this->assertWantedPattern('/undefined.*setfoo/i',
        $e->getMessage());
    }
  }
}
```

There's one other caveat: the $id attribute should be immutable once set.

Let's create a test for an immutable ID attribute. setId() can be called once to set the ID and retrieved innumerable times with getId(), but subsequent calls to setId() should have no effect.

```
class BookmarkTestCase extends BaseTestCase {
  //...

  function testUnsetIdIsNull() {
    $bookmark = new Bookmark;
    $this->assertNull($bookmark->getId());
  }

  function testIdOnlySetOnce() {
    $bookmark = new Bookmark;

    $id = 10; //just a random value we picked
    $bookmark->setId($id);
    $this->assertEqual($id, $bookmark->getId());

    $another_id = 20; // another random value, != $id
    //state the obvious
    $this->assertNotEqual($id, $another_id);
```

```
      $bookmark->setId($another_id);
      // still the old id
      $this->assertEqual($id, $bookmark->getId());
    }
  }
```

It's important to remember that methods explicitly defined in a class always override the catch-all __call(). You can define a specific, different behavior for any named method just by adding the named method to a class. Here, setId() overrides any fallback call to __call().

```
class Bookmark {
  protected $id;
  //...

  public function setId($id) {
    if (!$this->id) {
      $this->id = $id;
    }
  }
}
```

So far, all we have is a basic data object, so let's add some domain logic into the mix—after all, one of the reasons for applying the *Data Mapper* pattern is the separation of domain logic from the persistent storage of the domain object. In keeping with the design principal of "tell, don't ask", add a fetch() method to return the actual (HTML) contents of the bookmarked page.

Here's a test for this capability:

```
class BookmarkTestCase extends BaseTestCase {
  //...

    function testFetch() {
      $bookmark = new Bookmark;
      $bookmark->setUrl('http://www.google.com/');

      $page = $bookmark->fetch();
      $this->assertWantedPattern(
        '~<input[^>]*name=q[^>]*>~im', $page);
    }
  }
}
```

And here's an example implementation:

```
class Bookmark {
  //...

  public function fetch() {
    return file_get_contents($this->url);
  }
}
```

Now the full class looks like this:

```
class Bookmark {
  protected $id;
  protected $url;
  protected $name;
  protected $desc;
  protected $group;
  protected $crttime;
  protected $modtime;

  public function setId($id) {
    if (!$this->id) {
      $this->id = $id;
    }
  }
  public function __call($name, $args) {
    if (preg_match('/^(get|set)(\w+)/', strtolower($name), $match)
      && $attribute = $this->validateAttribute($match[2])) {
      if ('get' == $match[1]) {
        return $this->$attribute;
      } else {
        $this->$attribute = $args[0];
      }
    } else {
      throw new Exception(
        'Call to undefined method Bookmark::'.$name.'()');
    }
  }
  protected function validateAttribute($name) {
    if (in_array(strtolower($name),
      array_keys(get_class_vars(get_class($this))))) {
      return strtolower($name);
    }
  }
  public function fetch() {
    return file_get_contents($this->url);
  }
}
```

With a grip on the Bookmark class, let's get back to BookmarkMapper class. The core job of BookmarkMapper is to retrieve data from the database and create Bookmark objects.

The first task to accomplish with BookmarkMapper is the addition of new records to the database table.

In the *Data Mapper* pattern, the domain object is unaware of the *Data Mapper*, but contains all of the business logic, including potential rules regarding creation of the object. A logical way to create records then is to create a new instance of the Bookmark class, set the attributes, and then ask the BookmarkMapper to save the newly-created instance. Let's move forward with implementing this kind of an interface.

BookmarkMapper must interact with the database. As in the previous two chapters, let's use ADOdb as the database access layer. Furthermore, let's pass in an ADOdb connection during the construction of BookmarkMapper.

```
class BookmarkMapper {
  protected $conn;
  public function __construct($conn) {
    $this->conn = $conn;
  }
}
```

BookmarkMapper must also read the XML file shown earlier. To make the XML even more convenient to use, store the mappings as a hash of name => simplexml element for each field in the mapping file. Adding this to the constructor yields:

```
class BookmarkMapper {
  protected $map = array();
  protected $conn;
  public function __construct($conn) {
    $this->conn = $conn;
    foreach(simplexml_load_file('bookmark.xml') as $field) {
      $this->map[(string)$field->name] = $field;
    }
  }
}
```

Now you're ready to create a test case for the save() method.

```
class BookmarkMapperTestCase extends BaseTestCase {
  function testSave() {
    $bookmark = new Bookmark;
```

```
$bookmark->setUrl('http://phparch.com/');
$bookmark->setName('php|architect');
$bookmark->setDesc('php|arch magazine homepage');
$bookmark->setGroup('php');

$this->assertNull($bookmark->getId());

$mapper = new BookmarkMapper($this->conn);
$mapper->save($bookmark);

$this->assertEqual(1, $bookmark->getId());

// a row was added to the database table
$this->assertEqual(1, $this->conn->getOne(
  'select count(1) from bookmark'));
  }

}
```

Here, the test creates a new instance of the Bookmark class, sets the relevant attributes of the object, and then asks a BookmarkMapper instance to save() the Bookmark. Along the way, the test also validates that saving the object also sets its ID and inserts a row into the database.

Next, let's write some code to implement this.

```
class BookmarkMapper {
  //...
  const INSERT_SQL = "
    insert into bookmark (url, name, description,
      tag, created, updated)
    values (?, ?, ?, ?, now(), now())
    ";
  public function save($bookmark) {
    $rs = $this->conn->execute(
      self::INSERT_SQL
      ,array(
          $bookmark->getUrl()
        ,$bookmark->getName()
        ,$bookmark->getDesc()
        ,$bookmark->getGroup()));
  }
}
```

A class constant holds the statement to perform the insert, and the code "manually" maps the accessor methods of the Bookmark class to the correct bind values in the SQL statement.

This is all well and good, but two more things are needed: code to handle database errors and setting or modifying the $bookmark attributes that are initialized or changed by the database, respectively.

```
class BookmarkMapper {
  //...

  public function save($bookmark) {
    $rs = $this->conn->execute(
      self::INSERT_SQL
      ,array(
          $bookmark->getUrl()
        ,$bookmark->getName()
        ,$bookmark->getDesc()
        ,$bookmark->getGroup()));

    if ($rs) {
      $inserted = $this->findById($this->conn->Insert_ID());
      //clean up database related fields in parameter instance
      $bookmark->setId($inserted->getId());
      $bookmark->setCrtTime($inserted->getCrtTime());
      $bookmark->setModTime($inserted->getModTime());
    } else {
      throw new Exception('DB Error: '.$this->conn->errorMsg());
    }

  }
}
```

findById() is shown shortly, but its purpose is to find and return the Bookmark that matches the given ID. Essentially, the BookmarkMapper inserts the new Bookmark, extracts that record from the database, and sets the appropriate properties based on the new correct values. Nothing need be returned because the Bookmark instance itself was the parameter and it's already been updated to be correct.

Let's move on to the details of the findById() method. You can use the same BaseTestCase from the previous *Table Data Gateway* chapter:

```
class BookmarkMapperTestCase extends BaseTestCase {
  // ...

  function testFindById() {
    $mapper = new BookmarkMapper($this->conn);
    $this->addSeveralBookmarks($mapper);

    $this->assertIsA(
      $bookmark = $mapper->findById(1)
      , 'Bookmark');
    $this->assertEqual(1, $bookmark->getId());
  }
}
```

Technically, addSeveralBookmarks() won't work until findById() works (because of the code just shown in the save() method), but let's come to that in a minute.

```
class BookmarkMapper {
  // ...

  public function findById($id) {
    $row = $this->conn->getRow(
      'select * from bookmark where id = ?'
      ,array((int)$id)
    );
    if ($row) {
      $bookmark = new Bookmark($this);
      foreach($this->map as $field) {
        $setprop = (string)$field->mutator;
        $value = $row[(string)$field->name];
        if ($setprop && $value) {
          call_user_func(array($bookmark, $setprop), $value);
        }
      }
      return $bookmark;
    } else {
      return false;
    }
  }
}
```

Since every finder method in the mapper must transform a database row into a Bookmark instance, it makes sense to extract this capability into a separate method called createBookmarkFromRow().

```
class BookmarkMapper {
  // ...

  protected function createBookmarkFromRow($row) {
    $bookmark = new Bookmark($this);
    foreach($this->map as $field) {
      $setprop = (string)$field->mutator;
      $value = $row[(string)$field->name];
      if ($setprop && $value) {
        call_user_func(array($bookmark, $setprop), $value);
      }
    }
    return $bookmark;
  }
}
```

With this method, you can slim findById() down to just:

```php
class BookmarkMapper {
  // ...

  public function findById($id) {
    $row = $this->conn->getRow(
      'select * from bookmark where id = ?'
      ,array((int)$id)
    );
    if ($row) {
      return $this->createBookmarkFromRow($row);
    } else {
      return false;
    }
  }
}
```

All of this was all somewhat complicated, so a UML sequence diagram may be useful to help understand what is going on.

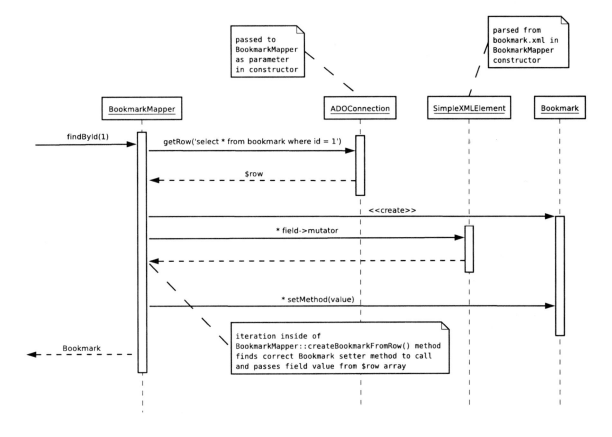

First, the data is retrieved from the database; next, an instance of the Bookmark class is created. Then, for each field in the mapping, the code finds the appropriate setter method and passes the row value to that setter. The Bookmark instance, now populated with database data, is then returned by findById().

Now let's look at the BookmarkMapper::add() method, used by BaseTestCase::addSeveralBookmarks(). Using a test case, verify that it both creates a row in the table and returns an instance of the Bookmark class with the correct data mapped in.

```
class BookmarkMapperTestCase extends BaseTestCase {
  // ...

  function testAdd() {
    $mapper = new BookmarkMapper($this->conn);
    $bookmark =
      $mapper->add(
        'http://phparch.com',
        'php|arch',
        'php|architect magazine homepage',
        'php');

    $this->assertEqual(1,
      $this->conn->getOne('select count(1) from bookmark'));
    $this->assertEqual('http://phparch.com', $bookmark->getUrl());
    $this->assertEqual('php|arch', $bookmark->getName());
    $this->assertEqual('php|architect magazine homepage',
      $bookmark->getDesc());
    $this->assertEqual('php', $bookmark->getGroup());
  }
}
```

Here's the relevant BookmarkMapper code.

```
class BookmarkMapper {
  // ...
  public function add($url, $name, $description, $group) {
    $bookmark = new Bookmark;
    $bookmark->setUrl($url);
    $bookmark->setName($name);
    $bookmark->setDesc($description);
    $bookmark->setGroup($group);

    $this->save($bookmark);
    return $bookmark;
  }
}
```

This is similar to to the Active Record `ActiveRecordTestCase::add()` convenience method, but here it's been added it to the mapper instead of the test case, making it available within the project code.

You can now move on to implementing additional finder methods, including methods that return collections of `Bookmark` instances.

```php
class BookmarkMapperTestCase extends BaseTestCase {
  // ...

  function testFindByGroup() {
    $mapper = new BookmarkMapper($this->conn);
    $this->addSeveralBookmarks($mapper);

    $this->assertIsA(
      $php_links = $mapper->findByGroup('php')
      ,'array');
    $this->assertEqual(3, count($php_links));
    foreach($php_links as $link) {
      $this->assertIsA($link, 'Bookmark');
    }
  }
}
```

Finding all bookmarks in a specific group can be implemented as:

```php
class BookmarkMapper {
  // ...

  public function findByGroup($group) {
    $rs = $this->conn->execute(
      'select * from bookmark where tag like ?'
      ,array($group.'%'));
    if ($rs) {
      $ret = array();
      foreach($rs->getArray() as $row) {
        $ret[] = $this->createBookmarkFromRow($row);
      }
      return $ret;
    }
  }
}
```

The `ADOConnection::execute()` method returns an `ADOResultSet` object. This result set has a `getArray()` method that returns an array of associative arrays (field => value) for each of the rows. These row arrays are in turn passed to the `createBookmarkFromRow()` method to create instances of the Bookmark class.

How about update in the mapper? The process of updating is also a collaboration between Bookmark and BookmarkMapper. Ensuring that bookmarks are indeed updated is best tested in BookmarkTestCase. Testing the round trip to the database belongs in the tests for BookmarkMapper.

```
class BookmarkTestCase extends BaseTestCase {
  // ...

  function testSaveUpdatesDatabase() {
    $mapper = new BookmarkMapper($this->conn);
    $this->addSeveralBookmarks($mapper);
    $bookmark = $mapper->findById(1);

    $this->assertEqual(
      'http://blog.casey-sweat.us/'
      ,$bookmark->getUrl());

    $bookmark->setUrl(
      'http://blog.casey-sweat.us/wp-rss2.php');
    $mapper->save($bookmark);

    $bookmark2 = $mapper->findById(1);
    $this->assertEqual(
      'http://blog.casey-sweat.us/wp-rss2.php'
      ,$bookmark2->getUrl());
  }
}
```

As it is now, the save() method inserts new bookmarks into the database via INSERT. However, as this test case implies, save() must now determine if the Bookmark parameter is new or has previously been added to the database. For the former, INSERT is appropriate; for the latter, an UPDATE is required.

That being the case, let's refactor the code performing the INSERT statement, which was in the save() method, into a new protected method called insert().

```
class BookmarkMapper {
  //...

  protected function insert($bookmark) {
    $rs = $this->conn->execute(
      self::INSERT_SQL
      ,array(
        $bookmark->getUrl()
        ,$bookmark->getName()
        ,$bookmark->getDesc()
        ,$bookmark->getGroup()));
```

```
      if ($rs) {
        $inserted = $this->findById($this->conn->Insert_ID());
        // clean up database related fields in parameter instance
        if (method_exists($inserted,'setId')) {
          $bookmark->setId($inserted->getId());
          $bookmark->setCrtTime($inserted->getCrtTime());
          $bookmark->setModTime($inserted->getModTime());
        }
      } else {
        throw new Exception('DB Error: '.$this->conn->errorMsg());
      }
    }
  }
}
```

With the existing save() method renamed to insert(), the (yet-to-be-written) save() method must check if the $id attribute has been set using getId():

```
class BookmarkMapper {
  //...

  public function save($bookmark) {
    if ($bookmark->getId()) {
      $this->update($bookmark);
    } else {
      $this->insert($bookmark);
    }
  }
}
```

Now you need an update() method that's similar to the insert() method. If you recall, the insert() method hard-codes mappings from attributes to field names. For update(), let's use a more dynamic approach, using the information gleaned from the bookmark.xml mapping file.

```
class BookmarkMapper {
  //...

  const UPDATE_SQL = "
    update bookmark set
      url = ?,
      name = ?,
      description = ?,
      tag = ?,
      updated = now()
    where id = ?
    ";
  protected function update($bookmark) {
    $binds = array();
```

```
    foreach(array('url','name',
      'description','tag','id') as $fieldname) {
      $field = $this->map[$fieldname];
      $getprop = (string)$field->accessor;
      $binds[] = $bookmark->$getprop();
    }

    $this->conn->execute(
      self::UPDATE_SQL
      ,$binds);
  }
}
```

Notice that the order of the elements in the array appear in the same order as what's needed in our SQL statement. The update() method captures the essence of the *Data Mapper*: it establishes relationships between attributes and fields.

Finally, let's look at an implementation of the "delete" CRUD capability. Let's write a method for the BookmarkMapper class that accepts a Bookmark and deletes it from the database.

First, a test:

```
class BookmarkMapperTestCase extends BaseTestCase {
  // ...

  function testDelete() {
    $mapper = new BookmarkMapper($this->conn);
    $this->addSeveralBookmarks($mapper);

    $this->assertEqual(5, $this->countBookmarks());

    $delete_me = $mapper->findById(3);
    $mapper->delete($delete_me);

    $this->assertEqual(4, $this->countBookmarks());
  }

  function countBookmarks() {
    return $this->conn->getOne(
      'select count(1) from bookmark');
  }
}
```

And the code:

```
class BookmarkMapper {
  // ...
```

```
    public function delete($bookmark) {
      $this->conn->execute(
        'delete from bookmark where id = ?'
        ,array((int)$bookmark->getId()));
    }
  }
```

And now you've implemented a *Data Mapper* pattern for the bookmark table with complete CRUD capabilities.

If your domain objects are particularly expensive to create, you'd probably want to write a `BookmarkMapper::deleteById()` method which did not required the domain object to be loaded prior to deleting it.

Issues

Clearly, adding a translation layer between a database schema and domain objects adds a bit of complexity. However, this complexity gives you tremendous flexibility in your code, as you're free to evolve your class independently from the table structure in the database.

You should also remember all of this is still a fairly simple translation mechanism. If you want to evolve this mechanism towards handling relationships between tables and their corresponding relationships in your domain model, you are headed towards the holy grail of ORM—Object Relational Mapping—which is not to be treaded lightly.

17

The Model-View-Controller Pattern

Web applications vary greatly and that variety causes a great deal of confusion about what pattern or patterns are best for architecting a certain application. Having said that, though, is there a "best" architecture for web applications?

The Problem

Can you deploy a single web site architecture to accommodate every common web application, including common presentation elements, authentication, form validation, and so on?

The Solution

The *Model-View-Controller* (*MVC*) pattern organizes and separates your software into three distinct roles:

- The *Model* encapsulates your application data, application flow, and business logic.
- The *View* extracts data from the *Model* and formats it for presentation.

• The *Controller* directs application flow and receives input and translates it for the *Model* and *View*.

The Origins of MVC

The *Model-View-Controller* pattern was originally developed by Trygve Reenskaug at Xerox's Palo Alto Research Center (PARC) in the late 1970s. The original reference implementation was coded in Smalltalk-80, and was originally designed to solve the GUI interaction problem in applications.

As you work with the *MVC* pattern, you'll appreciate its utility, especially for graphical user interface (GUI) applications. Moreover, *MVC* is also useful for web applications, albeit the discontinuities of accessing a server application through a series of stateless web connections present some unique challenges (and opportunities).

If you flipped to this chapter looking for the "one true way" to implement MVC for web applications, I hope you won't be too disappointed with the answers contained here. A perfect solution doesn't exist, but there are many "best practices" and related patterns that can surely help you realize an effective *MVC* implementation. Hopefully, the ideas presented here can serve as a springboard for your code and lead you to do more research.

The Model-View-Controller

Unlike other design patterns, the *MVC* pattern does not map directly to a class structure that you can code and deploy. Instead, MVC is more of a conceptual guideline or paradigm.

The conceptual MVC pattern is depicted as the relationship between three objects, the Model, the View, and the Controller. The Controller and the View both depend on the Model, because both the View and the Controller may request data from the Model. Any inputs to your system enter through the Controller, which selects a View to emit results. To put this in more concrete terms for you, a PHP developer, the Controller handles each incoming HTTP request and the View generates the HTTP response.

Here is the conceptual MVC pattern pictured as a diagram on the right:

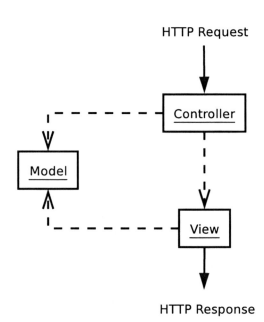

In this ideal MVC world, communication is straightforward, as expressed in this sequence diagram:

Of course the devil is in the details. When MVC is implemented in a web application, the *Model, View,* and *Controller* are never captured in single classes, but are instead implemented as closely-related groups of objects, where each group performs one specific *MVC* task. The *Controller* might be composed of several classes that combine to analyze the HTTP response and determine the desired action required by the application. The *Model* is almost certainly composed of many classes. And the *View* in a web application is usually some kind of a template system, and is likely composed of several objects.

In the following sections, let's dig a little deeper into each portion of the *MVC* triad to determine what design patterns exist in or facilitate each part and how they can help you organize your code.

The Model

The *Model* contains your application logic and data and is likely the primary driver of value in your application. The Model has no presentation-related features and is also completely decoupled from the responsibility to process HTTP requests. (As a quick rule of thumb, you should never see HTML tags or $_GET superglobals in any PHP *Model.*)

Domain Model

The *Domain Model* is a layer of objects that abstract the real world logic, data, and problems your application deals with. The *Domain Model* can be classified in two broad categories: a *Simple Domain Model* and a *Rich Domain Model.*

A *Simple Domain Model* tends to have a one-to-one correspondence between business objects and database tables. You've seen several patterns — *Active Record, Table Data Gateway,* and *Data*

Mapper, all database-related design patterns — that can help you organize your database-related logic into a *Domain Model* (although to keep examples reasonable, compact, and understandable in this book, the material never expanded beyond a one-to-one correspondence — an isomorphic mapping — of the simple *Domain Model*.)

A *Rich Domain Model* includes complex webs of tightly interwoven objects using inheritance, and leverages many of the design patterns covered in this book and the GoF book. *Rich Domain Models* tend to be supple, well-covered by tests, continuously refactored, and tightly coupled with the business needs for the domain they express.

Which style of *Domain Model* you adopt depends on the context of your application. If you're delivering a fairly simple form processing web application, it's not necessary to build a *Rich Domain Model*. However, if you're writing a library that's to be the core of a multi-million dollar enterprise's intranet infrastructure, then the effort you put into developing a *Rich Domain Model* is likely to pay off, providing you a platform to accurately express business processes and allowing you to rapidly deliver value.

Martin Fowler briefly covers both styles of the *Domain Model* in PoEAA, and Eric Evans's book, *Domain Driven Design*, is entirely devoted to the practices and process of developing a *Rich Domain Model*.

The View

The View manages all aspects of presentation. A *View* extracts data from a *Model* and might format it as HTML for a web page, as XML for a web service, or as text for email.

One good way to identify if you've succeeded in separating your code into well-defined roles is to try substituting (at least conceptually) another *View* that produces completely different output. For example, if you have a web application, what would you have to change to make your program work at the command-line prompt using the PHP CLI binary?

While the *View* has access to the *Model*, it is bad form for a *View* to call methods of the *Model* that change state—updates should only be performed by the *Controller*. The *Model* methods called by the *View* should be read-only data retrieval methods with no side effects.

There are two design patterns commonly used in Views: the *Template View* and the *Transform View*.

Template View

The primary pattern used in a *View* for a web application is the *Template View*. This pattern uses a template file (usually HTML) that includes special markers that are replaced with data from the *Model* when the *Template View* is executed.

PHP itself is an example of a specific type of *Template View* called a server page. A template system based on using PHP as the template itself is Savant (http://www.phpsavant.com/).

An example of using Savant is:

```php
// PHP4
require_once 'Savant2.php';

$tpl =& new Savant2();
$tpl->assign('title', 'Colors of the Rainbow');
$tpl->assign('colors', array('red', 'orange', 'yellow',
'green', 'blue', 'indigo', 'violet'));

$tpl->display('rainbow.tpl.php');
```

The file rainbow.tpl.php is a Savant template that resembles:

```php
<html><head>
<title><?php echo $this->title ?></title>
</head><body>
<h1><?php echo $this->title ?></h1>
<ol>
  <?php foreach ($this->colors as $color): ?>
    <li><?php echo $color ?></li>
  <?php endforeach; ?>
</ol>
</body></html>
```

There's always some temptation with complex template engines or even with Plain Old PHP Pages (POPP) to go beyond variable replacement and embed control structures and other logic into the pages. However, giving in results in business logic entangled within the presentation layer of your application, leading to a maintenance nightmare.

Writing Template Engines

It seems that writing a template engine is some kind of a right of passage in the PHP community, as a search for template engines in PHP reveals literally hundreds of them (see http://www.sitepoint.com/forums/showthread.php?t=123769 for an experiment in this area). If you choose to not use one of the popular engines and instead roll you own, there's a rich environment of example code to review.

The page http://wact.sf.net/index.php/TemplateView does a good job of outlining what styles of marker's can be used with a *Template View*. These include an attribute language, custom tags, HTML comments, and custom syntax.

The popular template engine Smarty (http://smarty.php.net/) is an example of a template engine that uses the custom syntax method. Loading a Smarty template might look like:

```
require_once 'Smarty.class.php';

$tpl =& new Smarty;
$tpl->assign(array(
  'title' => 'Colors of the Rainbow'
  ,'colors' => array('red', 'orange', 'yellow',
'green', 'blue', 'indigo', 'violet')
  ));
$tpl->display('rainbow.tpl');
```

The Smarty custom syntax of rainbow.html looks like:

```
<html><head>
<title>{$title}</title>
</head><body>
<h1>{$title}</h1>
<ol>
  {section name=rainbow loop=$colors}
    <li>{$colors[rainbow]}</li>
  {/section}
</ol>
</body></html>
```

The WACT (http://wact.sf.net/) template engine follows the *Custom Tag* pattern that Martin Fowler outlines in PoEAA. Although WACT supports a custom syntax similar to Smarty as a shortcut, WACT's custom tag array output might look like:

```
require_once 'wact/framework/common.inc.php';
require_once WACT_ROOT.'template/template.inc.php';
require_once WACT_ROOT.'datasource/dictionary.inc.php';
require_once WACT_ROOT.'iterator/arraydataset.inc.php';

// simulate tabular data
$rainbow = array();
foreach (array('red', 'orange', 'yellow',
'green', 'blue', 'indigo', 'violet') as $color) {
  $rainbow[] = array('color' => $color);
}

$ds =& new DictionaryDataSource;
$ds->set('title', 'Colors of the Rainbow');
```

```
$ds->set('colors', new ArrayDataSet($rainbow));

$tpl =& new Template('/rainbow.html');
$tpl->registerDataSource($ds);
$tpl->display();
```

The template rainbow.html might look like:

```
<html><head>
<title>{$title}</title>
</head><body>
<h1>{$title}</h1>
<list:list id="rainbow" from="colors">
<ol>
<list:item><li>{$color}</li></list:item>
</ol>
</list:list>
</body></html>
```

There are quite a number of included files for this WACT example. This is because the framework has a variety of components to address different portions of the web application problem and you only include the components you need. In the example above, the Template class is a *View*, the DictionaryDataSource is a proxy for the *Model*, and the PHP script itself is acting as the *Controller*. Many of the custom tags are designed to work with tabular data — like what you might extract from a database as a result set — hence the transformation of the simple array before using it in the template.

One last style is to have a valid XML file for a template and use attributes of the individual elements as the targets for your template replacements. Here's an example of this technique using PHP-TAL (http://phptal.motion-twin.com/).

```
// PHP5
require_once 'PHPTAL.php';

class RainbowColor {
  public $color;
  public function __construct($color) {
    $this->color = $color;
  }
}

// make a collection of colors
$colors = array();
foreach (array('red', 'orange', 'yellow',
```

```
    'green', 'blue', 'indigo', 'violet') as $color) {
        $colors[] = new RainbowColor($color);
    }

    $tpl = new PHPTAL('rainbow.tal.html');
    $tpl->title = 'Colors of the Rainbow';
    $tpl->colors = $colors;

    try {
        echo $tpl->execute();
    }
    catch (Exception $e){
        echo $e;
    }
```

The rainbow.tal.html template file might look like:

```
<?xml version="1.0"?>
<html>
  <head>
    <title tal:content="title">
      place for the page title
    </title>
  </head>
  <body>
    <h1 tal:content="title">sample title</h1>
    <ol>
      <li tal:repeat="item colors">
        <span tal:content="item/color">color</span>
      </li>
    </ol>
  </body>
</html>
```

Of course, the point of all of these solutions is to separate the presentation of *Model* data from the *Model* and from the application itself. Each of the prior examples produced essentially the same content, so the selection of which to use is largely a matter of personal preference.

The Transform View

The *Transform View* extracts data from your model and transforms the data into the desired output format. It essentially amounts to using a language to step through the elements of your data one by one, assembling the output along the way.

The difference between the *Template View* and the *Transform View* is the direction of data flow. In the *Template View* you start with a skeleton of your output and insert domain data into it. With the *Transform View* you start with the data and build the output from it.

The dominant technology for implementing a *Transform View* is XSLT.

The Controller

The *Controller* is the one role of *MVC* that most PHP MVC frameworks address. This is reasonable considering that *Models* are specific to the application and nearly every developer already has their favorite template engine, a major component of the *View*. That leaves interpreting the HTTP response, and controlling application flow (selecting the appropriate action to take or view to display), both approachable tasks for a generic framework.

Front Controllers

It's often helpful to centralize the control of application flow at a single point. Centralization can help you understand how a complex system operates and it also provides a single place where you can insert global code such as an *Intercepting Filter* pattern. A *Front Controller* is perfect for centralization.

Intercepting Filter

The *Intercepting Filter* pattern is an implementation of the *Chain of Responsibility* pattern from the GoF book. It allows for sequential processing of a request to apply common tasks such as logging or security.

There are two common implementations, one where the filters are applied sequentially in a chain until the application controller is reached, and another that resembles a series of decorators, useful for performing both pre- and post-filter actions (think of a whitespace removal or a compressing filter where you might start output buffering in pre-processing and perform your filter in the post-processing action).

As a simple example of what an *Intercepting Filter* might look like integrated with a *Front Controller*, assume we have in interface for our Filters which has both `preFilter()` and `postFilter()` methods. We can then build a means of adding filters to our `FrontController`:

```
class FrontController {
  var $_filter_chain = array();
  function registerFilter(&$filter) {
    $this->_filter_chain[] =& $filter;
  }
}
```

And then we can apply the `preFilter()` methods in sequence, prior to running the actual work of the `FrontController` (page generation, dispatching, etc). After the `FrontController` has performed its task, the postFilter() methods could be called in reverse order.

```
class FrontController {
  //...

  function run() {
    foreach(array_keys($this->_filter_chain) as $filter) {
      $this->_filter_chain[$filter]->preFilter();
    }
    $this->_process();
    foreach(
      array_reverse(array_keys($this->_filter_chain)) as $filter) {
      $this->_filter_chain[$filter]->postFilter();
    }
  }

  function _process() {
    // do the FrontController work
  }
}
```

As an example, this HtmlCommentFilter class would remove all HTML comments from the resulting output of the page.

```
class HtmlCommentFilter {

  function preFilter() {
    ob_start();
  }

  function postFilter() {
    $page = ob_get_clean();
    echo preg_replace(
      '~<!-.*->~ims'
      ,''
      ,$page);
  }
}
```

Application Controllers

Front Controllers often delegate control to an *Application Controller* and the *Application Controller* pattern is really the heart of what the *MVC Controller* is all about. The primary responsibility of the *Controller* is deciding what the application should do in response to an incoming request.

A typical way of implementing a *Controller* is using the *Command* pattern. The *Command* pattern encapsulates an action in an object so you can parameterize a request, queue it, log it, or support operations like undoing an action. In the context of a web application, they are useful as the target of code that dispatches to a concrete *Command* to carry out the work of a particular HTTP request. Essentially, the *Command* pattern lets you break down the discrete behaviors of your application and code, each as a small, manageable class, with a uniform API to allow the *Controller* to dispatch to a specific concrete *Command* to implement the desired application functionality.

Don't let this buzzword-laden talk of controllers and dispatching confuse you. If you've spent even a few hours with PHP, you've likely written some kind of an *Application Controller*. For example, a simple form that posts back to itself, such as...

```php
if (count($_POST)) {
  // do form handling code
} else {
  // display the form
}
```

... is a form of *Application Controller*. A somewhat more complex *Application Controller* is something like this:

```php
switch ($_POST['action']) {
case 'del': $action_class = 'DeleteBookmark'; break;
case 'upd': $action_class = 'UpdateBookmark'; break;
case 'add': $action_class = 'InsertBookmark'; break;
case 'show':
default:
  $action_class = 'DisplayBookmark';
}

if (!class_defined($action)) {
  require_once 'actions/'.$action_class.'.php';
}
$action =& new $action_class;
$action->run();
```

Another possible way to implement dispatching is to have a configuration that loads an associative array. You might end up with:

```php
$action_map = array(
    'del' => 'DeleteBookmark'
```

```
    ,'upd' => 'UpdateBookmark'
    ,'add' => 'InsertBookmark'
);

$action_class = (array_key_exists($_POST['action'], $action_map))
    ? $action_map[$_POST['action']] : 'DisplayBookmark';

if (!class_defined($action)) {
   require_once 'actions/'.$action_class.'.php';
}
$action =& new $action_class;
$action->run();
```

My experience with web applications has shown that a "double dispatching" architecture can be a useful mental map to compare frameworks' dispatching mechanisms against. The first dispatch is to an "action," any event that needs to perform an action using your *Model*. After any visible action, an HTTP redirect would be issued to instruct the client to fetch a particular *View*. The second dispatch is to select a specific *View*. (In early procedural incarnations of this methodology, I used a case statement, but the MVC paradigm lends itself to using the *Command* pattern to perform this dispatch.)

The "real life" version of a *Model-View-Controller* sequence diagram looks fairly similar to the "ideal" sequence diagram shown above. The main addition is an ActionFactory to produce each Action, which is a concrete *Command*.

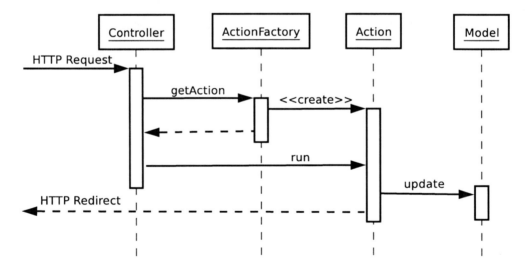

In many of the MVC implementations I have developed, the second dispatch is performed by the default ShowViewAction.

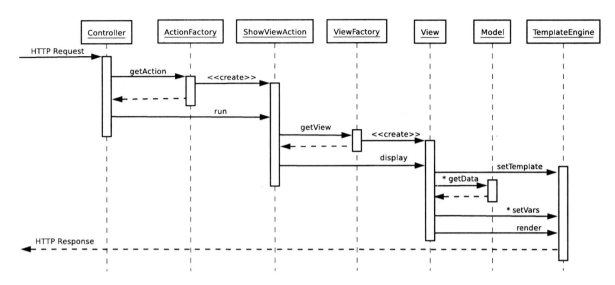

This diagram shows the first dispatch creating the concrete *Command* ShowViewAction. This action would in turn use a ViewFactory to create a concrete View class, which is an example of what Martin Fowler calls a *View Helper* in the PoEAA section on *Views* in *MVC*. This View would use your preferred TemplateEngine to select and parse a template file, populate template variable: from data in the Model, and render the resulting content from the template and return it to the client.

It is this kind of a diagram that can give *MVC* a reputation for bloat, but in fact, each element of this diagram was added in response to a need to organize the code to make it easier to maintain.

In general, I have found the most significant hurdle to using a specific framework is gaining an understanding of how that framework operates and how to add application-specific features. The actual organization is typically straightforward once understood, but it seems at first daunting and unapproachable with no context to work from.

Cross-Cutting MVC Concerns

There seems to be a number of "what goes where" questions surrounding *MVC*, and you can receive substantially different answers from different *MVC* proponents.

Where does $_SESSION belong? One argument says that sessions are a persistent data store, usually implemented as files on the server and are therefore best kept in the *Model*. A second set of developers argues that like the other PHP superglobals, session data is an input to the system and therefore belongs in the *Controller*. Yet another set of developers say sessions are implemented using cookies, a technology that only works with HTML over HTTP and therefore sessions are *View* related.

Where does authentication belong? It seems like it's part of application logic and would therefore belong to the *Model*. But what if you want to limit certain actions (part of the *Controller*) to only authenticated users? Well, the *Controller* can access the *Model*, so it seems a perfect place. But what about HTTP authentication? Does it too go into the *Controller*?

Where does the browser fit in this whole concept? Clearly the *View*, right? What if you try to implement Javascript validation? Doesn't validation belong in the *Controller* and the *Model*? How do you get it into the *View*?

None of these issues are show stoppers, but each can cause some thought provoking, even gut-wrenching moments when trying to figure out just how to align these concerns in your *MVC* implementation.

Non-MVC Frameworks

Clearly not every framework is centered on the separation of concerns and ideas embodied by the *MVC* pattern. Here is a small sampling of non-MVC framework ideas.

Event Handling

When you work in a GUI environment, the tools are generally set up to responsd to events. Think `button.click()`. Several PHP frameworks have tried to adopt this as a core idea.

Prado was recently recognized in Zend's PHP5 coding contest and has event handling as a core concept. WACT has the concept of using the *Composite* pattern to aggregate controllers, each of which has "listeners" that can approximate an event handling perspective.

Inversion of Control Containers

A hot topic in Java circles is *Inversion of Control* (IoC) *Containers*, also known as the *Dependency Injection* pattern. A good introductory article on this pattern is available at http://www.martin-fowler.com/articles/injection.html.

There is a promising PHP5 project that's a port of the original Java PicoContainer at http://www.picocontainer.org/.

Dependency Injection is a pattern I personally am very interested in using in my own development efforts because it inherently works well with the Test Driven Development methodology, allowing you to more readily test your code because it is designed to play nicely with other components right from the start.

This pattern is really orthogonal to *MVC*—one of the areas I am most interested in is combining a *Dependency Injection* container like Pico and a *MVC* framework like WACT to produce an application that "autowires" itself. Ideally this will create easy to assemble web applications, and at the same time allow for easily testable code by instructing the container to inject *Mock Objects* instead of real dependencies.

Conclusion

This has been a whirlwind tour of MVC and of related design patterns. If you want to look at fully developed PHP MVC frameworks, I would recommend reviewing Mojavi (http://www.mojavi.org/); it's a good example of the pattern and the project has active development and a robust community.

As you should know by now, I am partial to WACT (http://phpwact.org/), which has the distinction of having framework components for all three parts of the *MVC* triad: a *Composite Controller* mechanism, a *Custom Tag* template system for *Views*, and the DataSource (see *Chapter 10 — The Specification Pattern*) as a generic proxy for the *Model*.

While this chapter may not have solved any web architecture problems you have, hopefully it has provided you with some ideas—starting points for further research—and perhaps even the inspiration for you to write the Magic Web Application Architecture that revolutionizes PHP development. If you do, please make sure to let the rest of us know.

18
Conclusion

WE HAVE COME TO the end of our brief journey together. It is my hope we have accomplished something together, both the overt goal of introducing the concepts of Design Patterns with specific examples in PHP, but also more subtle accomplishments, such as the introduction of Agile Development techniques like Test Driven Development.

Design Patterns are a useful tool for you to have in your programming toolkit, to be pulled out and applied appropriately to complicated design problems. Design patterns give you the possibility to quickly add flex points to your design, using time-worn, proven techniques. Using Design Patterns also gives you an additional ability to communicate with other developers, with the names of the each patterns now acting as a short cut for a whole body of knowledge.

It is possible to go overboard with any technique, including OOP or Design Patterns. This is where it's important to apply other Agile Development practices, specifically *"Do the simplest possible thing that will work."* If the task at hand doesn't require the flexibility or warrant the complexity of the Design Pattern based solution, then don't use it. Design Patterns are mean to solve specific problems in your code, not to create problems.

Testing your code is incredibly powerful. There has been clear evidence of this throughout the book, with each chapter heavily emphasizing the testing of the patterns as well as the coding of the pattern implementation itself. No other practice has influenced the design, stability, and maintainability of the code I have written as much as adopting the practice of testing.

The code in this book was developed by first writing the unit test cases and the code, and only when the code passed the tests did I migrate it into the body of each chapter. The full source code for each of these tests is available for you in the source code download for the book. I encourage you to review these tests, understand them, even see their shortcomings. But most of all I encourage you to take the step of testing your own code if you're not doing so now.

The Design Patterns presented in this book are by no means comprehensive, but were instead intended to provide you with a sample of some of the most commonly applicable patterns in the PHP/Web Application context. This book is a starting point for you begin your own journey of understanding and application of Design Patterns.

One of my personal goals in writing this text was to gain better clarity and understanding of the patterns myself, under the assumption there is no better way to learn than to teach. I believe I have achieved this goal, and I hope you find as much utility in reading this work as I had in authoring it.

I wish you the best in applying Design Patterns to your PHP applications.

Happy coding.

A

Pattern Quick Reference

One of the downsides of design patterns is that there are so many of them—this book covers almost twenty of them in great detail, and there are several more that are not directly relevant to PHP.

Therefore, I thought that it might have been handy to have a simple (and, thankfully, relatively short) reference table that can help you jog your memory when you're looking for a pattern to solve a particular problem but can't quite remember which pattern you should use.

The table in the following pages provides you with a short overview of every pattern covered in this book, together with the chapter in which it is covered and pointers to external resources like books. Together with the index, it will hopefully provide you with a quick way to locate the pattern for every occasion.

AbstractFactory

Summary	Facilitates the building of families of related objects.
Reference Chapter	3
Other Resources	*GoF*—Page 87

ActiveRecord

Summary	Creates an object that wraps a row from a database table or view, provides database access one row at a time, and encapsulates relevant business logic.
Reference Chapter	14
Other Resources	*PoEAA*—Page 160 *Data Access Patterns*—Page 33

Adapter

Summary	Allow classes to support a familiar interface so you can use new classes without refactoring old code.
Reference Chapter	13
Other Resources	*GoF*—Page 139 *Agile Software Development*—Page 317 *Roles, Responsibilities and Collaborations*—Page 340 *Design Patterns Explained*—Page 95 *Advanced PHP Programming*—Page 44

Application Controller

Summary	A central point for handling navigation for an application, typically implemented in an index.php file dispatching based on URL query parameters.
Reference Chapter	17
Other Resources	*PoEAA*—Page 379

Builder

Summary	Facilitates the initialization of complex object state.
Reference Chapter	3
Other Resources	*GoF*—Page 97

Command

Summary	Encapsulate a request as an object.
Reference Chapter	17
Other Resources	*GoF*—Page 233

Composite

Summary	Manage a collection of objects where each "part" can stand in as a "whole". Typically organized in a tree hierarchy.
Reference Chapter	10, 17
Other Resources	*GoF*—Page 163 *Agile Software Development*—Page 293

Custom Tag

Summary	Improve presentation separation by encapsulating components to appear as new HTML tags.
Reference Chapter	17
Other Resources	*GoF*—Page 139 *PoEAA*—Page 374 http://wact.sf.net/index.php/TemplateView

DataMapper

Summary	An object that acts as a translation layer between domain objects and the database table that contains related data.
Reference Chapter	16
Other Resources	*PoEAA*—Page 165 *Data Access Patterns*—Page 53

Decorator

Summary	Attach responsibilities to an object dynamically. Can simplify class hierarchies by replacing subclasses.
Reference Chapter	12
Other Resources	*GoF*—Page 175 *Design Patterns Explained*—Page 241

Dependency Injection

Summary	Construct classes to accept collaborators through the constructor or setter methods, so that a framework can assemble your objects.
Reference Chapter	17
Other Resources	*PoEAA*—Page ??? http://www.martinfowler.com/articles/injection.html

Domain Model

Summary	An object model of business logic that includes both data and behavior.
Reference Chapter	17
Other Resources	*PoEAA*—Page 116 *Evans DDD*

FactoryMethod

Summary	Facilitates the creation of objects.
Reference Chapter	3
Other Resources	*GoF*—Page 107 *Agile Software Development*—Page 269 *Design Patterns Explained*—Page 285 *Advanced PHP Programming*—Page 54

Front Controller

Summary	A controller that handles all requests for a web application.
Reference Chapter	17
Other Resources	*PoEAA*—Page 379

Handle-Body

Summary	A collective name for design patterns that hold a reference to a subject object (for example, Proxy, Decorator, and Adapter).
Reference Chapter	N/A
Other Resources	*http://www.c2.com/cgi/wiki?HandleBodyPattern*

Iterator

Summary	Easily manipulate collections of objects.
Reference Chapter	8
Other Resources	*GoF*—Page 257

MockObject

Summary	Supplies a stub that validates whether certain methods were or were not called during testing.
Reference Chapter	6, Appendix B
Other Resources	*http://www.lastcraft.com/mock_objects_documentation.php* *http://www.mockobjects.com/MocksObjectsPaper.html*

Model-View-Controller

Summary	An application layering pattern that separates concerns between your domain model, presentation logic and application flow.
Reference Chapter	17
Other Resources	*PoEAA*—Page 330 *http://wact.sf.net/index.php/ModelViewController*

MonoState

Summary	Allow all instances of an object to share the same state.
Reference Chapter	4
Other Resources	*Agile Software Development*—Page 177 *http://c2.com/cgi/wiki?MonostatePattern*

Observer

Summary	Register objects for later callback. Event-based notification. Publish/Subscribe.
Reference Chapter	9
Other Resources	*GoF*—Page 293 *Agile Software Development*—Page 297 *Design Patterns Explained*—Page 263

Proxy

Summary	Provide access to an object through a surrogate object to allow for delayed instantiation or protection of subject methods.
Reference Chapter	11
Other Resources	*GoF*—Page 207 *PoEAA*—Page 200 *Agile Software Development*—Page 327

Registry

Summary	Manages references to objects through a single, well-known, object.
Reference Chapter	5
Other Resources	*PoEAA*—Page 480

ServerStub

Summary	Simulates a portion of your application for testing purposes.
Reference Chapter	6
Other Resources	*PoEAA*—Page 504

Singleton

Summary	Provide global access to a single instance of an object.
Reference Chapter	4
Other Resources	*GoF*—Page 127 *Agile Software Development*—Page 177 *Design Patterns Explained*—Page 255 *Advanced PHP Programming*—Page 56

Specification

Summary	Flexible evaluation of objects against dynamic criteria.
Reference Chapter	10
Other Resources	*Evans DDD*—Page 224, 273

State

Summary	Have an object change its behavior depending on state changes.
Reference Chapter	7, 8
Other Resources	*GoF*—Page 305

Strategy

Summary	Allows for switching between a selection of algorithms by creating objects with identical interfaces.
Reference Chapter	6
Other Resources	*GoF*—Page 315 *Agile Software Development*—Page 161 *Roles, Responsibilities and Collaborations*—Page 338 *Design Patterns Explained*—Page 229

TableDataGateway

Summary	An object that acts as a gateway to a database ta ble or view, providing pro-vide access to multiple rows.
Reference Chapter	15
Other Resources	*PoEAA*—Page 165

Template View

Summary	Render a page by replacing embed-ded markers with domain data.
Reference Chapter	17
Other Resources	*PoEAA*—Page 361

TemplateMethod

Summary	Define an algorithm with "hook" methods allowing subclasses to change the behavior without chang-ing the structure.
Reference Chapter	7, 12
Other Resources	*GoF*—Page 325 *Roles, Responsibilities and Collaborations*—Page 330 *Design Patterns Explained*—Page 279 *Advanced PHP Programming*—Page 49

Transform View

Summary	Process domain data sequentially to transform it to some form of output.
Reference Chapter	17
Other Resources	*PoEAA*—Page 361

ValueObject

Summary	Handles objects whose equality is determined by the value of the objects' attributes, not by the identity of the objects.
Reference Chapter	2
Other Resources	*PoEAA*—Page 486 *Evans DDD*—Page 99

View Helper

Summary	A class that helps the view by collecting data from the Model.
Reference Chapter	17
Other Resources	*PoEAA*—Page 355

Visitor

Summary	Defines an algorithm as an object that "visits" each member of a aggregate performing an operation.
Reference Chapter	7,10
Other Resources	*GoF*—Page 331

Book References

- **GoF** - Erich Gamma, Richard Helm, Ralph Johnson, John Vlissides *Design Patterns: Elements of Reusable Object-Oriented Software*. Addison-Wesley, 1995.

- **PoEAA** - Martin Fowler *Patterns of Enterprise Application Architecture* Addison-Wesley, 2003.

- Harry Fuecks, *PHP Anthology: Object Oriented PHP Solutions*, SitePoint Pty. Lt., 2003

- Allen Holub, *Holub on Patterns: Learning Design Patterns by Looking at Code*, Apress, 2004.

- Robert Martin, *Agile Software Development*, Prentice Hall, 2003.

- Clifton Nock, *Data Access Patterns*, Addison-Wesley, 2004.

- George Schlossnagle, *Advanced PHP Programming*, SAMS, 2004

- Alan Shalloway and James R. Trott, *Design Patterns Explained*, Addison-Wesley, 2005

- Rebecca Wirfs-Brock and Alan McKean, *Roles, Responsibilities and Collaborations*, Addison-Wesley, 2003.

- Matt Zandstra, PHP 5 Objects, Patterns, Practice, Apress, 2004.

B

SimpleTest
Testing Practices

THOUGH TESTING YOUR CODE is not specifically related to the implementation of design patterns, testing your code is such a powerful coding tool, it's tightly integrated into the text of this book. The tests shown in this book ensure the code's accuracy, but also implicitly describe how a section of code is supposed to work.

The most practical way to approach automated testing is with a *testing framework*, most of which are derived from the design of JUnit (http://junit.org/). There are quite a number of PHP unit testing frameworks in existence, with 90 percent of them named PHPUnit (see http://www.google.com/search?q=phpunit). Sebastian Bergmann's PHPUnit2 seems to be under the most active development, supporting PHP5 since July 2004 (http://pear.php.net/package/PHPUnit2/download).

This book uses SimpleTest (http://sf.net/projects/simpletest/). It has excellent tutorials and documentation, and it supports web testing and the *Mock Object* testing pattern (covered in *Chapter 6—The Mock Object Pattern*).

This appendix includes additional material that can help ramp up your testing skills. Specifically, there's a section about "scaffolding" and how to best structure and execute your test code; a section on the WebTestCase feature of SimpleTest, which allows you to test your entire web application as a "black box" just as an end-user would; and you can read about the *Partial Mock Object* technique, which can be used effectively to introduce *Mock Objects* into test code by systematically replacing internal *Factory* methods.

Best Practices for Using SimpleTest

SimpleTest is a unit testing framework developed by Marcus Baker. The current version of SimpleTest is coded for PHP4, but it runs on PHP5 with very minimal issues. You can look at the SimpleTest documentation and tutorials either on <u>http://simpletest.org/</u> or <u>http://www.last-craft.com/simple_test.php</u>. These provide a very thorough introduction to using the tool.

The first step in building a test suite for a reasonable size project is to make a project-specific testing include file. The primary content of this file should be a subclass of UnitTestCase written specifically for your project.

The first line of code should be a definition of the SIMPLE_TEST constant. SIMPLE_TEST is both a historical artifact and a useful feature: in past versions, SimpleTest used this constant itself, but this dependency has now been removed. Otherwise, for practical reasons, the constant can be used as an indication that you're currently running a test (normally it's not a good practice to alter your code's behavior under testing conditions, but an example of where you might is to guard against exit() inside of your projects when running test cases) and can be used to record a library path.

```
/**
 * relative path to SimpleTest
 *@ignore
 */
if (!defined('SIMPLE_TEST')) define('SIMPLE_TEST', 'simpletest/');
```

Once this constant is defined, include the SimpleTest files you use in every test case:

```
/**#@+
 *     SimpleTest includes
 */
require_once SIMPLE_TEST.'unit_tester.php';
require_once SIMPLE_TEST.'reporter.php';
require_once SIMPLE_TEST.'mock_objects.php';
require_once SIMPLE_TEST.'web_tester.php';
/**#@-*/
```

Another best practice I have is to place all of my test cases in a subdirectory "tests/" immediately below my project root. (One problem with this practice is any code that relies on relative includes from this project root may break under test conditions. This can be solved by adding the parent directory "../" to the include path.) I also include any common setup for the application (such as base library includes, constant definitions, and so on).

```
/**
 * modify php include path to include parent directory
 *
 * this is required because the tests are run from
 * the tests subdirectory and the application is run from
 * (and coded for) the parent directory
 * @ignore
 */
if (!defined('TEST_PATH_MODIFIED')) {
ini_set('include_path', '..:'.ini_get('include_path'));
define('TEST_PATH_MODIFIED', true);
}
/**
 *include standard setup file for this application
 */
require_once 'setup.php';
```

Finally, I create a project-specific subclass of the UnitTestCase class to use for testing. You can then include assertions and utility functions unique to this project inside this class and have them available in all of your test cases.

```
/**
 *UnitTestCase for myProject application
 *@packagemyProject
 *@subpackagetests
 */
class MyProjectUnitTestCase extends UnitTestCase {
function projAssertSomething() {}
function projHelperUtil() {}
}
```

I also highly recommend that you make your test cases as easy to run as possible. That means several things. First, you should be able to run a specific unit test case or a collection of cases for one aspect of your code, and you should be able to run every test that you've written.

It is also helpful to be able to run your tests through the browser or via the command-line. Handling the latter is straightforward: detect if you are using the CLI interface and select the appropriate test runner to execute the test:

```
if (TextReporter::inCli()) {
  exit ($test->run(new TextReporter()) ? 0 : 1);
}
$test->run(new HtmlReporter());
```

The ability to select and run individual tests or the entire test suite depends on how you organize your test case files and how you organize your tests.

If you don't include an index file and have auto indexing enabled in your web server, you can run an individual test case just by clicking on its filename. Here, each test case has to differentiate if it's running singly or as part of a larger suite and behave appropriately.

In addition, I find that I typically define more than one test case in each file, because I may define one *UnitTestCase* for the actual unit test and another as an integration test. Because of this possibility, I define even a single test case in standalone test files as *group* tests. Here is a trimmed down example:

```
require_once 'myprojunittestcase.php';

class TestSomething extends MyProjUnitTestCase {
    function TestSomething($name) {
        $this->UnitTestCase($name);
    }
    function setup() {}
    function teardown() {}
    function TestSomething() {
        $this->assertTrue(true, 'this should pass');
    }
}
class TestSomethingIntegration extends MyProjUnitTestCase {
    //...
}

//run if stand alone
if (!isset($this)) {
    $test =& new GroupTest('Something Unit Test');
    $test->addTestCase(new TestSomething );
    $test->addTestCase(new TestSomethingIntegration);

    if (TextReporter::inCli()) {
        exit ($test->run(new TextReporter()) ? 0 : 1);
    }
    $test->run(new HtmlReporter());
}
```

You also need a file to run the entire test suite for your project. I usually name this file the highly imaginative "run.php". In this file, add each of the individual test case files to a single group test, using $this->addTestFile(...) for each test. A stub of this file looks like:

```
define('SIMPLE_TEST', 'simpletest/');
require_once 'myprojunittestcase.php';

$test =& new GroupTest('My Project Application Tests');
$test->addTestFile('testsomething.php');
//...

set_time_limit(0);
if (TextReporter::inCli()) {
        exit ($test->run(new TextReporter()) ? 0 : 1);
}

$test->run(new HtmlReporter());
```

If your testing needs are more complicated than this, you might want to take a look at the scripts that run the Web Application Component Toolkit (WACT) test suite at http://wact.sf.net/test/ and http://cvs.sf.net/viewcvs.py/wact/wact/tests/.

Mock Objects

We covered *Mock Objects* in some depth in *Chapter 6*, but let's review the concept again as part of this discussion on test practices.

Mock Objects follow a five-step testing pattern:

- Create the *Mock Objects* (generate the *Mock Object* code, instantiate).
- Setup the state of the *Mock Objects* (return values, etc.).
- Establish expectations for the *Mock Objects* (method X() is called with parameter 'Y', method Z() should never be called, and so on).
- Invoke the code you are testing with the *Mock Objects* as parameters.
- Verify the expectations of the *Mock Objects*.

The classic example of how a *Mock Object* can be used is simulating database interactions inside of a class. The following example shows how to simulate the Oracle driver provided by the popular ADOdb (http://adodb.sf.net/) database access library (used as the database access layer for the database-related patterns presented in *Chapters 14—16*).

```
// PHP5 code
Function TestGetData() {
  $this->assertTrue(defined('SomeModel::DATA_FUNCT')
        , 'DATA_FUNCT constant defined');
  $c = new MockADODBConnection($this);
  $rs = new MockADORecordSet($this);
  $test_parm = 5;
  $test_array = array(
          array('testkey'=>'testval1')
          ,array('testkey'=>'testval2')
          );
  $rs->SetReturnValue('GetArray', $test_array);
  $rs->ExpectOnce('GetArray');

  $c->SetReturnReference('execute', $rs);
  $expect = array(new WantedPatternExpectation(
          '/'.preg_quote(SomeModel::DATA_FUNCT,'/').'/')
          ,array('FOO' => $test_parm));
  $c->ExpectOnce('execute', $expect);

  $o = new SomeModel($c);
  $this->assertEqual($o->getData($test_parm), $test_array);

  $rs->tally();
  $c->tally();
}
```

Notice that the example—like your code—must introduce the mock database connection object somewhere in the code. There are many ways to do this, and you have probably used one or more of them in the past: global variables, a *Singleton* class, or always passing the connection into the retrieval method. This code uses a hybrid approach, passing the connection to the object at the time of instantiation. (My personal approach has been to allow for an optional connection parameter, otherwise retrieving the object from a *Factory*).

Lets walk through this test method step by step.

The first assertion verifies a particular class constant exists. Both the class method being tested and the test case make use of this constant.

The next two lines create $c and $rs, which are the Mock database connection and Mock result set, respectively. The test case itself is passed as an argument to *Mock Objects* when they are instantiated.

The next two lines of code create variables to hold values used in the test. I don't spend a lot of time getting creative here, just slap in some values that approximate the right type. (I did not model the number of records or the real field names of the records with reasonable values in the test data, I just put together an array or an associative array and used those simplified values for testing.) In most cases, you are just verifying that the expected value—meaning the one you put into the server stub—was returned by your tested code. (You can get into more specifics around the details of the real returned structure when you do integration testing.) Sometimes I add random values to the test data, particularly if I've implemented some kind of caching in the tested code and I want to verify that the cache is being cleared.

The next line, `$rs->SetReturnValue('GetArray', $test_array)` instructs the mock result set to return the `$test_array` any time it's `getArray()` method is called, followed immediately by telling the mock to expect the `getArray()` method to be called exactly once in the tested code.

The line `$c->SetReturnReference('execute', $rs)` tells the mock database connection to return the mocked result set if anyone calls the `execute()` method.

Where *Mock Objects* really kick into overdrive is in simulating failure. (Just how gracefully does your application handle the database returning an error instead of the expected result set?)

SimpleTest uses the static method `Mock::generate()` to create a class definition for a *Mock Object*. The `generate()` method takes the class name you want to mock and generates and evaluates the PHP code for the mock class. You then create *Mock Objects* inside of the test case by `$mock =& new MockOriginalClass($this)`, where `$this` is the test case itself.

Web Testing

SimpleTest includes a `WebTestCase` class, similar in scope to jWebUnit (http://jwebunit.source-forge.net/). `WebTestCase` provides a browser in a script, capable of fetching, validating, and manipulating the end content of your PHP application.

> **WebTestCase**
> The SimpleTest WebTestCase allows you to test the end result of your PHP application, with the web site with your PHP script acting as the user and browser. It is a PHP implementation of a web testing framework, like http://htmlunit.sourceforge.net/. The WebTestCase can fetch pages, follow links, validate the presence and default values of form elements, and submit forms, frames, HTTP response codes, and more.

You can easily script actions like browsing to a main page, clicking on a "login" link, retrieving a form, and submitting a username and password. The features of `WebTestCase` are beneficial for both integration testing (of your final application), as well as for working with legacy code (providing you a test harness for major work at restructuring older scripts, ones that probably do not have unit tests of their own).

Let's build a `WebTestCase` for the "legacy" web application developed in *Chapter 6—The Mock Object Pattern*. The tests will serve as a safety harness as the sample code is refactored.

Our Legacy Application

The simple script below is typical and could appear in any number of PHP applications. The page generates a login for if the user has not yet logged in, acts as a form handler for the form, shows different content after a successful login, and provides a logout feature.

Here's the code to display a login form if the user is not yet logged in:

```
<html>
<body>
<form action="<?php echo SELF; ?>">
Name:<input type="text" name="name">
Password:<input type="password" name="passwd">
<input type="submit" value="Login">
</form>
</body>
</html>
```

Or, if the user is logged in, here's the content to display:

```
<html>
<head>
<script type="text/javascript">
function logout() {
   document.location = "<?php echo SELF; ?>?clear";
}
</script>
<body>Welcome <?=$_SESSION['name']?>
<br>Super secret member only content here.
<button onClick="logout();">Logout</button>
</body>
</html>
```

Adding in the form handling capabilities, session startup and logout feature, and the whole script might look like:

```
session_start();

define('SELF',
  'http://'.$_SERVER['SERVER_NAME'].$_SERVER['PHP_SELF']);

if (array_key_exists('name', $_REQUEST)
  && array_key_exists('passwd', $_REQUEST)
  && 'admin' == $_REQUEST['name']
```

```php
        && 's3cr3t' == $_REQUEST['passwd']) {
        $_SESSION['name'] = 'admin';
        header('Location: '.SELF);
    }

    if (array_key_exists('clear', $_REQUEST)) {
        unset($_SESSION['name']);
    }

    if (array_key_exists('name', $_SESSION)
        && $_SESSION['name']) { ?>
        <html>
        <head>
        <script type="text/javascript">
        function logout() {
            document.location = "<?php echo SELF; ?>?clear";
        }
        </script>
        <body>Welcome <?=$_SESSION['name']?>
        <br>Super secret member only content here.
        <button onClick="logout();">Logout</button>
        </body>
        </html> <?php
    } else { ?>
        <html>
        <body>
        <form action="<?php echo SELF; ?>">
        Name:<input type="text" name="name">
        Password:<input type="password" name="passwd">
        <input type="submit" value="Login">
        </form>
        </body>
        </html> <?php
    }
```

So how can you get a handle on this legacy code to start restructuring it?

One method is to create a WebTestCase covering all of the aspects of the application you are about to restructure. This is a step removed from unit testing and is more like "acceptance testing" where you simulate how the end-user is expected to interact with the application via the browser.

Include WebTestCase from SimpleTest and base your test cases on the WebTestCase class instead of the UnitTestCase class. I also like to define a constant for the URL to the page I am testing. With all of this, your test script contains this code:

```php
<?php
require_once 'simpletest/unit_tester.php';
require_once 'simpletest/reporter.php';
require_once 'simpletest/web_tester.php';

define('TEST_URL', 'http://www.example.com/path/to/page.php');
```

```
class PageWebTestCase extends WebTestCase {
  function TestInitalFetchNoSecretContent() {
    $this->assertTrue($this->get(TEST_URL));
    $this->assertNoUnwantedPattern('/secret.*content/i');
  }
}
```

The $this->get() method fetches a URL into the testing script's simulated browser. Later assertions, like the assertNoUnwantedPattern() by default apply to the content of the page fetched into the browser.

assertNoUnwantedPattern()

The assertion **assertNoUnwantedPattern()** fails if the specified PCRE regular expression is present in the tested content. This allows you to verify content you do not want present is indeed missing.

One powerful use is to validate there are no PHP errors in the page (assuming the default error handler is still in place for the application).

Run the test and verify it passes with a green bar. Let's check some more of the application's features with further test methods.

```
class PageWebTestCase extends WebTestCase {

  function TestInitalFetchNoSecretContent() { /*...*/ }
  function TestInitalFetchContainsLoginForm() {
    $this->assertTrue($this->get(TEST_URL));
    $this->assertField('name');
    $this->assertField('passwd');
    $this->assertWantedPattern('/<form.*<input[^>]*text[^>]*'
      .'name.*<input[^>]*password[^>]*passwd/ims');
  }
```

assertField()

The assertion **assertField()** detects if a particular form input is present in the page. The assertion takes one-three parameters: the name of the input and, optionally, the expected value and the message to display for failure.

These tests establish a fresh connection to the application and verify that it has a login form and does not contain the "secret content".

Next, lets move on to validating that the login form works, starting with a failure (bad credentials submitted) condition:

```
class PageWebTestCase extends WebTestCase {
  function TestInitalFetchNoSecretContent() { /*...*/ }
  function TestInitalFetchContainsLoginForm() { /*...*/ }
  function TestBogusLoginFailure() {
    $this->assertTrue($this->get(TEST_URL));
    $this->setField('name','foo');
    $this->setField('passwd','bar');
    $this->clickSubmit('Login');
    $this->assertNoUnwantedPattern('/secret.*content/i');
    $this->assertWantedPattern('/<form.*<input[^>]*text[^>]*'
      .'name.*<input[^>]*password[^>]*passwd/ims');
  }
}
```

The `WebTestCase::setField()` allows you to fill in the values of form elements. `WebTestCase::clickSubmit()` lets you submit the form, performing an HTTP GET or POST operations, as specified by the form. After submitting the form, the test verifies that the login form is redisplayed.

Next, test the successful login case:

```
class PageWebTestCase extends WebTestCase {
  function TestInitalFetchNoSecretContent() { /*...*/ }
  function TestInitalFetchContainsLoginForm() { /*...*/ }
  function TestBogusLoginFailure() { /*...*/ }
  function TestSucessfulLogin() {
    $this->assertTrue($this->get(TEST_URL));
    $this->setField('name','admin');
    $this->setField('passwd','s3cr3t');
    $this->clickSubmit('Login');
    $this->assertWantedPattern('/welcome\s+admin/i');
    $this->assertWantedPattern('/secret.*content/i');
    $this->assertNoUnwantedPattern('/<form.*<input[^>]*text[^>]*'
      .'name.*<input[^>]*password[^>]*passwd/ims');
  }
}
```

This validates that after posting the correct credentials, the "secret content" is present and the login form is no longer present in the document.

You can also verify that new browsers do not have valid credentials, which is proof that you're using the session to cache the login information. SimpleTest essentially creates a new instance of the browser for each test method, so an additional test and a subsequent method should create a new session, and therefore go back to the login form.

```php
class PageWebTestCase extends WebTestCase {

    function TestInitalFetchNoSecretContent() { /*...*/ }
    function TestInitalFetchContainsLoginForm() { /*...*/ }
    function TestBogusLoginFailure() { /*...*/ }
    function TestSucessfulLogin() { /*...*/ }
    function TestNewBroswerDoesNotCarrySession() {
        $this->assertTrue($this->get(TEST_URL));
        $this->assertField('name');
        $this->assertField('passwd');
        $this->assertWantedPattern('/<form.*<input[^>]*text[^>]*'
            .'name.*<input[^>]*password[^>]*passwd/ims');
    }
}
```

Lastly, you can test "logout".

```php
class PageWebTestCase extends WebTestCase {

    function TestInitalFetchNoSecretContent() { /*...*/ }
    function TestInitalFetchContainsLoginForm() { /*...*/ }
    function TestBogusLoginFailure() { /*...*/ }
    function TestSucessfulLogin() { /*...*/ }
    function TestNewBroswerDoesNotCarrySession() { /*...*/ }
    function TestLogoutWorks() {
        $this->assertTrue($this->get(TEST_URL));
        $this->setField('name','admin');
        $this->setField('passwd','secret');
        $this->clickSubmit('Login');
        $this->assertWantedPattern('/welcome\s+admin/i');
        $this->assertWantedPattern('/secret.*content/i');
        $this->assertTrue($this->get(TEST_URL.'?clear'));
        $this->assertNoUnwantedPattern('/secret.*content/i');
        $this->assertWantedPattern('/<form.*<input[^>]*text[^>]*'
            .'name.*<input[^>]*password[^>]*passwd/ims');
    }
}
```

With an adequate WebTestCase for the application, you can proceed to restructure it with a reasonable confidence that you're achieving the same result, which was the end result of the testing performed in *Chapter 6*.

Partial Mock Objects

To use *Mock Objects*, you must make sure that you can inject the *Mock Object* into your code with minimal intrusion. If you're used to creating objects in the middle of your code with a `new` operator, this may seem problematic.

One simple restructuring you can do is to instead call an internal *Factory* that returns the newly created instance. You can then use the *Partial Mock Object* technique to replace your target code's normal internal *Factory* with a replacement method that returns the *Mock Object* instead. This allows you to inject an instance of an object where you otherwise could not get it into the flow of the code, but otherwise be testing all of your actual code.

The next series of code examples show a simple case where you might find this kind of trick useful. The example, using the `Color` class from *Chapter 2—The Factory Method Pattern*, is perhaps overly simple, but it does convey all of the concepts; hopefully you can extrapolate this technique to your own work.

This simple class manipulates text to add a `<span>` tag to highlight some text.

```
class TextWriter {
  var $_buffer = '';
  function addText($text) {
    $this->_buffer .= $text;
  }

  function addHighlightedText($text) {
    $color = new Color(255,255,0);
    $this->_buffer .= '<span style="background-color: '
      .$color->getRgb().'">'.$text.'</span>';
  }

  function render() {
    $ret = $this->_buffer;
    $this->_buffer = '';
    return $ret;
  }
}
```

A simple example of this class in action is shown in this test case:

```
class TestTextWriter extends UnitTestCase {
  // ...

  function TestSimpleText() {
    $o =& new TextWriter;
    $test_string = 'this is some text';
    $o->addText($test_string);
```

```
        $this->assertEqual($test_string, $o->render());
        $this->assertEqual('',$o->render());
    }

    function TestHighlightNoColorChange() {
        $o =& new TextWriter;
        $o->addText('This is a string with a ');
        $o->addHighlightedText('yellow');
        $o->addText(' highlight');
        $this->assertWantedPattern(
        '~string.*<span.*background.*#FFFF00.*yellow</span>.*highlight~i'
            ,$o->render());
    }
}
```

This class works, but isn't very flexible.

The next requirement is to allow for the highlighted text color to change, but still allow for the yellow default color. A first attempt at this might be to change the addHighlightedText() method as follows:

```
class TextWriter {
  // ...

  function addHighlightedText($text, $color=false) {
    if (!(is_object($color)
      && method_exists($color, 'getRgb'))) {
      $color = new Color(255,255,0);
    }
    $this->_buffer .= '<span style="background-color: '
      .$color->getRgb().'">'.$text.'</span>';
  }
}
```

This code works, but has one flaw—if you tried to pass in a *Mock Object* in the $color parameter, the testing would function correctly, but because PHP4 passes copies of objects by default, the tally() capability of the *Mock Object* would be broken. In this example, you can't just change the $color parameter to be pass by reference because a by reference parameter can not have a default value (and would therefore be required, violating our requirements).

One way to get around this is to have the addHighlightedText() method accept an object in an "envelope". An array, which contains an object reference, can be passed by value and yet still contain the object reference. The addHighlightedText() method could be altered to accept this convention as follows:

```
class TextWriter {
  // ...
  function addHighlightedText($text, $color=false) {
    if (is_array($color)
      && is_object($color[0])
      && method_exists($color[0], 'getRgb')) {
      $color =& $color[0];
    }
    if (!(is_object($color)
      && method_exists($color, 'getRgb'))) {
      $color = new Color(255,255,0);
    }
    $this->_buffer .= '<span style="background-color: '
      .$color->getRgb().'">'.$text.'</span>';
  }
}
```

Now a test like the one that follows passes because the *Mock Object* is passed by reference and is yet still optional.

```
class TestTextWriter extends UnitTestCase {
  // ...
  function TestHighlightBlueWithMock() {
    $o =& new TextWriter;
    $o->addText('This is a string with a ');
    $test_color =& new MockColor($this);
    $test_color->setReturnValue('getRgb', '#0000FF');
    $test_color->expectOnce('getRgb');
    $o->addHighlightedText('blue', array(&$test_color));
    $o->addText(' highlight');
    $this->assertWantedPattern(
    '~string.*<span.*background.*#0000FF.*blue</span>.*highlight~i'
      ,$o->render());
    $test_color->tally();
  }
}
```

You might think this is altering your code to allow for testing, but with more complex systems, you nearly always want to make sure that you're operating on "the" object, not a copy, and this code is one way to allow for an *optional* pass by reference mechanism anywhere in your code.

But all of this is still somewhat dissatisfying, after all, the many lines of code added to addHighlightedText() simply deal with the optional passing of an object by reference. In addition, there is still no way to test the default color as a *Mock Object* if that were necessary.

There is another way to structure your code that combines the CrayonBox Color Factory with a

Factory Method internal to the `TextWriter` class that reduces the number of lines of code and deals with the default object testing issue.

```
class TextWriter {
  // ...
  function &getNamedColor($color_name) {
    return CrayonBox::getColor($color_name);
  }
  function addHighlightedText($text, $color_name='yellow') {
    $color =& $this->getNamedColor($color_name);
    $this->_buffer .= '<span style="background-color: '
      .$color->getRgb().'">'.$text.'</span>';
  }
}
```

This code introduces the protected factory method `getNamedColor()`, which returns by reference a `Color` object created from the `CrayonBox` *Factory*. The second, optional, parameter to `addHighlightedText()` is now $color_name, which is a string and can easily be passed by value.

Let's take a look at the "traditional" means of testing this: hand code a subclass of `TextWriter`, which allows you to replace the `getNamedColor()` method with code returning a *Mock Object*. Such a subclass might look like:

```
class TextWriterWithMockFactory extends TextWriter {
  var $_test_color;
  function setColor(&$color) {
    $this->_test_color =& $color;
  }
  function &getNamedColor($color='') {
    if ($this->_test_color) {
      return $this->_test_color;
    } else {
      return parent::getNamedColor($color);
    }
  }
}
```

A test using this `TextWriterWithMockFactory` class might look like:

```
class TestTextWriter extends UnitTestCase {
  //...
  function TestHandCodedParticalMock() {
    $col =& new MockColor($this);
```

```
        $col->setReturnValue('getRgb', '#00FF00');
        $col->expectOnce('getRgb');
        $tw =& new TextWriterWithMockFactory;
        $tw->setColor($col);
        $tw->addText('This is a string with a ');
        $tw->addHighlightedText4('lime', 'lime');
        $tw->addText(' highlight');
        $this->assertWantedPattern(
          '~string.*<span.*background.*#00FF00.*lime</span>.*highlight~i'
          ,$tw->render());

        $col->tally();
    }
}
```

Fortunately, similar to how `Mock::generate()` can save you time hand coding *Mock Object*s for testing, you can use `Mock::generatePartial()` to generate a "partial" *Mock Object* of your class which "knocks out" selected methods, similar to the hand coded example above. You can instead test the `TextWriter` code by creating a *Partial Mock Object* of the `TextWriter` class and replacing the `getNamedColor()` method with your own method which returns *Mock Objects*. The resulting test might look like:

```
class TestTextWriter extends UnitTestCase {
    // ...
    function TestHighlightWithFactoryMethodMocked() {
      Mock::generatePartial('TextWriter',
        'MockTextWriterNamedColor',
        array('getNamedColor'));
      $col =& new MockColor($this);
      $col->setReturnValue('getRgb', '#00FF00');
      $col->expectOnce('getRgb');
      $tw =& new MockTextWriterNamedColor($this);
      $tw->setReturnReference('getNamedColor', $col);
      $tw->expectOnce('getNamedColor', array('lime'));
      $tw->addText('This is a string with a ');
      $tw->addHighlightedText('lime', 'lime');
      $tw->addText(' highlight');
      $this->assertWantedPattern(
      '~string.*<span.*background.*#00FF00.*lime</span>.*highlight~i'
        ,$tw->render());
      $tw->tally();
      $col->tally();
    }
}
```

Internal *Factory Methods* are a powerful tool to reduce the complexity of your code, add flexibility, and allow for detailed testing using the *Partial Mock Object* technique.

Index

Printed in the United States
211717BV00002B/7/A

9 780973 589825